Politics in Western Europe today:

Perspectives, policies and problems since 1980

*Edited by D. W. Urwin
and W. E. Paterson*

LONGMAN
London and New York

Longman Group UK Limited,
Longman House, Burnt Mill, Harlow,
Essex CM20 2JE, England
and Associated Companies throughout the world.

Published in the United States of America
by Longman Inc., New York

First published 1990

British Library Cataloguing in Publication Data
Politics in Western Europe today: perspectives,
  policies and problems since 1980.
  1. Western Europe. Politics
  I. Urwin, Derek (Derek William), 1939–II. Paterson,
  William E. (William Edgar), 1941–320.94

ISBN 0-582-05824-4 CSD
ISBN 0-582-00295-8 PPR

Library of Congress Cataloging in Publication Data
Politics in Western Europe today: perspectives, policies, and problems
  since 1980/edited by D. W. Urwin and W. E. Paterson.
      p. cm.
    Bibliography: p.
    Includes index.
    ISBN 0-582-05824-4.

    ISBN 0-582-00295-8
    1. Europe – Politics and government – 1945–2. European Economic
  Community. I. Urwin, Derek W. II. Paterson, William E.
JN94.A2P634 1990
940.55′8–dc20   89-8289
                                                                    CIP

Set in Linotron 202 10/12 pt Bembo

Produced by Longman Singapore Publishers (Pte) Ltd.
Printed in Singapore

Contents

Contents

List of abbreviations

BSI	British Standards Institution
CAP	Common Agricultural Policy
CDU	Christian Democratic Union (West Germany)
CEOE	Spanish Confederation of Employers' Associations
CGTP	General Confederation of Portuguese Workers
CIPI	Interministerial Committee for the Co-ordination of Industrial Policy (Italy)
COREPER	Committee of Permanent Representatives
CSU	Christian Social Union (West Germany)
DC	Christian Democrats (Italy)
ECSC	European Coal and Steel Community
ECU	European currency unit
EMS	European Monetary System
EP	European Parliament
EPC	European political co-operation
GMBATU	General, Municipal, Boilermarkers and Allied Trades Union
GSEE	General Confederation of Greek Workers and Employers
IDA	Industrial Development Authority
INF	Intermediate-range Nuclear Forces
IKV	Dutch Inter-church Peace Council
LO	Trade Union Confederation (Sweden)
MCA	Monetary Compensation Amounts
MEP	Member of the European Parliament
ND	New Democracy Party (Greece)
PASOK	Panhellenic Socialist Movement (Greece)
PCI	Italian Communist Party
PRD	Democratic Renewal Party (Portugal)

List of abbreviations

PSD	Social Democratic Party (Portugal)
PSOE	Spanish Socialist Workers' Party
SEA	Single European Act
SPD	Social Democratic Party (West Germany)
UCD	Union of the Democratic Centre (Spain)
UGT	Socialist Union Confederation (Spain)
USDAW	Union of Shop, Distributive and Allied Workers
WAC	Women's Action Committee
WEU	Western European Union
WLM	Women's Liberation Movement

List of tables

Preface

The origins of this book lay in our feeling, as teachers of comparative European politics, that there was a noticeable lack of comparative material on the politics of the 1980s to which students could be directed for background reading. We should like to thank the contributors to this volume for responding so positively to our invitation to participate in the project and for accepting so generously our advice and comments on earlier drafts of their chapters. We should also like to thank other of our colleagues in the Department of Politics at the University of Warwick for their many helpful comments. Finally, we should like to thank Dorothy Foster and Iris Host for their valuable and necessary secretarial assistance.

Derek W. Urwin and William E. Paterson
Coventry, England

CHAPTER ONE

Introduction: Western European Developments

Derek W. Urwin and William E. Paterson

In 1945 the outlook for Western Europe appeared rather bleak. Two major military conflicts, separated in time by a severe economic depression, had culminated in a scenario where there were no European victors. Europe was to be dominated and constricted by the new ideological and political competition of the two superpowers, the United States and the Soviet Union. The new reality was symbolised by the *de facto* partition of the Continent; and the dividing line between East and West that was drawn after the defeat of Hitler's Reich was to remain very largely undisturbed across the ensuing decades. While the eastern half of the Continent fell under Soviet influence, Western Europe became, in essence, a client of the United States, a status which, at least in terms of defence and security, the countries themselves had been desperate to have formalised in the immediate post-war years.

The Western European countries drew several lessons from the experiences of the past, and these were compounded by their interpretation of the new reality of the cold war. The concerns of government had to be greater international co-operation, collective security, and economic growth and prosperity. Together, these would provide the necessary basis for securing the goals of a strong liberal democracy and the construction of the welfare state.

Over the next twenty years or so, Western Europe seemed to have largely achieved these goals. With the exceptions of Greece, where a fragile democratic structure was toppled by an army coup in 1967, and of Spain and Portugal, where right-wing authoritarian regimens survived undisturbed and seemingly unaffected by the world around them, the commitment to liberal democracy was strengthened. Challenges from the political extremes withered or remained effectively isolated. The political systems seemed to have settled down, as it were, in a comfortable middle age, displaying a high degree of political stability and consensus where little of note appeared to separate the political parties from one another. Political competition seemed to have become muted, to be concerned more with who could more effectively manage a prosperous economy and the distribution of state benefits than with matters of principle.

Political consensus and stability were paralleled by, and to some extent an effect of, economic satisfaction. Despite the gloomy prognostications of 1945, Western Europe tripled its wealth within a generation, with rapid economic growth and unprecedented levels of prosperity that extended across most segments of society. Keynesian techniques of economic management, it was believed, provided governments with the means of ensuring that this sustained growth would continue, so enabling the further dispensation of benefits to the whole population through the extensive welfare state structures and provisions that had been established.

Sheltering behind the American nuclear umbrella, Western Europe was also largely satisfied about its security. The establishment of the North Atlantic Treaty Organisation (NATO) in 1949 provided it with a collective defence system and valuable experience in collaborative security. The gradual thaw in the cold war and the new interest in *détente* that emerged after the mid-1950s did not seem to undermine the essential bipolarity of the Continent. While Western European governments welcomed any improvement in superpower relations, fearing that the Continent would be the major military arena in any future war, they continued to regard the American presence in Europe as the fundamental guarantee of their own freedom.

The acceptance of a common concern in security, of the interdependence and reduced status of Western Europe, was matched by a very tight growing involvement of the states in political and economic co-operation. Western European countries became entangled in a growing web of international and European organisations. For some, co-operation between states was a way of curbing any future resurgence of German militarism. For others, it was seen as a way of boosting European economic strength in a world economy dominated by the United States. For yet others, however, co-operation was but a stepping-stone towards, and a means of securing, full-blooded political union in Western Europe. Within this complex of collaboration, the European Community stands out as the most ambitious attempt at economic and political union. While its establishment in 1957 effectively divided the countries of Western Europe on the merits and objectives of membership, it was not long before all had to take greater cognisance of it. On the other hand, the internal arguments within the Community in the mid-1960s seemed to have placed strict limits upon its development as a political organisation.

Within the space of a few years, the picture of European stability and contentment, even complacency, seemed to have been shattered. Two dates stand out as symbols of critical turning-points in Western European development: 1968 and 1973. The former is remembered as a year of student protest, especially in France where it seemed likely at one point to bring about the downfall of the government. The latter was the year when oil prices were quadrupled, plunging Western Europe into economic recession.

Although there were already signs that the post-war economic boom, which had benefited from cheap energy, was slowing down, the 1973 action by the oil-producing states was a severe shock to Western Europe. Inflation became a severe problem, and high levels of unemployment increasingly became accepted as a fact of life. Governments wrestling with these problems also found themselves exposed to severe competition on the world's industrial markets from rapidly industrialising countries in other parts of the world, spearheaded by Japan. The net result was a new mood of economic pessimism and doubt. Retrenchment rather than expansion was the new economic reality. The unquestioning faith in Keynesianism as an effective tool of economic management was severely dented, permitting the espousal of alternative philosophies. The most important of these was monetarism, which became most closely associated with the Conservative government under Margaret Thatcher which came to power in Britain in 1979. One of the consequences of previous economic beliefs was a growth in government as an important actor in the economy and society. Retrenchment cast doubts upon the validity of big government, not least because it seemed to have encouraged an inflated, rigid and impersonal bureaucracy and to have stifled individual initiative and responsibility.

Retrenchment also had consequences for the greatest recipient of economic growth, the welfare state; and a more critical eye was cast upon its efficiency, costs and merits. Economic recession reduced the amount of revenue that could be made available for welfare services, while at the same time loading the system with extra demands, for example because of increasing unemployment. Simultaneously, there emerged a greater ambivalence about the virtues of the welfare state. On the one hand, people had been socialised into accepting the state as the great provider of a whole range of services without having had to pay too much regard to their costs; on the other, there was a growing dislike of its bureaucratic structures and impersonality.

Long before the oil crisis of 1973, Western Europe had had to come to terms with waves of protest from groups which seemed to reject the political consensus of the past and its precepts. The student unrest of the late 1960s was the first of these; it was the forerunner of several later movements, mainly but not entirely fuelled by young well-educated middle-class people, that rejected what they saw as the complacency, materialism and bureaucratic nature of contemporary society. The 1970s saw an injection into politics of a new idealism, of new demands and new principles, of arguments for new forms of democratic participation. Many of the activists in these movements had been politically socialised during the student unrest of previous years. In that sense too, there was a degree of overlap in participation and thematic concern across the several feminist, ecology, terrorist, anti-nuclear and peace movements that characterised the decade, and that sooner or later obliged governments to take on board some of their arguments and even at least to consider the validity and utility of some of the precepts upon which the post-war political framework and economic society had been based.

Western European states and governments faced additional challenges from other directions. One was a flowering of peripheral nationalism, a political mobilisation of people who felt that they possessed an identity different from that of the state-defined citizenship, who argued for the right to govern themselves, and who on occasions were prepared to resort to violence as a means of achieving their goals. Another challenge arose from past economic success. One consequence of economic growth had been a labour shortage. To overcome the deficit, governments had encouraged immigration from other parts of the world. Whether or not the governments had believed that the immigrants would only be temporary residents is irrelevant. By the 1970s their numbers were such, with a second generation knowing only Western European life, that they had turned many countries into multicultural societies, forcing governments to consider problems of discrimination and assimilation.

Changes also occurred on the international front during the 1970s. The retirement and subsequent death of President de Gaulle opened the way for an enlargement of the European Community, and Britain, Ireland, and Denmark duly became members in 1973. An expanded membership only made co-ordination and consensus more difficult, a problem heightened by the further accession of Greece, Spain and Portugal in the 1980s. This, plus the worsening economic situation, had the paradoxical effect of strengthening the inter-governmental element of the Community, as states strove to defend their national economies, while simultaneously demanding that it achieve a higher and more effective level of political co-ordination and integration to combat common problems. While there were strongly differing views within the Community on the desirability of a closer political union, that was the basic, if at times unspoken, theme of virtually all Community discussions on future plans and progress after 1972.

One area where the Community members did have some success in co-ordination was in foreign policy. Defence matters were ex-cluded from the brief, yet they were something that could not be ignored as they related to the security of the Community and its relationship with the United States. *Détente* seemed to have reached a pinnacle of achievement with the Moscow Agreement of 1972. Sub-sequently, however, Western European governments became in-creasingly alarmed by a growing disparity between the superpowers. While Soviet military strength continued to grow, the United States, introspective after the trauma of Vietnam, seemed to have slumped into a vacillating weakness. No matter how much an American presence in Europe might constitute a 'fire hazard', Western Europe worried that the American commitment to a Western European defence had been seriously diminished. It was the Western European governments that urged a strengthening of NATO in the late 1970s; the outcome was the 1979 agreement on modernisation and the stationing of American intermediate-range nuclear missiles on the Continent. More importantly, it contributed to a breakdown of the old consensus on defence, as several political parties, usually on the left, took issue with the new NATO decisions. The election of Ronald Reagan, with his more hawkish stance, to the American presidency in 1980 merely provided a further twist to the story, caus-ing some to worry that the United States might be swinging too strongly to the other extreme.

Finally, the 1970s saw the disappearance of another well-established feature of the European scene. Human mortality was the victor in Spain and Portugal where, within the space of a year, the long-standing authoritarian regimes collapsed. At the same time, the military junta in Greece simply disintegrated, primarily because of its own incompetence. The interesting question was what would take their place, and judgement on whether the desire to establish liberal democracy would succeed was perhaps in doubt for some time. This was particularly so in Portugal, which was swept by revolutionary fervour and where the Communist Party seemed to be making a firm bid for power. In Spain a question mark had to be placed against whether the still powerful army would stay out of the political arena, while in Greece it was a question of whether effective political parties could be established and endure. All three states would have to strive for democratic consolidation at the same time as having to cope with the more uncertain economic conditions and atmosphere of the decade.

While the 1950s and 1960s were not perhaps as politically static as is sometimes suggested, Western Europe is undeniably one of the more politically stable areas of the world, with a durable set of institutions and practices. Yet the challenge of change and its generation of, and impact upon, political issues and decisions has been as great as, for example, that of technological change. At no time, perhaps, was this as obvious in the 1970s, a decade which forced countries into a more fundamental reassessment of their situation and of the course of development since 1945. In the 1980s governments have had to wrestle with many of the problems and issues that surfaced during the previous decade. The contributions to this book are designed to offer to a student readership an introduction to some of the policy issues and concerns with which contemporary governments have had to contend. Each author was invited to provide analysis of recent developments and to indicate the problems that still wait to be resolved.

Two chapters focus specifically upon economic problems. That by Stan Taylor deals with the issue of persisting unemployment in the 1980s, and reviews the effect of differing government strategies. His conclusion is that no panacea is in sight, at least in the short term. In his discussion of relationships between government and industry, Wyn Grant discusses how the changing economic climate led to a switch away from interventionism towards a more market-oriented emphasis. He shows that this cannot be entirely explained by the political party make-up of government, and argues that one of the lessons for the future is to be more circumspect about distinguishing what is socially desirable from what is economically justified. Richard Parry tackles the broad theme of the welfare state in a period of economic retrenchment. He evaluates the different policy responses that have been made in the 1980s, as well as the more fundamental problems of the welfare state concept and its objectives. Peter Byrd discusses the re-emergence of defence as a political issue in the 1980s in terms of the interplay between external and domestic factors, between the relationship with the United States and the desire for political unity. Despite the moves that have been made towards arms reduction, Byrd sees defence remaining a major policy problem for governments, not least because old certainties have gone without their being replaced by new ones.

A second set of contributions deal with the aftermath of some of the challenges to the established political order that emerged in the 1970s. In her chapter on feminism and politics, Joni Lovenduski undertakes a stocktaking of two decades of agitation. She sees the 1980s as essentially being a period of consolidation, but suggests that while gender equality has gained some successes, these have created a future dilemma for feminist groups: how to campaign within the organised world of politics while still retaining the characteristics – spontaneity, lack of organisation and hierarchy – of a social movement, characteristics which many feminists believe provided the movement with its fundamental vitality. The same dilemma of movement versus organisation is a central theme of Derek Urwin's chapter on the green wave. The establishment of Green parties was perhaps an admission that there were limits to what ecology movements could achieve. But while Green parties have made an impact upon the political agenda, they have not been able to determine that agenda. Zig Layton-Henry's chapter traces the pattern of immigration and the problems it has created for Western European governments. He points out that the immigrant presence raises the question of what membership in a modern state means. The problem of political and civic rights and the nature of citizenship are issues which governments may well have to address in the near future.

Richard Gillespie evaluates the performance of the new liberal democracies in southern Europe. His analysis suggests that consolidation of democracy has been reasonably successful, but that one should be wary of judging them against the standards of some ideal-type democracy. His conclusion is that while there are problems and dangers, the prospects seem bright for further democratic consolidation. Two chapters offer different perspectives upon the European Community. That by Juliet Lodge adopts a Community perspective and looks at past policy areas and future development in the light of the Single European Act of 1987. She argues that the move towards 1992 demands a greater level of understanding and co-operation between the institutions of the Community, with a particular emphasis upon the need to improve the status and role of the European Parliament. William Paterson's perspective is more national. Through a selection of important policy areas dealt with by the Community in recent years, he examines the role and attitudes of the three major states of Britain, France, and West Germany. His analysis suggests that while all wield considerable influence, none can effect decisive direction over the Community, and that the opportunity of the future perhaps lies more with the Commission.

The final chapter, by Gordon Smith, is a broad review of Western European developments, with a specific focus upon the party systems. Modern government in Western Europe is party government. Political parties dominate the electoral process, legislatures and governments. Hence, no matter what the issue or challenge, attention will ultimately be focused upon party reactions and strategies. Against this background, Smith sees post-war European politics moving in stages from cleavage-based party systems to a stage dominated by party adaptation, and finally to a stage of diffusion and deconcentration.

What, then, might the future hold? By the late 1970s the intellectual and social underpinnings of the post-war political consensus had been largely eroded. With the electoral victories of Mrs Thatcher, the break with the consensus was perhaps sharpest in Britain. But throughout Western Europe the political agenda of the 1980s has been dominated by the implementation of the changed policy focus. The most obvious feature has been the redefinition of the role of the state. The post-war consensus had been based upon a central role for the state in the provision of welfare and the maintenance of full employment. The new agenda envisages a much less ambitious role for the state in terms of both the desirability and possibility of state action. A secondary theme that has emerged in the 1980s has been the absorption of new political demands first raised, at least forcefully, during the previous decade. Both processes would seem still to have some distance to go.

The leitmotif of the 1980s, then, has been rapid and far-reaching change in the domestic political agenda. Changes in the external political agenda, while not insignificant, were rather less dramatic. It is, however, very probable that the years could see equally dramatic shifts in the external environment. The move towards 1992 has already affected some changes in the balance between member states and the European Community. Were 1992 to be fully implemented and the new co-operation procedure envisaged by the Single European Act to function effectively, the consequences for the autonomy of the member states would be dramatic indeed. Some of these consequences are already beginning to emerge, and if other proposals, for example the establishment of a European Central

Bank, were to reach fruition, then the implications for the role of the state will be extremely far-reaching. Moreover, no European state can ignore the existence of the Community. The move towards 1992 has also exerted a powerful pull on the European non-members of the Community, forcing them to re-evaluate their relationship with it, even perhaps to consider applying for membership. In short, Western Europe might well be on the threshold of a dramatic step towards a much closer union. And if that is the case, it will also have enormous potential implications for Western Europe's relations with other states, most especially the United States and Japan.

A major element of the post-war West European consensus was fear of the Soviet Union. Almost all of the security arrangements that were constructed after 1945 and some of the impetus behind West European integration were motivated by this fear. Here, too, past certainties have gone, with new ones still to materialise. Since the advent of Mikhail Gorbachev to the Soviet leadership, Western Europe has found it increasingly difficult to perceive the Soviet Union as a threat in the same way as in the past. The possibility of a firmer superpower accord and a more 'amiable' Soviet Union has weakened the credibility of the Western Alliance's nuclear deterrent. In this new climate it will be much more difficult for NATO to effect the proposed modernisation of short-range nuclear weapons or even to justify increased expenditure on conventional forces. The implications of these international developments could create severe problems for Western European security policy. If the new Soviet line persists, there could well be a large-scale reduction in both NATO and Warsaw Pact forces. If the Soviet position reverts back to a hard-line stance in the future, Western Europe would be placed in a difficult position, since any response to Soviet initiatives will have involved defence cuts. Either way, Western Europe might well have to face up to difficult choices.

More widely, the defence and security arrangements of post-war Western Europe were designed to contain not just a manifest Soviet threat, but also any possible resurgence of German aggression. Integration of West Germany was the means by which German re-armament was to be contained. The consequent lack of autonomy was acceptable to West Germany because of its fear of the Soviet threat. The political stability of post-war Europe, in fact, has been contingent to a large extent upon the absorption of the two German states into their respective power blocs. A *rapprochement* between East and West could therefore be a two-edged sword. It may offer greater stability to the Continent; alternatively, it could reopen the German question, with all the attendant dangers that could have for European stability.

While the Soviet Union will continue to loom large in the circulations of Western European governments, albeit perhaps in a different way from the past, the influence of the United States could well decline. Its own changing economic situation as well as developments occurring within both Europe and the Soviet Union would suggest that it is unlikely that the United States will be able to continue as the overwhelming producer and guarantor of Western European security. One consequence of the changing superpower relationship could be that the United States will argue, with even more vigour than in the past, that Western Europe should shoulder more of the costs of the defence burden. On the other hand, the shift within Western Europe in the perception of the Soviet Union would make it difficult for governments to accept such a policy. The political agenda of Western European government in the 1980s was largely structured around the domestic role of the state. That of the future may well have to pay more attention to the changing external environment, for there too old certainties seem to have begun a process of erosion.

POLICY AREAS AND ISSUES

CHAPTER TWO
The viability of the welfare state

Richard Parry

Modern European states are welfare states. The term describes political systems which try to secure the welfare of their citizens in order to win consent and votes as well as improving the quality of personal and social life. This welfare takes the form of income support, or replacement, for those with a weak position in the labour market, and services in kind at times of need or economic incapacity. All European nations provide welfare of this kind. What differs is how it is provided (by the state, the private sector, or intermediate bodies like churches and charities); who is eligible for it (all or part of the population); who pays (the state, the beneficiary, or employers); how much of national resources it consumes; and whether it has a wider moral vision or is a pragmatic set of policies. These alternatives provide European nations with many policy choices which this chapter explores – but to renounce social policy altogether is not a realistic option for advanced industrial societies.

Between 1945 and 1970, post-war peace allowed European nations to go through a social revolution. Population moved from rural to urban areas; employment shifted from agriculture to manufacturing and then to service industries; family patterns were fragmented; the possibilities of life were extended. Social policies were developed both to facilitate economic development and to protect citizens from its consequences. Pension, sickness and unemployment benefits were extended to most of the workforce. Education came to be seen as an individual right and a wise social investment. Social care previously entrusted to family or friends became part of state welfare. The rapid economic growth of most European countries produced higher earnings and consumption. These in turn were taxed, yielding higher tax revenues without any increase in tax rates.

During the 1970s, European welfare states ran into a crisis (OECD 1981). This took two forms: loss of finance and loss of consent. When economic growth slowed in the mid-1970s, because of a world recession caused by an increase in oil prices, automatic revenue growth was no longer available. Either taxes had to be increased – which voters were resisting – services would have to be cut or states would run a deficit. This latter course could not be sustained in the long run. In James O'Connor's phrase of 1973, there was a 'fiscal crisis of the state', in which services had become politically and economically indispensable but could no longer be financed painlessly through public mechanisms.

At this time, many citizens started to become ambivalent about state welfare. At one level, they had come to take for granted high-quality health and education services, and income support in times of sickness, unemployment or old age. At another, they resented the power of welfare bureaucracies and sought more freedom of choice. Many people – around 20 per cent of the workforce in some countries – depended upon welfare state jobs for their livelihood; but the 80 per cent who did not had less reason to challenge political programmes promising more to the private sector.

In the early 1980s voters experimented with a variety of governments and broke with many political patterns of the post-war years. Britain elected a Conservative government in 1979 which, against evidence of a lack of consent to its social programmes, won office again in 1983 and 1987. France returned a Socialist government (with a Communist health minister) in 1982 but dismissed it in 1986. West Germany stayed with the Social Democrats throughout the 1970s but then swung Conservative in 1983. Italy flirted with the Communists in the late 1970s but had governments dominated by the Christian Democrats throughout the period. Spain's new democracy embraced socialism of a right-wing kind. Norway, Sweden and Denmark had periods of Conservative-dominated governments for the first time in decades. Many governments had hopes or rhetoric of restructuring the welfare state, but nearly all of them left the social policies of their nation intact when they departed from office.

By the mid-1980s, Europe had entered a post-crisis state. Economic growth had recovered and inflation had been sharply reduced. Unemployment was a serious problem, but the earnings of those in jobs were higher than ever. No longer could social scientists speak of a crisis of the welfare state which has yet to be resolved. Whether a lasting new stability had replaced it, however, was less clear. It is only by putting recent experience in the context of the growth of the welfare state that we can understand the challenges it now faces and assess its viability into the 1990s.

THE HISTORICAL ROOTS OF THE WELFARE STATE

Recent writing on the welfare state (Wilensky 1975; Flora and Heidenheimer 1981; Flora 1981, 1985) has emphasised that it must be seen as an aspect of the national development of European states. The definition of national boundaries in the nineteenth century, the decline of agricultural employment, the birth of industrial capitalism, the emergence of the trade union movement, the extension of the franchise and the birth of mass political parties – all were part of an interconnected process that led to the first social policies. Governments needed to win the consent of an industrial workforce and 'reproduce' a reasonably healthy and educated population. Social policies were tangible offerings to the electorate from parties in all parts of the political spectrum. Over time, social policies became an intrinsic part of the social and economic structure of Western nations, surviving changes of regimes and even wars. For instance, the present-day social insurance schemes of West Germany and Italy inherited changes made in the Nazi and Fascist period.

European thinking on the Welfare State, especially in West Germany, has taken a theoretical position influenced by critical sociology. Early in the century, Max Weber spoke of 'life chances' (Flora 1986; I, xv) in which social policy alters the structures through which individuals obtain possessions, a position in life and personal fulfilment. Later writers have viewed the entire social and political order as a system. For instance, Claus Offe's book of essays *Contradictions of the Welfare State* (1984) sees welfare state institutions as instruments of co-ordination and management, guiding capitalism through its crises and trying to bring the economic, political, and social systems into some sort of harmony. As his title suggests, Offe is pessimistic about whether this can be achieved. 'Decommodification' (the weakening of the value of labour and capital in the economic market by state regulation) undercuts the premises of the Western economic order. A system designed to make capitalism work paralyses it. A similarly wide-ranging approach marks the work of other German gurus like Jurgen Habermas and Niklas Luhmann.

British writing (notably by Richard Titmuss and T. H. Marshall), sets a quite different tone. It emphasises the way that social policies can enhance social solidarity and improve the quality of social values. Titmuss drew a distinction between 'residual' and 'institutional' welfare, the former dealing with the casualties of capitalism, the latter integrating social welfare into the fabric of society. In this view, the perception of social need alongside economic wealth inspires altruistic behaviour which underwrites public consent for 'social rights' which go beyond the individual's position before the state. This is guaranteed by sound and fair administrative procedures. Many British writers admire welfare systems (Mishra calls them 'integrated' (1984; Table 4.1)) in which there is bargaining between corporate interests such as employers, trade unions, and the professions. But the tradition in most European countries is of a far more pluralistic and conflict-based approach.

A further strand, derived from Catholic theology, sees the welfare state as a promoter of social solidarity through intermediary bodies like the church and the family. It tries to relate the operation of state welfare to the moral position of the individual on society. The building-up of state institutions is seen as artificial, and subversive of natural human motivations which are more than a calculation of costs and benefits. This has influenced Christian Democracy, notably in Italy, West Germany and the Netherlands. There is nothing quite comparable to it in Britain and the United States; it is not necessarily a conservative force, for it may involve generous social expenditures, especially on education and family benefits.

All of these positions have had some influence in the history of European social policy. In some countries, the welfare state is associated with left-wing governments, but in most it predates their entry into power and was indeed designed to keep them out of it. The welfare state is conventionally stated to start in Germany with Bismarck's proposal for an insurance scheme for sickness in 1881. This was part of his attempt to demonstrate that conservative as well as socialist political forces could respond to the needs of the urban industrial workforce. It led to the enactment of insurance schemes covering sickness, invalidity and old age during the 1880s, consolidated in 1911 (Alber 1986: 6). This set the principle that employees and employers should contribute to the schemes as a kind of price-tag for being part of the capitalist economic system. Benefits should be earned, not handed out; the state should regulate and subvent, but not administer directly.

Flora and Alber (1981: 54) identify four stages in the extension of eligibility to social insurance. A gradual introduction before 1914 was followed by an extension between the wars which added new risks (especially unemployment) and new groups (especially families). The completion of coverage took place in most states soon after the Second World War, and in the 1960s there was a consolidation in which schemes were unified and broadened, to express some idea of national solidarity. But the insurance principle had not lost its force. Other European states have gone less far than Britain in the direction of income maintenance by the state solely on the basis of need.

Education and health services have different traditions. Public education systems had taken over from the church during the nineteenth century (Germany in 1872, France in 1886), being seen in most places as part of the framework of the state rather than as a social policy. But it was well into the twentieth century before state provision superseded charities in health and social services. Insurance schemes extended their coverage over the whole working population, but entitlement to benefit depended on contributions rather than need. Health services never came under full state control, and involve in most countries the independence of doctors and financial contributions from patients.

SOCIAL POLICY AND NATIONAL RESOURCES

An international study published in 1985 showed that in 1981 social policy consumed between 24 and 38 per cent of national resources in European nations (Table 1). The definition of 'social' includes public expenditure on education, health and welfare, pensions, and other income maintenance (but not housing or tax reliefs). This ratio has been increasing throughout the post-war period, but it only began to take off during the 1960s. The decade from 1965 to 1975 was crucial in most countries. The biggest spenders are four medium-sized nations – Belgium, the Netherlands, Sweden, and Denmark. West Germany, France, and Italy cluster at about 30 per cent, well ahead of Britain on 25 per cent.

This spending is a major contribution to total public expenditure as a proportion of the national economy (measured by gross domestic product (GDP)). On the latest figures, for 1985, this is 52 per cent for Western Europe as a whole, but the range is wide. At the top, four countries stand out: Sweden at 65 per cent, and the Netherlands, Denmark and Italy at 58–60 per cent. West Germany and Britain are below average at 47–48 per cent (*OECD Economic Outlook*, June 1987:

Table 1 Social expenditure as a percentage of GDP, Western European nations, 1960 and 1981

	1960	1981	Elasticity	
			1960–75	1975–81*
Belgium	17.4	37.6	2.1	3.6
Netherlands	16.2	36.1	2.3	0.8
Sweden	15.4	33.4	2.0	4.7
Denmark	n/a	33.3	n/a	2.5
West Germany	20.5	31.5	1.8	0.8
France	13.4	29.5	1.6	2.2
Italy	16.8	29.1	1.7	1.6
Ireland	11.7	28.4	2.1	2.0
Austria	17.9	27.7	1.5	1.7
Norway	11.7	27.1	2.4	1.1
Finland	15.4	25.9	1.7	1.7
United Kingdom	13.9	23.7	2.2	1.8
Switzerland	7.7	14.9	2.2	2.6
Average (unweighted)	14.8	29.1	2.0	2.1

* The relationship of average annual social expenditure growth to GDP growth in two periods – 1960–75 and 1975–81. For example, 1.0 represents growth at the same rate, 2.0 social expenditure growing twice as fast as GDP.

Source: Based on OECD (1985: Tables 1 and 2).

Table R8). But if we exclude transfer payments spent by individuals (such as pensions) and consider only government final consumption (such as education and health services and defence), two countries stand out: Sweden at 27.5 per cent of GDP, Denmark at 25 per cent. The European average is 19 per cent (Table R6). On the other hand, the Netherlands and France have the most generous social security transfers. Three European nations have worryingly large public sector deficits – Italy at over 12 per cent of GDP, and the Netherlands and Belgium at over 6 per cent. But in all three cases these proportions are on a downward track in 1987–88.

Table 2 shows how the social expenditure share of GDP increased on average from 17 per cent in 1960 to 27.5 per cent in 1975. Thereafter growth slowed, reaching 30 per cent in 1981. Growth in social expenditure has been much faster than in gross national product: the 'elasticities' (Table 1) are almost all greater than 1. Two countries – Belgium and Italy – stand out as increasing their relative expansion after 1975. But three – West Germany, the Netherlands, and Norway – have held the rise in social spending to less than economic growth.

Table 2 The slowing of expenditure growth, OECD Europe

	1960–75	1975–81
Social expenditure as % GDP, start of period	16.9	27.5
Annual average percentage growth rate	7.3	4.6
Of which:		
more costly services	0.4	0.7
Real growth	6.8	3.9
Of which:		
More people	1.8	0.8
Wider coverage	1.0	0.2
Real improvement in services	4.6	3.3
Social expenditure as % GDP, end of period	27.5	30.0

Source: Based on Colin Gillian and Richard Hemming, 'Social expenditure in the United Kingdom in a comparative context' in Rudolf Klein and Michael O'Higgins (eds), *The Future of Welfare* (Oxford: Basil Blackwell, 1985).

However, Table 2 notes that much growth was accounted for by an increased population or a wider coverage. These have now slowed, leaving the annual real improvement in services at 4.6 per cent in the earlier period, 3.3 in the latter.

There are four major components of total social spending: education, health, pensions, and other social security. Education is less important that it once was: its share fell from 26 per cent in 1960 to 21 per cent in 1981. The other categories all slightly increased their share: in 1981 pensions were 35 per cent and health 21 per cent (OECD 1985: Table 3). All these categories have shown growth in real expenditure; it is the rate of increase that differs. The main lesson from this is that on average only about 40 per cent of social spending is on service in kind – that is, delivered to clients by employees (such as teachers, nurses and doctors) whose pay is the main item of expenditure. The 'in kind' proportion varies (1981) from 31 per cent in Austria, 34 in Belgium, and 37 in West Germany, to 47 in Britain and 55 per cent in Ireland.

There has been a similar increase in public employment but rather different experiences between the European states. Table 3 shows that in every case the proportion of the workforce employed on public social policy at least doubled between 1950 and 1980. But in Sweden it increased nearly four times, to the point where one worker in five is in this sector. The principal occupational groups are teachers

Table 3 Public social employment as percentage of workforce

	1950	1981
Sweden	4.8	20.7
United Kingdom	5.6	14.2
France	3.4	12.3
West Germany	4.5	9.7
Italy	2.5	9.3

Source: Adapted from Rose (1985: Table 1.5).

and nurses. West Germany and Italy stand at less than half the Swedish level, with Britain and France in between.

Despite this evidence of growth, we should be wary of putting political interpretations on it, such as that expenditure is too high or out of control. Much spending is on transfer payments (notably pensions) which individuals are free to spend as they wish. Moreover, public social programmes bear upon only a part of social experience. Religion, the family and the law have a greater influence upon social behaviour; foreign, defence and economic policy are pre-eminent in the actions of states and the fate of governments. International league tables of public spending are of doubtful political salience, because of measurement problems and because the strong national identities of European states limit the place accorded to international comparisons in political debate.

THE GOVERNMENT OF SOCIAL POLICY

One result of the way that the welfare state has grown is that it does not have a uniform administrative structure. Only in very few countries are all the main services paid for out of taxes and delivered by public employees. Britain and Sweden come closest to pure welfare states in this respect. Other nations have mixed patterns often dominated by insurance schemes. There is no need to dwell on the administration of social policy in the major countries, but we should note briefly some salient points.

First, the role of central government is rather limited. It employs teachers in France and, in most countries, the central administration of social security. When effective regional government exists, social policy responsibilities are an important part of their power: they run education in West Germany and health in Italy. Finally, local government is in most places the direct employer in education and social services and often of hospitals. Local administration is usually subject to much central guidance and financing.

Taking these service by service, education stands outside the usual welfare state services, because it was accepted early by Conservatives as a precondition for national solidarity, requiring to be inside the public sector. It also tends to be a rather centralised service: in France this is formally so, with teachers and civil servants liable to work anywhere in the country (though it was never true that the Education Minister in Paris could look at his watch and know what was being taught throughout France at that moment). In West Germany education is the responsibility of the *Länder*; in Britain the influence of central ministries and the teaching profession is strong. In most countries it is an élitist service, selecting schoolchildren for either an intellectual (*Gymnasien* in West Germany, *lycées* in France) or a technical education. Britain and Sweden are the only major countries to have reorganised their secondary education on comprehensive, non-selective lines. The incomplete evidence on private provision suggests that there is virtually none in Sweden, the Netherlands, and Italy, but that in France and West Germany around 10 per cent of secondary pupils are educated privately.

In health, most countries operate through insurance schemes which both reimburse health care charges and pay sickness benefit. Usually, patients pay doctors direct and are reimbursed for less than the full cost. But Britain (1948), Denmark (1973), and Italy (1980) have National Health Services without insurance funds and with free access for all. Whatever the structure, the position of doctors as free professionals tends to be guaranteed, and the regulation of the relationship between doctor, patient and government is a perennial problem. The private share of health expenditure in Western European countries is of some significance: it varies between 8 per cent in Belgium and 28 per cent in Austria.

In social security, all nations have insurance schemes in which contributions paid while in work guarantee an income when work is prevented by sickness, accident, old age, and, in most countries, unemployment. Employers and employees contribute heavily to these schemes, so adding to personal and corporate taxation; for instance, in France contributions are 40 per cent of state revenue. The main variable is whether schemes cover all occupational groups (as in Britain or Sweden), or draw distinctions between blue-collar, white-collar, and agricultural workers and public and private sectors (as in France and West Germany). In many countries, civil servants have a privileged position.

Most benefits are earnings-related. Sweden and Britain both introduced flat-rate pensions in 1948, but later political pressure added an earnings-related element (Sweden in 1960, Britain in 1975). Annual indexation in line with the cost of living has become the rule – in West Germany in 1957, Italy in 1969. The standard pension given a full contribution record is often high: 67.5 per cent of average earnings in West Germany and 80 per cent in Italy, but the actual average payment is less (in 1980 47 per cent in West Germany, 39 per cent in Britain, 32 per cent in Sweden, and 31 per cent in Italy (Flora 1986–88, Vols 1,2)). The coverage of invalidity pensions is notably variant – in 1978 8 per cent of the population in France, Sweden and Britain but 13 per cent in the Netherlands, 15 per cent in West Germany and 18 per cent in Italy (Stone 1985: Table 1). This is a reminder that need is never absolute but is an expression of political and professional judgement.

There are three weak links in European income maintenance. First, unemployment is often treated separately and less favourably. Typically, it covers only a limited period of unemployment (such as one year), leaving the long-term unemployment dependent on means-tested social assistance. Secondly, child benefit or family allowances are a poor relation. They were introduced for all children in Sweden in 1948 but not until 1974 in West Germany or Italy. France, by contrast, has always encouraged families by a high level of child benefit. Thirdly, social assistance, the successor to the Poor Law, provides an inadequate substitute for those not covered by insurance schemes. Britain's income support system is a rather generous and comprehensive one by European standards.

Housing has often not been regarded as a public social service at all, and it shows the most complex patterns of public–private mix. Only Britain has a high (but now diminishing) public rented sector; elsewhere, public support is channelled through rent subsidies to tenants and loan subsidies to private builders or co-operative associations. An example of the latter is *Neue Heimat* in Germany, the subject of a financial scandal in 1986. Public expenditure on housing and the regulation of the housing market have in general been declining. The emphasis tends to be on owner-occupation – usually accompanied by generous tax reliefs – but in many places the supply of reasonably priced housing is inadequate. Governments seem to have found it difficult to find a satisfactory role in the provision of the most important item of capital investment in people's lives.

Two countries, West Germany and Sweden, have made labour market services an integral part of their social policy through industrial training and the regulation of labour practices. Sweden's National Labour Market Board (1948) has sought to replace unemployment compensation with a more positive policy. There is still no comprehensive unemployment insurance in Sweden. This contrasts, for instance, with the high earning replacement ratio in the Netherlands. In West Germany, the Federal Labour Market Organisation has a similar though less ambitious policy. Italy has tried another, more opportunistic, approach. The rate of unemployment benefit is very low, leading to the system of *Cassa Intergrazione Guadagni* (CIG), which pays people for working short-time or not at all while leaving them on a firm's books: at its peak in 1984 this was supporting half a million workers.

VARIABLES IN THE POLITICS OF WELFARE STATES

In seeking to understand the recent history of these policies, several cross-cutting variables need to be isolated. The primary questions are of cost and affordability. Despite Mrs Thatcher's preferred analogy, social policy cannot be approached in terms of housekeeping economics. There is no ultimate level of income support, taxation or public expenditure. But two variables may cause social policies to be economically destabilising. The first is the 'relative price effect', in which wages or benefits rise faster than the rate for economy as a whole. This is a particular problem where there are many public employees in social policy whose wages drift upwards without their productivity increasing. As Table 2 shows, this has eaten into real growth, especially in the late 1970s, but in the 1980s most governments have contained it by resisting public sector wage demands.

The second is the 'Dutch disease', deriving from the experience of the Netherlands, in which social expenditures (in this case financed by oil and gas revenues) become so generous that they crowd out industrial investment and become a barrier to economic adjustment. Certainly, from a low base the Netherlands became one of the world's biggest social spenders. Most of these were transfer payments (passing money to individuals for them to spend), creating problems of work incentives. Economic analysis can provide no firm guide in these cases, though there is a long tradition of hostility to social welfare by free-market economists. The answer lies in the self-regulating character of the political system, in which a 'welfare backlash' signals the opinion of the 'middle mass' that welfare has gone too far.

A further issue is that of professional and corporate power. The structure of social policy becomes an important part of the way that governments accommodate important groupings in society. In Sweden, the influence of the trade union confederation (LO) has been crucial in entrenching generous social benefits and extending economic democracy (such as workers' shareholdings in the 'wage-earner funds'). Throughout Europe, teachers and doctors are major interest groups. Teachers were an important component of the Socialist parliamentary majority in France in 1982, and doctors have secured high earnings out of socialised health care. A possible exception is Italy, where partisan control and clientelism are much stronger, to the point where various public offices are in the nomination of one party or another.

Political scientists are particularly interested in the role of party government in social policy; does it alter according to the political colour of the government, or does it develop in a cross-party way? The evidence favours the latter view. This is because social policies grow incrementally and to an extent irreversibly (once the age of retirement or of school-leaving, and the rules about inflation-linking, have been set); and because all governments have to prove their credentials in terms of bread-and-butter issues. The most politicised system is Italy, where the imminence of elections is a key element in the improvement of social policy. It seems that, while left-wing governments such as West Germany's Social Democrats in the early 1970s put more effort into increasing social expenditure independently of economic growth, right-wing parties have shared in the expansion of state welfare.

The overriding social problem for most European governments in the 1980s has been unemployment (Table 4). All European countries experienced an increase in unemployment during the 1970s from a starting base where it seemed a trivial problem (except in Italy). The reasons for this were two relatively predictable developments. The size of the labour force was increased by the coming of age of those born during the baby boom of the 1960s, adding to the greater economic participation of married women. At the same time, many industries were either reducing or failing to increase their employment levels. But some countries have had markedly better records than others. Spain is on its own in terms of the severity of the problem, but Britain, Belgium, Italy, France, and the Netherlands have had periods of double-digit unemployment in the 1980s. West Ger-

Table 4 Unemployment in major European Countries

% of labour force	1971	1980	1986
Spain	3.1	11.2	21.0
United Kingdom	3.6	5.0	11.5
Belgium	2.1	8.8	10.8
Italy	5.3	7.5	10.5
France	2.6	5.9	10.3
Netherlands	1.3	6.0	9.9
Denmark	0.7	6.5	7.8
West Germany	0.9	3.0	6.9
Finland	2.2	4.6	5.4
Austria	1.3	1.9	3.6 (85)
Sweden	2.5	2.0	2.7
Norway	1.5	1.7	1.9

Source: Based on *OECD Economic Outlook*, June 1987, Tables 20 and R12; *OECD Historical Statistics 1960–84*, Table 2.15, *1960–80*, Table 2.14.

many has a poor record by its past standards. But Sweden, Austria, and Norway have contained unemployment to under 5 per cent through a combination of economic growth, retraining, and higher public employment. The Swedish example has attracted particular interest, as it treats unemployment as a central economic circumstance for the individual, to be prevented by social policies, and not just a by-product of economic policy.

Many would see the ultimate aim of social policy as being the relief of poverty, but it is no accident that the concept and its measurement are bedevilled by confusion. We must distinguish between absolute poverty – lack of resources to buy a minimum subsistence – and relative poverty – falling short of average income levels. Many British and Scandinavian writers have emphasised the latter approach, but it remains controversial for it implies that 'the poor will always be with us' even as income levels rise. The concept embraces aspects of social alienation which may not only be caused by lack of income. The European Community has promoted comparative studies of the problem of poverty, so far rather inconclusively. For what it is worth, one recent analysis found that the proportion of households receiving less that 60 per cent of average income was 28 per cent in France, 16.5 per cent in Germany, 14 per cent in the Britain, and 9.1 per cent in the Netherlands (Walker *et al.* 1984: Table 2.25). This suggests that states with a social security system uneven in its generosity according to occupation and employment record run the risk of leaving many households well short of the income of the average.

Here we should mention the 'black economy', or economic activity that does not enter into official statistics – mostly paid work that is concealed from the tax authorities. By definition, it cannot be measured accurately, but it seems to be most substantial in Italy at perhaps 25 per cent of GNP. This makes some people better off than they seem, but it also marginalises them into a sector without rights of social citizenship like pension and sickness benefits. The social implications of the black economy are complex, because it may also give people more control of their lives, working for themselves or in a small group rather than for a large organisation.

This relates to income distribution. Once the notion of the welfare state was extended (first in Scandinavia) from social protection to economic democracy, one implicit objective became the reduction of differentials between income groups. The state plays an important part in this process, for it both gives and takes away. In addition to market income (earnings from work), people receive direct transfers (like pensions and child benefits) and services in kind (education, health). But they also pay taxes (on income and consumption). A high level of transfers and taxes may involve much money changing hands without many being better off. Summarising the inadequate cross-national evidence, it appears that tax–benefits systems are only moderately redistributive. Taxes, taken as a whole, do not transfer much from the rich to the poor. Services in kind are often consumed disproportionately by the middle class. The most important shift is through direct transfers from the economically active to the inactive (especially pensioners). Sweden stands out for the level and relative success of its transfer system (Ringen 1987: 174–5).

A final question relates to social disturbance. Part of the function of the welfare state has been the management of social relationships within a nation. During the first half of the twentieth century many European states had tense and often violent conflicts between social and occupational groups. After quiescence in the 1950s, these flared up in the late 1960s, with student unrest and industrial trouble. These protests were often bought off by more generous social benefits. It is noteworthy that the economic recession after the mid-1970s was overcome much more peaceably. Class conflict has diminished, but qualities of tolerance have scarcely improved. Foreign workers have inspired resentment (notably *Gastarbeiter* in West Germany). Racial tension became explicit in France in 1986 with the election to Parliament of deputies from Jean-Marie Le Pen's National Front. Ironically, the generosity of social transfers to economically weak groups can promote resentment of this kind.

POLITICAL RESPONSES IN THE 1980s

The crisis of welfare is the conjunction of these problems with a slowdown of economic growth. But has it led to a dismantling of the welfare state? The evidence discussed earlier does not suggest a major retrenchment. However, a pattern does emerge in the early 1980s of a political acceptance that benefits were too generous. For the first time, governments with a policy of cuts have not necessarily suffered an electoral penalty. In a technical sense, it is easy to trim the value of benefits without disturbing their structure. Indexation of benefits or pay rises to employees can be restricted; earnings replacement rates of benefits can be reduced; eligibility in terms of contributions paid can be tightened; and user charges for services can be raised. These have been tried in many countries, notably the Netherlands, Belgium, and Denmark. Where financial deficits have threatened the solvency of social security schemes, as in France in the mid-1980s, there has been a political consensus for action and increased contributions.

A particularly interesting case is the Netherlands. A left-wing government in 1973 coincided with the peak of gas revenues. By 1982 the country had the most generous income maintenance system in Europe. For instance, unemployment benefit replaced 80 per cent of income for six months, and 75 per cent for the next two years. In 1982 a right-wing government led by Ruud Lubbers came to power. In 1983 it trimmed these replacement rates, and forced a 3 per cent cut in welfare benefits and public sector pay. It was returned to office in 1986.

Similarly in Belgium. As Table 1 showed, this had risen to the top of the social spending league by 1981. A succession of short-lived governments had been preoccupied by the language issue and had conceded welfare benefits to defuse it. By 1981 the public sector deficit was 16 per cent of GDP. In December 1981 a new right-wing government led by Wilfried Martens took office and reduced the indexation of benefits and public sector wages; Martens remained in office until the end of 1987.

Other examples may be cited. The new Socialist government in France increased benefits on coming to office in 1981, but embarked upon an austerity programme after a second devaluation of the franc in 1982. Its defeat by the right in 1986 was only a narrow one. In Italy, the Socialist-led government of Bettino Craxi from 1983 to 1987 had, by Italian standards, modest success in containing the demands of the public sector. In 1986, a referendum voted against the maintenance of the full *scala mobile* system of wage indexation. In West Germany, retrenchment started in the mid-1970s, a testament to the German preoccupation with economic stability. After the election of 1983, benefits were trimmed further by the Christian Democratic-led government of Helmut Kohl, which was re-elected in 1987. In Denmark, Poul Schlüter's Conservative-led welfare-cutting government was returned in 1987. And, of course, the Thatcher government in Britain won impressive election victories in 1983 and 1987. The only clear case where a welfare-cutting government was removed from office is Sweden, where the Social Democrats were returned to power in 1982.

Another of the great policy responses of the 1980s is privatisation, the withdrawal of the state from the direct production of service. Privatisation can mean many things, and usually less of a change in patterns of consumption and production than in those of distribution and costs. Many European states – Britain, France, West Germany, Italy, Austria – have privatisation programmes which are effectively withdrawing the state from profitable industrial enterprise. The disposal of shares involves their marketing to individual shareholders in a way claimed by right-wing governments to extend 'popular capitalism'. This notion has taken off in Britain since the successful flotation of British Telecom in 1984, and a comparable programme began in France in 1986. In this process the socialised values of the welfare state begin to lose their resonance. But wholesale privatisation of social policies is much less practicable. Most European social policies cannot be privatised because they already represent a delicate compromise between social interests, and most European countries safeguard private provision, especially where the churches are involved. Even industrial privatisation was checked by the sharp fall in share prices in October 1987.

THE DEEPER PROBLEMS OF THE WELFARE STATE

In recent years, new kinds of writing about the welfare state have paralleled our understanding of it as a concept. Much of the older writing was relentlessly optimistic about human nature, or read like a government report; it prompted the German sociologist, Ralf Dahrendorf, to ask in a book review in 1980, 'Must social policy be boring?' Now the literature is richer and less naive. Politically, it is prepared to recognise the tactical considerations that make governments favour some policies over others (for instance, manipulating unemployment to fit in with the cycle of elections). Sociologically,, there is a willingness to consider concepts like fulfilment, happiness and love: for instance, Erik Allardt presents, alongside indicators of expenditure and coverage, ones on friendship, political participation, leisure-time activities, and even 'relations to nature' (like the frequency of country walks) (Allardt 1986). This approach is also prepared to consider seriously why, for instance, the suicide rate in Norway is half that of other Nordic countries.

Above all, there are analyses of the welfare state as a cause of problems rather than a cure for them. The social state may be both inefficient and oppressive. In West Germany, a growing body of literature is preoccupied with concepts like duty, obligation and practical ability in everyday life. These may be threatened by one-sided transfers from the state, which give generously but demand in return certain norms of action and of relations between producers and consumers. In Finland, J. P. Roos has analysed the autobiographies of Finns to uncover a great deal of alienation among the 'new middle class'. These children of the welfare state were, in the phrase coined by Neil Kinnock, the first in their family for a thousand generations to go to university and are now in welfare state jobs like teachers and social workers. Uprooted from their family backgrounds, they feel a sense of loss and disruption despite, or even because of, being cradled in the welfare state. In short, people are thrown into a world they did not create themselves and which limits the possibilities in their lives.

So there is a choice, both intellectual and political. In one view, the welfare state has regained its stability: its services are valued and can be afforded. Survey evidence in many countries suggests a solid consensus in favour of the welfare state despite some wavering in the 1970s. The most notorious instance of a taxpayer's backlash – the 15 per cent vote won by the Progress Party in the 1973 Danish election – has not been repeated in any national poll.

The context has stabilised in resources terms, too. The pressure of demographic change in education, health and pensions has slowed in the period analysed by the Organisation for Economic Co-operation and Development (OECD), and it will be into the twenty-first century before the ageing of the population becomes a major issue. The OECD (1985: 49) makes the sometimes overlooked point that prosperous nations at a time of economic growth should have no difficulty in affording their social policies, especially now that relative prices have been brought under control. To a large extent, Europe has come through the instability of the late 1970s and early 1980s.

The alternative view is that Western Europe is entering a new kind of crisis in which social protection will rest on an individual's own resources and economic position. The leading edge of this is in Britain, where the Thatcher government has ambitious plans to give more discretion to individual parents and tenants in the management of state housing and education. Public disquiet with education policies was demonstrated in France in 1984, when street protests in Paris against plans to amalgamate private schools with the state system led to the withdrawal of the plans and a more conservative school curriculum. The Thatcher government in Britain has the political power to push through radical challenges to the welfare consensus. But there is little evidence in the rest of Europe that such bold reappraisals of social policy could be carried through. In particular, coalition government is a powerful brake on any change that might harm the economic position of important interest groups.

There are also new forms of social relationships. Female participation in the workforce has continued to grow even with high unemployment. In Europe 49 per cent of the female working-age population are economically active, but this ranges from 77 per cent in Sweden to 41 per cent in the Netherlands and Italy, and 33 per cent in Spain (*OECD Historical Statistics 1980–84*, Table 2.8). In Sweden, this has been made possible by a highly developed version of what Martin Rein has called the 'social welfare industry'. One-third of women work in the public social services, often caring for other people's children. The feminist movement has forced a redefinition of relations between the genders, and contributed to the spread of 'post-industrial values' in which economic power will seem less important than the quality of social life.

The ultimate viability of the welfare state is guaranteed by the fact that around one-third of economic activity passes through it. Protecting it is the surest way that a political party can entrench its position with the electorate. This is true in both clientelistic political systems like Italy, and those based on a balancing of social interests like the Netherlands. The taxpayers' revolt of the 1970s was an ephemeral matter, for an immediate sense of grievance expressed in a protest vote cannot compare with the guarantees of social protection which the welfare state has extended to all citizens. Economically, too, the disruptions of the 1970s were not the start of a long slump. Oil prices fell, inflation was conquered. By the mid-1980s, it was possible once again to take a more detached view of the welfare state, in terms of the quality of social life it was producing.

But when we move out of the political and economic sphere, questions are less easy to answer. Increasingly, the form of the welfare state, its institutions and rules, has become detached from the substance of welfare (what people feel and experience about their security and well-being). The former is partly a matter of playing games with political tactics and bureaucratic rules. Every position can be defended and justified, especially when its consequences cannot yet be known. Values and qualities may be lost, not least because politicians and officials may lack contact with the social circumstances that underlie their policies. In order to treat issues politically, the preferences and needs of individuals must be aggregated. The political level may become quite blind to the failures and unintended consequences of social policies.

Europeans are worriers about both the character of their societies and the proper role of their governments. Until the middle of the twentieth century, basic questions of national and personal survival were at the forefront of their minds. The unprecedented peace and prosperity of the post-war era opened up concerns about welfare and social functioning. Phenomena of the 1980s like drug abuse, AIDS, football hooliganism, the destruction of forests by pollution, higher divorce rates, and the disintegration of the family all pose questions about the kind of society we have created after decades of high social spending. The crisis of the 1975–85 decade was on the familiar ground of economies and politics, and it concluded with an acceptance that the welfare state had grown to its limits but should in its essential form be maintained. The next crisis may be one about the sociological reality of what the welfare state has done to human beings, and it will be far less easy for politicians and voters to resolve.

REFERENCES AND FURTHER READING

Academic experts, let alone students, find it difficult to produce satisfactory comparative accounts of European social policy. Data are hard to obtain and compare; national definitions of what constitutes social policy vary; it is difficult to have a grasp of both factual detail and broader political trends. Two useful and in many ways pioneering accounts are Heidenheimer *et al.* (1983) and Jones (1985), but they are not fully systematic and have uneven detail. A stimulating edited collection, dealing with both theoretical issues and the factual position is Rose and Shiratori (1986); a similar approach but less successful overall is Eisenstadt and Ahimeir (1985). Mishra (1984) is a well-presented, admirably clear argument in the British tradition. John Keane's introduction to Offe (1984) is a way into the necessarily complex German literature.

Comparative statistics have been improved by the work of the OECD (OECD 1981, 1985). These are official publications, though, and the treatment is dry. Rose's volume of public employment (1985) contains much of interest on the operation of the welfare state. More interesting still is the work of Peter Flora (1981 and 1985 for concise accounts). Flora and Heidenheimer (1981) broke new ground in the rigour of its attempt to obtain comparative data and its attention to political and sociological change. Flora subsequently led the Growth of Limits project (published in five volumes 1986–88), which has long country chapters for twelve Western European nations (sadly excluding France) and a comparative volume by Peter Flora. Volume 4 is the data handbook for the set and gives a factual account of the government and financing of the twelve Welfare States in the early 1980s.

For current developments, social policy is rather ill-served. The *Journal of Social Policy* and *West European Politics* have some articles; and *The Economist* is better than most newspapers in noting social policy developments, especially in its country surveys.

REFERENCES

Alber, Jens (1986) 'Germany', in Flora (1986) Vol. 2, pp. 1–154.

Allardt, Erik (1986) 'The civil conception of the Welfare State in Scandinavia', in Rose and Shiratori (1986), pp. 107–125.

Eisenstadt, S. M and Ahimeir, Ora (1985) *The Welfare State and its Aftermath* (London: Croom Helm).

Ferrera, Maurizio (1986) 'Italy', in Flora (1986), vol. 2, pp. 385–458.

Flora, Peter (1981) 'Solution or source of crisis? The Welfare State in historical perspective', in W. J. Mommsen (ed.), *The Emergence of the Welfare State in Britain and Germany* (London: Croom Helm), pp 343–389.

Flora, Peter (1985) 'On the history and current problems of the welfare state', in Eisenstadt and Ahimeir (1985), pp. 11–30.

Flora, Peter (ed.) (1986–88) *Growth to Limits*, vols 1–5 (Berlin: de Gruyter).

Flora, Peter and Alber, Jens (1981) 'Modernisation, democratisation and the development of welfare states in Western Europe', in Flora and Heidenheimer (1981) pp 37–80.

Flora, Peter and Heidenheimer, Arnold J. (eds) (1981) *The Development of Welfare States in Europe and America* (London: Transaction Books).

Heidenheimer, Arnold J., Heclo, Hugh and Adams, Caroline Teich (1983) *Comparative Public Policy* (London: Macmillan).

Jones, Catherine (1985) *Patterns of Social Policy* (London: Tavistock).

Mishra, Ramesh (1984) *The Welfare State in Crisis* (Brighton: Wheatsheaf).

Offe, Claus (1984) *Contradictions of the Welfare State* (London: Hutchinson).

OECD (1981) *The Welfare State in Crisis*. (Paris: OECD).

OECD (1985) *Social Expenditure 1960–1990* (Paris: OECD).

Ringen, Stein (1987) *The Possibility of Politics* (Oxford: Clarendon Press).

Rose, Richard (ed.) (1985) *Public Employment in Western Nations* (Cambridge: Cambridge University Press).

Rose, Richard and Shiratori, Rei (eds) (1986) *The Welfare State East and West* (New York: Oxford University Press).

Stone, Deborah (1985) *The Disabled State* (London: Macmillan).

Walker, Robert, Lawson, Roger and Townsend, Peter (eds) (1984) *Responses to Poverty: Lessons from Europe* (London: Heinemann).

Wilensky, Harold (1975) *The Welfare State and Equality* (Berkeley: University of California Press).

CHAPTER THREE
The politics of unemployment
Stan Taylor

As the Second World War drew to a close, political leaders throughout Western Europe began to turn their attention to the forthcoming peace. Many thought that, once the inevitable post-war boom was over, there would be a return to the conditions of the 1930s, i.e. stagnating capitalism and mass unemployment. Such a development would, it was feared, undermine political stability in the region in so far as people who had fought and sacrificed for a better world would never again tolerate millions out of work: as *The Economist* (2 October 1943) put it: 'If liberal democracy is not compatible with full employment, then it is liberal democracy that will go.'

This possible scenario focused political attention upon the contention, usually associated with the British economist John Maynard Keynes, that state intervention in the economy was necessary to secure full employment. In a series of publications culminating in 1936 with *The General Theory of Employment, Interest and Money* (Keynes, 1967), Keynes had argued that unemployment was centrally caused by a flaw inherent in the capitalist system, namely the absence of any mechanism to ensure that consumption and investment would generate a level of aggregate demand sufficient to support full employment. The remedy was, Keynes suggested, for the state to step in and assume this role, using its power over taxation, spending, and interest rates to maintain an appropriate level of demand.

Keynes's ideas had, in general, attracted a sceptical response in the 1930s, largely because they involved governments in deliberately unbalancing their budgets to finance reflation and were likely, given short-run constraints on the ability of economies to expand, to accelerate inflation. Neither of these consequences appealed to a

33

political generation which had been brought up to believe that states, like households, should balance their expenditure and revenue, and which was terrified of inflation, especially after the economic and social dangers had been so graphically illustrated by the experiences of Germany in the 1920s. However, these concerns were assuaged by the apparent success of Keynesian-type policies during the Second World War, and after 1944 this, coupled with the need to satisfy popular aspirations, led to governments, political parties, unions and resistance movements issuing declarations of intent that full employment must be the first priority of policy in the post-war era.

In the event, even after the expected post-war boom had begun to fade in the early 1950s, the commitment of Western European governments to full employment was scarcely tested for the best part of twenty years: the region as a whole enjoyed an unprecedented spell of virtually unbroken growth, which sustained the underlying demand for labour at an exceptionally high level through to the early 1970s. In this buoyant climate, the maintenance of full employment was taken for granted, demanding little more than marginal adjustments of demand by governments to forestall what, by pre-war standards, were relatively trivial cyclical downturns. Such intervention was, in the main, conducted within the framework of a budget surplus because of the fiscal dividend of growth; and, while boosts to the economy were associated with spurts of inflation, the latter was modest and regarded as the acceptable price of maintaining full employment.

The strength of the demand for labour in Western Europe in the earlier part of the post-war period can be seen from the first column of Table 5 which gives the standardised average rates of unemployment for a range of countries over the 1956–74 period. Apart from Italy with its exceptional regional problem in the backward and agrarian south of the country, the vast majority of West European states experienced unemployment rates of 2.5 per cent or less.

However, the long boom was brought to an abrupt halt in the mid-1970s following the decision of the Organisation of Petroleum Exporting Countries (OPEC) to use oil as a political weapon, which resulted in a quadrupling of oil prices in 1973–74. This hit the heavily oil-dependent West European economies hard – only Norway had its own oil flowing ashore and then in minuscule quantities – and sent them into the first large-scale recession of the post-war period. Virtually all West European governments responded to the crisis in the approved Keynesian manner by deliberately unbalancing their budgets and pumping new demand into their economies to avert the

Table 5 Standardised unemployment rates in selected Western European
countries

	1956–86 (period averages)		
	1956–74	*1975–79*	*1980–86*
Austria	2.0	1.9	3.3
Belgium	2.6	7.0	11.2
Denmark	1.8	6.5	9.1★
Finland	2.0	5.1	5.2
France	1.9	4.9	8.6
Germany	1.3	3.5	6.1
Italy	6.1	6.8	9.2†
Netherlands	1.7	5.3	10.0
Norway	2.0	1.9	2.4
Spain	2.4	5.8	17.2
Sweden	1.9	1.9	2.8
Switzerland	0.1	0.4	0.6
United Kingdom	2.9	5.8	10.6

★ National figures for the 1980s.
† Average 1980–85.

Sources: Based on Bean *et al.* (1987: 1); OECD (1987: 28–9).

threat to employment. However, as can be seen from the data on
1974–79 average unemployment rates in Table 5, only four states –
Austria, Norway, Sweden and Switzerland – succeeded in maintaining rates of unemployment comparable to those in the earlier part of
the post-war period; the others experienced average rates varying
from 3.5 per cent (West Germany) to 7.0 per cent (Belgium).

The widespread, if not total, failure of demand management in
Western Europe after 1973 prompted a reappraisal of Keynesianism,
particularly because in many countries deficit-financed reflation had
been followed not only by rising unemployment but also by accelerating inflation. This combination was not, according to
Keynesian theory, supposed to happen – unemployment should not
have risen in the first place, but even if it had, inflation should have
declined – and Keynesian economists were at something of a loss to
explain what had gone wrong and why. However, there were other
economists who believed that they had the answers; the so-called
'monetarists'.

While the origins of monetarism lay in the classical and neo-clas-
sical economics of the nineteenth and early twentieth centuries, the
term itself was coined in the late 1960s to describe the theories of a
group of economists, centred around Milton Friedman and his col-

leagues at the University of Chicago, who questioned Keynes's entire approach to economic analysis. In particular, in the present context, they challenged his ascription of unemployment to a deficiency of aggregate demand. Contrary to Keynes, the monetarists argued that there were mechanisms within the capitalist system itself which could maintain the demand for labour and so secure full employment in the sense that all who were willing to work, and who were prepared to accept what pay employers could afford, would be able to do so. From this it followed that unemployment was caused primarily by rigidities on the supply side of the labour market, in particular from a lack of incentive to work, something which reflected the generous benefits available in most countries and the acquisition by trade unions of monopoly powers in maintaining wages about the level at which employers would take on more workers. These factors, they argued, gave rise to a 'natural' rate of unemployment for each country, one that was appropriate to the degree of benefits-induced or institutional rigidity in the labour market, and which could not be permanently reduced by raising aggregate demand in the economy.

The implication of this view was that Western European governments had, since the war, been following entirely inappropriate policies that had led, via rapid and sudden expansions of the money supply ahead of the growth of output, to inflation becoming embedded in their economies, posing a threat to competitiveness and ultimately jobs. The solution was, the monetarists argued, for governments to concentrate on anti-inflationary objectives by constraining the growth of the money supply, cutting public spending, reducing budget deficits and confining action on employment to measures designed to reduce the 'natural' rate, e.g. cutting benefits and tackling union monopolies.

While, in the early 1970s, after twenty years in which full employment had seemingly been guaranteed by Keynesian policies, few politicians were prepared to take monetarism seriously, attitudes began to change following the apparent failure of demand management amid mounting unemployment and inflation in 1975–76, and in the mid- and late 1970s a number of governments made gestures in the direction of a monetarist macroeconomic stance. Most, however, fell well short of endorsing it in full. The hope was still that the problems of unemployment, inflation and budget deficits would soon go away of their own accord as the West European economies absorbed the shock of the oil price crisis and returned to the path of economic growth.

However, the Western European economies were still in a relatively parlous condition when they were hit by a second use of the oil price weapon by the OPEC states in 1979–80, which plunged them back into deep recession. But worse was to come on both the demand and supply sides. With regard to the former, the second oil price shock caught the international economy on the brink of a cyclical downturn and this, in conjunction with a rapid rise in US, and then world, interest rates in 1981–82 in the wake of the Reagan administration's early experiments with monetarism, sent the capitalist economies into the worst slump for half a century. The problem was compounded on the supply side because many West European economies experienced exceptionally rapid labour-force growth in the early 1980s as the extra-large generation of children born in the 'baby boom' of the 1960s became an extra-large generation of new entrants to the labour market. The twin factors of a slump in the demand for labour and a sharp rise in its supply combined to put employment under even more severe pressure.

Whereas in earlier post-war decades, Keynesianism had been the only option, by the 1980s the governments of Western Europe – except in Italy where late industrialisation caused a spurt of economic growth – seemingly faced a strategic choice between continuing with demand management and so risking inflation and even higher budget deficits, or opting for monetarist policies with their attendant political risks of an electoral backlash or even disorder as unemployment was allowed to rise unchecked. In the event, most governments, including those of Britain, Belgium, Denmark, the Netherlands, and West Germany, opted for the monetarist road. As the final column of Table 5 shows, these were among the states which experienced the highest average rates of unemployment over the 1980s. Of the others, France, Austria, and Norway all attempted to pursue Keynesian-style full employment strategies: although, as Table 5 again shows, France proved unable to achieve this objective, the latter two countries enjoyed considerable success. Finally, there were two countries, Switzerland and Sweden, which attempted to combine both financial discipline with full employment; and both succeeded on the latter count with average unemployment rates of 0.6 and 2.8 per cent respectively. Thus, during the 1980s, the West European states fell into four broad groups, the first following a monetarist path to high unemployment, the second a Keynesian path to the same end, the third a Keynesian path to relatively full employment, and the fourth an at least quasi-monetarist path of full employment. In the remainder of the chapter, these four paths are discussed before the political impact of employment is analysed and a conclusion reached.

THE MONETARIST PATH TO HIGH UNEMPLOYMENT

The first West European country explicitly to follow the monetarist road was Britain. Early in the post-war period, all British parties had been staunch advocates of Keynesian policies. However, their application had, from the late 1950s onwards, been associated with surges of inflation and balance of payments problems, leading to a 'stop–go' cycle whereby the raising of demand for employment purposes had been followed by retrenchment to control inflation and bring the external accounts into line. The end result had been a rise in unemployment, and the whole process had begun all over again. Successive governments had attempted to cure this cycle and establish a stable framework for economic growth and full employment. But all efforts had foundered on the twin rocks of the external constraints that arose from Britain's international monetary role and the intransigence of Britain's decentralised and ill-disciplined trade union movement. Britain's economy was thus in difficulties even before the crisis of 1975–76 and the dramatic failure of the Labour government's bid to protect employment by reflating the economy while relying upon a 'social contract' with the unions to contain wage rises. The policy resulted in rising unemployment, accelerating inflation, spiralling public spending, and a huge increase in the public debt. The latter forced the government to go cap in hand to the International Monetary Fund which, as a condition of bailing Britain out, insisted on the adoption of deflationary policies which the Labour government had implemented despite their consequences for employment.

This episode discredited both the Labour Party and Keynesianism, and opened the way for the election in 1979 of a Conservative government, led by Margaret Thatcher, that was committed to monetarism, i.e. the pursuit of anti-inflationary objectives via controlling the money supply and lowering public spending. Employment was to be left to the market except for measures designed to reduce the 'natural' rate of unemployment, including cuts in benefits and restrictions on the power of the unions. Considerable progress was made in these directions in the government's first eighteen months in office, but this was not matched by similar progress on inflation. Soaring public spending stoked a doubling of the rate of increase in prices and this, coupled with a strong pound and high interest rates, crippled British industry: unemployment began to rise rapidly during 1980, well in advance of the rest of Western Europe. When, later that year, the numbers out of work topped 2 million or 10 per cent of the workforce, with the forecast that they would rise still higher as the international recession began to bite, it was generally expected that the government would 'U-turn' and attempt to promote recovery by using the proceeds of Britain's North Sea oil to finance industrial rejuvenation while seeking a deal with the unions to contain inflation.

In the event, Mrs Thatcher was, in her own words, 'not for turning' and in March 1981 the Chancellor of the Exchequer introduced a massively deflationary budget intended to demonstrate, once and for all, the government's determination to break inflationary expectations irrespective of the consequences for jobs. The diminution of domestic demand that followed from the budget measures was compounded by the deepening external recession. As a result, the numbers out of work rose sharply to pass 3 million, or 13 per cent of the workforce, in early 1982, despite a Pauline conversion by senior ministers towards the use of labour market programmes to tackle unemployment. The few largely experimental schemes inherited from Labour had been derided as inefficient and ineffective, and cut back in 1980–81; but towards the end of 1981 the government abruptly changed its stance and indulged in a rapid and large-scale expansion of job programmes, particularly for the young and, reflecting Britain's early start in the growth of unemployment, the by now considerable total of the long-term unemployed.

However, neither the expansion of the special employment measures nor a succession of changes in the method of counting the official total of the unemployed proved sufficient to halt the rise in the unemployment figures. In June 1983 Mrs Thatcher became the first Prime Minister in history to go the electorate with over 3 million people out of work. But this dismal record failed to disadvantage the Conservatives at the polls; despite a slight slippage in their share of the vote, the fact that the opposition was divided between Labour and the new alliance of Liberals and the recently formed Social Democratic Party meant that, under Britain's 'first-past-the-post' electoral system, Mrs Thatcher romped home to a second term of office with a more than trebled parliamentary majority. During the next two years there was a strong underlying economic recovery, but also higher unemployment: the number of new jobs created failed to keep pace with continuing job losses as well as the growing number of entrants or, as the upturn gathered momentum, re-entrants to the labour market.

It was only in 1986 that the official statistics began to show a fall in the numbers out of work, and even this was in part artificially induced through expansion of labour market programmes, further adjustments to the method of counting the unemployed (there were nineteen revisions in all between 1979 and 1986). and by placing pressure on the unemployed to accept jobs or a placement on a scheme or forfeit their right to benefit. By these means, as well as by engineering a pre-election consumer boom, unemployment was set on a downward course well before Mrs Thatcher sought re-election in June 1987. The numbers out of work dipped just below the 3 million mark (10.8 per cent of the workforce) in time for the election, and this took the edge off continuing public concern to the extent that the opposition parties stressed other themes and issues; for example, the Labour Party cancelled an election broadcast that would have attacked the government on unemployment in favour of rerunning an earlier successful film eulogising the qualities of the party's leader. Unemployment was thus the forgotten issue of the 1987 election campaign, when the Conservatives won a historic third term in office.

While in 1979–80 the Thatcher administration had stood virtually alone in Western Europe in its monetarist outlook, in 1981–82 it was joined by newly formed or elected right-wing governments in a number of other countries: Belgium, Denmark, the Netherlands and West Germany. Belgium had, like Britain, seen inflation, public spending and public debt spiralling upwards in the wake of the reflation of the mid-1970s, although not to the extent of having financial discipline externally imposed. Instead, a succession of governments had wrestled ineffectively with the crisis, largely because of fears of the effect of cutbacks in spending on what was already a high level of unemployment. However, in late 1981 the success of the monetarist Liberals in winning seats at the expense of the centre had persuaded the leader of the Christian Democrats, Wilfried Martens, to form a coalition incorporating the Liberals but excluding the Socialists. The new government acted immediately to cut public spending, including Belgium's generous unemployment benefits, and to lessen union influence through a combination of the de-indexing of wages and the imposition of wage reductions in the public sector.

As in Britain, the removal of demand from the economy in the teeth of a major recession sent unemployment soaring to reach 15 per cent of the workforce by the mid-1980s, the highest level of any major industrial country in Western Europe. The government's response was the establishment of large-scale labour market programmes. These included a highly successful apprenticeship scheme for the young, coupled with coercion in the form of the so-called 'troisième circuit du travail' whereby the long-term unemployed were given the option of taking whatever work, menial or otherwise, was available or losing their entitlement to benefit. But neither what the Socialist opposition bitterly decried as conscription nor continuing austerity and high unemployment proved a barrier to re-election, and the Martens coalition won a second term of office in 1985, only to fall on a matter unrelated to its economic record in 1987.

The Belgian experience in the 1980s was closely paralleled in Denmark and the Netherlands. In the former, there had been two decades in which the growth of public spending, particularly on welfare, had outstripped the growth of output, leading to inflation, balance of payments deficits and job losses. Successive Social Democrat governments had been unable to tackle these problems, with a consequent loss of electoral support. In September 1982 Poul Schlüter's Conservative-led minority government stepped into the breach with a package that included spending cuts targeted on benefits – including those of the unemployed – and the de-indexing of wages to control inflation. The numbers out of work were allowed to grow rapidly, averaging over 10 per cent of the workforce by 1984, when the government secured re-election, before falling between 1985 and 1987 when, despite left-wing gains, the coalition continued in office. The story was much the same in the Netherlands. The massive reflation of 1975–76 that was meant to project employment was not only followed by a rapid growth in the numbers out of work; it also resulted in inflation and rising public spending seemingly becoming embedded in the economy, leaving the left in a dilemma when faced with a further need to reflate in the recession of 1981–82. The beneficiary was the Christian Democrat-led coalition of Ruud Lubbers which came to office in late 1982 and imposed cuts in public spending, unemployment benefits, and pay in the public sector. Unemployment packed at 12 per cent of the workforce in 1983 and then subsided somewhat, although it was still 10 per cent when the Lubbers government was re-elected in 1986.

All of these four countries had a poor record in protecting employment in the 1970s. They had experienced severe problems with inflation, spiralling public spending, and large budget deficits, and suffered from declining competitiveness. But the fifth country in this category, West Germany, shared none of these characteristics. Despite attempts by the independent Bundesbank to impose monetarist policies in the mid-1970s, the Social Democrat (SPD)/Free Democrat coalition had, using Keynesian policies, kept unemployment down to around 3.5 per cent in the late 1970s. It had maintained – courtesy of links with the trade unions – low inflation, constrained the growth of the budget deficit and generally preserved the health of what was by far the strongest industrial economy in Western Europe. This achievement was one reason why the coalition was able to improve its position substantially in the 1980 election and win a fourth term in office.

However, within a year of the election, the coalition had begun to distance itself from Keynesianism and full employment objectives in favour of a more monetarist stance. The central reason for this departure appeared to be fears that reflation would result in a substantial worsening of the budget deficit, by then running at 4.6 per cent of gross domestic product (GDP). While this figure was low by comparison with many West European countries and probably could have been allowed to go higher, the latter prospect was sufficient to cause widespread alarm in West Germany where budget deficits were of recent origin and where there had been, ever since the hyperinflation of the early 1920s, a collective paranoia over sound finance. Constrained, then, in his ability to fulfil employment objectives by the perceived need to halt the growth of the budget deficit, the SPD Chancellor, Helmut Schmidt, announced in late 1981 that the coalition would henceforth seek to find a 'middle way' between Keynesianism and monetarism which would preserve employment in so far as that was consistent with financial objectives.

But the outcome of this rethink, as revealed in the savings package presented to the Bundestag in December 1981, leaned more towards financial than employment aims. At a time when 1.6 million people, or 6 per cent of the workforce, were out of work, the government announced its intention of slashing public spending, with one-fifth of the cuts to come from labour market programmes – far more than was justified on a pro rata basis. The main reason for the unexpected severity of the package and the emphasis upon trimming labour market programmes appears to have been a shift to the right by the minority partner in the coalition, the Free Democrats, who were fearful of being outflanked by other right-wing parties. Their demands were reluctantly acceded to by the SPD as the price of maintaining the coalition, although not without considerable misgivings, particularly by the party's left wing, and attacks by the latter on the leadership mounted as unemployment soared in 1982. But paradoxically, higher unemployment pushed up the budget deficit, which led to further demands by the Free Democrats for cuts in public spending. As the SPD left became more vociferous and the Free Democrats more intransigent, the Chancellor was placed in a 'no-win' situation. Rather than preside further over the disintegration of the coalition, Schmidt terminated it in September 1982. Following a constructive vote of no confidence in the Bundestag on 1 October, Schmidt resigned and a new coalition was formed with the Free Democrats supporting the Christian Democratic Union (CDU) and its Bavarian allies, the Christian Socialists. The CDU leader, Helmut Kohl, became Chancellor. He immediately called an election for March 1983 in which the SPD, hamstrung by their record, were unable to make political capital out of the by then 1.8 million people (8 per cent of the workforce) out of a job, and this contributed to the party's heavy defeat at the hands of the right.

The new government's general economic strategy was monetarist in so far as it was essentially aimed at reducing the budget deficit via cuts in public spending, in the belief that this would enable interest rates to be lowered and free resources for use by the private sector. The latter would, it hoped, then act as the engine of recovery, and in the process create the new jobs necessary to bring unemployment down. Accordingly, in June 1983 a rolling programme of major spending cuts was initiated – including a cut in benefits for claimants without children – although the Chancellor reined in his free market instincts enough to preserve job-related industrial policy and labour market spending, partly to massage the unemployment figures. Then, with the liberalisation measures in place, the government sat back to await what was called *die Wende* (the turn), the rejuvenation by private enterprise of the economy and employment.

By early 1984, assisted by the rapid decline of oil prices and the slide of the dollar against the Deutschmark, the economy began to grow rapidly, although 2.3 million people (9.5 per cent of the workforce) were still unemployed. It was at this juncture that the largest trade union. IG Metall, advanced a scheme for the introduction of a 35-hour week which, union economists had calculated, would created enough jobs effectively to halve the numbers out of work. This scheme was backed reluctantly by the SPD but failed to attract the support of some other unions and was actively opposed both by the employers' federation and the government. The latter offered instead legislation which would allow, subject to a collective agreement, retirement at 58, but this was insufficient to defuse the issue. When in the late spring of 1984, negotiations on the 35-hour week failed, the metalworkers embarked upon a series of strikes which were only settled by the promise of a phased reduction in working hours, starting with an immediate cut to a 38.5-hour week. Thus ended what was to prove the major instance in Western Europe of a union using the strike weapon in the 1980s to pressurise government and employers over unemployment.

The combination of a booming economy, earlier retirement, shorter working hours and minor increases in the numbers of special employment schemes in 1985 all contributed to a slight fall in unemployment during 1986; by the end of the year the numbers out of work stood at 2.2 million or 8.9 per cent of the workforce. This drop was cited as evidence of the success of its policies by the coalition government in the 1987 election. Despite counter-claims by the SPD that the numbers out of work were still 400,000 up on when Kohl had entered office in 1982, the issue failed to make a significant impact. Thus, in West Germany, as in the other countries discussed, high unemployment proved no barrier to the re-election of a monetarist right-wing government.

THE KEYNESIAN PATH TO HIGH UNEMPLOYMENT

High unemployment did, however, prove a barrier to the re-election of a right-wing neo-monetarist government in France in 1981. At the start of the 1980s, France was governed, as it had been since 1958, by the right or centre–right, with the presidency occupied by Valéry Giscard d'Estaing and the premiership by Raymond Barre. The latter had been appointed in 1976 in place of Jacques Chirac, the architect of the Keynesian strategy to protect employment in the recession of 1975–76 which had, as in most of the cases discussed earlier, culminated in high unemployment, rising inflation, and a growing budget deficit. His successor, a well-known Conservative, had in many respects anticipated the monetarist revolution by redrafting the national plan to eliminate all reference to full-employment objectives, focusing instead upon anti-inflationary targets to be met by reducing the budget deficit. While his government succeeded on the budgetary front, so much so that by the early 1980s France had one of the lowest deficits in Western Europe, inflation remained a chronic problem while unemployment, rising since the early 1970s, continued on its upward trend. The reversal of this was not accorded high priority until 1981 when, on the run-in to the presidential and National Assembly elections, the French Socialist Party began to campaign on the issue. Untainted by the record of failure which had hampered the left in so many other West European countries, the party was able to gain considerable mileage from promises to put people back to work. Its success on the issue was implicitly acknowledged in March 1981 when Giscard announced a policy goal of cutting the total of the unemployed, then standing at 1.7 million (7 per cent of the workforce) by 1 million, mainly through schemes to encourage early retirement. However, Giscard's conversion came too late to save the right, and promises to bring down unemployment played an important role in the election of the Socialist candidate, François Mitterrand, to the presidency in May and to the return of a left majority in the National Assembly the following month.

The Mitterrand strategy for the economy and employment had four main elements. The first was what may be termed 'redistributive Keynesianism', involving a massive release of new demand into the economy, targeted at raising the incomes of the poor who, it was assumed, would increase their spending and so generate a consumer boom that would create new jobs. The second element was a rapid enlargement of the public sector, directly to create employment, and indirectly to provide a stimulus that would lift the French economy as a whole out of recession. Thirdly the strategy envisaged a significant expansion of labour market programmes; and fourthly jobs were to be created by major reductions in working hours. The government acknowledged that this programme would have major implications for inflation, the budget deficit, and, if higher incomes were spent on imports, for the balance of payments, but was confident that these problems could be dealt with. Inflation was to be contained by co-operation with the trade unions, relieved after so long in the political wilderness to have a sympathetic administration in office. The budget deficit was to be tackled by a combination of higher taxes on the rich and an increase in tax receipts and reduction in benefits as people returned to work. And any balance of payments problem would be solved by the ability of firms, given a head start by domestic reflation, to take advantage of the widely expected upturn in the world economy.

The new government immediately began to implement the four elements of its strategy. With regard to redistribution, family allowances were raised by 81 per cent for parents with two children, housing allowances for lower-paid workers were increased by 25 per cent, both health benefits and pensions were increased substantially, and the minimum wage was pushed up by 15 per cent in real terms. In the public sector, during 1981–82 the government hired an extra 240,000 workers. The third component, an expansion of labour market programmes, was catered for by extending 'contracts of solidarity', allowing workers to retire at 55 on 70 per cent of their salaries, subsidising workers who went half-time and released work for the unemployed, and exempting employers who took on new staff from social security contributions. The fourth objective, a reduction in working time, was achieved in July 1981 when the working week was cut from 40 to 39 hours and workers were given a statutory fifth week of holidays.

By these means, the government managed to keep around 150,000 people off the unemployment register in 1981, 400,000 in 1982, and nearly 700,000 in 1983. However, this did no more than slow down the rate of growth of unemployment, and even then at a very high cost. The budget deficit increased sevenfold as a proportion of GDP in 1980–82, inflation remained substantially above international levels, and the trade deficit nearly doubled. This was clear evidence that the government had been over-optimistic in assuming that it could control the reflationary forces that it had unleashed, and it led to massive international speculation against the franc; partly to ease this and partly to help French exports and jobs, the franc was devalued in October 1981 and again in June 1982. On the latter occasion devaluation was, at the insistence of France's partners in the European Monetary System, accompanied by a mild deflationary package, but this failed to halt the lurch of the economy into financial chaos or to stem speculation against the franc. After a brief internal debate over whether the government should try to preserve its employment strategy by adopting protectionism – a suggestion ill received by France's European Community partners – Mitterrand bowed to the inevitable and his government prepared an austerity package which was introduced in March 1983. This included a massive devaluation of the franc, a freeze on the budget, and a standstill on public sector recruitment, all of which signified that the Mitterrand government had effectively abandoned redistributive Keynesianism and public sector expansion as a means of tackling the problem of unemployment. This was now to be dealt with primarily by labour market programmes, to which end the package contained a new measure guaranteeing a safety net of benefits and training for those out of work, the so-called 'traitement social du chômage'.

The new monetarist policies succeeded in reducing inflation, the budget deficit and the trade deficit over 1983–85, but they did not help unemployment which rose from an average 8.1 per cent of the workforce in 1983 to 9.9 per cent in 1984 and 10.2 per cent in 1985, the last figure representing 2.4 million people. In order to try and turn the tide, the government, much like its counterparts elsewhere in Western Europe, brought in a batch of labour market measures, including funding for school-leavers and young workers to set up in business, as well as a large-scale 'make-work' scheme providing socially useful part-time work for the unemployed. These new measures helped to stabilise unemployment over 1985 but the numbers out of work rose again at the start of 1986. Hence, in the elections for the National Assembly held in March of that year, the Socialists were not even able to salvage their reputation by claiming that unemployment was on downward trend, and this was a major factor contributing to their defeat and the return of a right-wing government in the Thatcherite mould. Thus the Mitterrand experiment, probably the most ambitious attempt to tackle unemployment in any West European country, ended in economic failure and then a political rebuff for the left, although the President himself survived to win a second term of office in 1988 and install a new, but decidedly right-wing, Socialist administration.

THE KEYNESIAN ROAD TO LOW UNEMPLOYMENT

If Keynesianism proved unworkable in France in the 1980s, it was applied more successfully in two other West European countries, Norway and Austria. Norway was a special case in so far as it possessed very large reserves of North Sea oil and gas – much larger in relation to the size of the economy than those of Britain or the Netherlands – which doubled in value with the oil price hike of 1979–80, so generating a considerable surplus on both the budget and the balance of payments in the early 1980s. Thus, although after 1981 there was a bourgeois government in office dedicated towards at least a partial dismemberment of the system of massive industrial subsidies used by its Labour predecessors in the mid-1970s to project employment, it was able to move towards this objective without resorting to monetarism by using oil-financed tax cuts to maintain full employment. However, in the mid-1980s this strategy came under increasing strain because of seemingly endemic inflation, problems arising from the failure of the non-oil sector of the economy to adjust to the post-oil crisis international environment, and finally the fall in oil prices in the mid-1980s which diminished the room for fiscal expansion. These cast a shadow over the government's record and, full employment notwithstanding, it lost support in the 1985 election. Subsequently, the government suffered a parliamentary defeat on its budget proposals and was replaced by a minority Labour administration which has continued, amid mounting difficulties, to pursue full employment, albeit not via tax cuts but through extra public spending.

The other country which pursued a Keynesian strategy with a high degree of success was Austria, which began the 1980s under a Social Democrat government that arguably had the best economic record in Western Europe. Not only had it succeeded in preserving full employment in the 1975–76 recession, but at the same time it had secured a reduction in inflation. The credit for this remarkable achievement was widely attributed to Austria's unique 'social partnership' between the state, capital, and labour, a partnership which had been forged during the Allied occupation after the war and then survived both independence in 1955 and the return, after two decades of all-party government, to single- party rule from 1966 onwards. In the realm of economic policy, the partnership had taken the form of voluntary and close co-operation in setting and implementing economic goals, and it was this which had allowed the Social Democrat government to run an expansionary fiscal policy to preserve full employment in 1975–76 while relying on the social partners to constrain the effects upon inflation. In the case of labour, this task was made manageable by the ability of union leaders to impose wage discipline via a centralised union structure, and by their ready acceptance of the ultimate anti-inflationary discipline of a hard currency policy. This mixture of expansionary fiscal policy, voluntary prices, and incomes restraint, and a hard currency policy had been labelled 'Austro-Keynesianism', and it was to form the basis of the government's response to unemployment in the early 1980s.

The world recession hit Austria rather later than elsewhere, and it was not until early 1982 that, with unemployment standing at 3 per cent of the workforce, the government decided to intervene. With the full backing of its social partners, it reduced taxes and increased spending, with the extra resources being concentrated on measures designed to stimulate new investment and create jobs. When, in the face of unexpectedly rapid labour force growth – mainly stemming from the return of expatriates in the wake of high unemployment in West Germany – the numbers out of work continued to rise, the government introduced a second employment package in September 1982. This included a major construction programme for regions with high unemployment, additional infrastructure investment, subsidies for private investment, and a new labour market programme for the young. By these means, the growth of unemployment was restrained so that by early 1983 only 4 per cent of the workforce was out of a job. This achievement, however, failed sufficiently to impress the Austrian electorate; in the 1983 election the Social Democrats lost ground and were forced to form a coalition with the conservative Free Democrats.

The coalition took a more cautious fiscal stance over 1984–85 for fear of worsening a budget deficit already swollen to record levels by the reflations of the 1970s and the 1980s, and unemployment was allowed to drift up towards the 5 per cent mark. Yet this was still, by the standards of most of the rest of Western Europe, a remarkable achievement, accompanied as it was by a balance of payments surplus and falling inflation, courtesy of the operation of the social partnership. However, these positive aspects of the coalition's economic performance were overlain by concern about what came to be seen as a structural imbalance in the budget and by the inability of industry, particularly the large public sector, to adjust to the economic realities of the post-oil crisis world. After a series of political crises the Social Democrat Chancellor, Franz Vranitsky, called an early election for January 1987 partly in the hope that this would resurrect a grand coalition with the conservative People's Party which might command a consensus over measures to tackle the country's industrial and budgetary problems. With no party winning a majority, such a coalition was formed in March 1987 although, at the time of writing, it remains to be seen how successful it will be in preserving full employment in the face of financial exigencies, an achievement secured by few Western European countries in the 1980s.

THE QUASI-MONETARIST PATH TO FULL EMPLOYMENT

The two countries which did manage to protect full employment while sustaining or restoring financial discipline were Switzerland

and Sweden. In the former the explanation is comparatively simple; successive governments ran tight fiscal and monetary policies while mopping up unemployment largely by restricting the supply of labour. In particular, the government failed to renew the work and residence permits of thousands of migrant workers – who made up a quarter of the workforce – and released their jobs for domestic employees. In addition, pressures were applied to diminish female participation in the workforce via an employer's code for hiring workers which discriminated against 'second earning marriage partners'; this left families with the choice of having one or the other partner in work, which was almost the male in view of his higher earnings. By these means, neither of which could have legally applied in countries in the European Community, Switzerland secured the lowest rate of unemployment in Western Europe in the 1980s.

Sweden, however, resorted neither to cuts in the migrant labour force nor to penalising women to maintain full employment. At the start of the 1980s, Sweden was governed by a centre–right coalition which had come to power in 1976, terminating forty-four consecutive years of Social Democrat rule. The latter had been hallmarked by a concentration on full employment as one of the overriding priorities of policy and, in the belief that any failure on this score would condemn them to another prolonged spell in the wilderness, the coalition had striven to keep the unemployment figures down, using every weapon in its arsenal. This included expanding the labour market programmes which Sweden had pioneered to international acclaim in the 1950s and 1960s, but also providing industrial subsidies and pump-priming of the economy on a scale unknown under the Social Democrats, who had been noted for both their acceptance of the primacy of market forces in the industrial field and their fiscal conservatism.

The centre–right coalition's all-about attack certainly succeeded in keeping the numbers out of work down in the late 1970s and the opening years of the 1980s, when the rate of unemployment hovered around the 2 per cent mark. But this was achieved at a significant cost; between 1975 and 1981 the trade deficit increased from 0.5 to 2.5 per cent of GDP, the inflation rate accelerated from 9.8 to 12.1 per cent, government spending rose from 48 to 67 per cent of GDP, and the gross public debt more than doubled from 29 to 66 per cent of GDP. Moreover, the massive feather-bedding of Swedish industries for employment purposes prevented adjustment to change, with the result of sluggish growth in output, productivity, and investment, and a decline in the country's share of world trade. Thus by 1981 the Swedish economy was, largely because of the indiscriminate pursuit of full employment, in serious trouble, and the coalition began to reverse tack. Despite the severe impact of the oil price rise of 1979–80 upon the Swedish economy, the government refused to unbalance the budget further or to vote additional funding for labour market programmes, i.e. it signalled its intention of accepting a higher rate of unemployment. The latter rose to 2.5 per cent over 1981 and then passed the 3.5 per cent in the late summer of 1982, where it remained at the time of the election held in September. With their credibility badly damaged by the state of the economy, the centre–right parties lost support in the election and a minority Social Democrat goverment took office.

Faced with similar economic problems, governments in many other European countries had, as has been seen, opted for full-blooded monetarism. Instead, the Swedish Social Democrat opted for a variant which might be described as left-wing quasi-monetarism. This involved accepting that further deficit-financed reflation for employment purposes was out of the question, as was the continuation of massive industrial subsidies to support uneconomic jobs, i.e. the government saw the need to pursue a broadly deflationary macroeconomic strategy and a much less interventionist microeconomic one. But instead of them sitting back and allowing unemployment to rise while cutting benefits and dismantling trade union monopolies – which were all antithetical to the Swedish Social Democrat tradition – an attempt was made to preserve employment by other means. In the short term, the employment fall-out from cutting the budget deficit and allowing previously subsidised firms to go to the wall was to be mopped up by expanding the already extensive network of labour market programmes to improve the skills of the unemployed and enhance their job prospects. This was backed by the strong sanction of losing benefits in the event of reluctance to participate in schemes or take the employment offered, i.e. what has been termed 'workfare'. In the longer term, the strategy was to use the freedom to devalue virtually at will – a freedom not of course available to members of the European Monetary System – to generate growth and jobs.

The government set the ball rolling in October 1982 by announcing a massive 16 per cent devaluation and this was shortly followed by a package of tax increases and cuts in public spending, particularly on industrial subsidies. To contain the employment effects of these measures, spending on labour market programmes was increased to the tune of kr. 3.7bn, and this was supplemented by a further kr.

2.7bn appropriation in early 1983. With its strategy for the economy and employment in place, the government then awaited the results which, overall, were extremely gratifying; the current account moved back into surplus in 1984, the public sector deficit began to fall, inflation came down, and the rate of unemployment declined from an average of 3.5 per cent over 1983 to 2.8 per cent over 1985. Despite this record, however, the Social Democrats lost ground in the September 1985 election and were left reliant upon Communist support to stay in office.

Inflation continued to fall over 1986, averaging out at a historic low of 3.3 per cent for the year, while at the same time unemployment also dropped slightly, the annual average being 2.7 per cent. To a considerable extent, this remarkable conjunction of a fall in both inflation and unemployment was attributable to the success of the government's strategy in preventing what has been termed 'hysteresis', the effective isolation of the unemployed from the labour market and hence from exerting an influence on wage bargaining. Whereas in other countries, the unemployed had been left largely to their own devices and had often dropped out of the workforce, Sweden's 'workfare' politics had kept the unemployed in touch with work and so preserved their influence upon wages. It would seem that, just as in the 1930s when the Swedish Social Democrats had pioneered the use of Keynesianism to secure full employment, so their counterparts in the 1980s had shown that financial stringency could be adapted so as to be compatible with low unemployment.

THE POLITICAL IMPACT OF UNEMPLOYMENT

Perhaps the most striking feature of a review of Western European countries in the 1980s is the extent to which, irrespective of whether governments followed routes to high or low unemployment, this – except in France in 1981 – failed to stimulate political reaction. Whereas, as was noted earlier, it was fear of potential political unrest that had been one of the primary factors in motivating West European politicians to pursue full employment after the war, in the event the return of high unemployment in many countries passed off virtually without incident or even electoral censure of the governments concerned. Thus, despite opinion polls recording widespread public concern over unemployment, parties presiding over record numbers out of work in Britain, Belgium, Denmark, the Netherlands, and West Germany all secured second, and in some cases third, terms of office in the 1980s. Similarly, whereas on the basis of the salience of the unemployment issue earlier in the post-war period, it would have been expected that governments with a relatively good employment record would have been rewarded by the voters, the highly successful Social Democrat parties in Austria and Sweden and the bourgeois parties in Norway all suffered rebuffs at the hands of their electorates.

To turn first to the absence of unrest in the countries with high unemployment, there can be little doubt that, if the unemployed of the 1980s had been absolutely deprived to the extent that their forebears were in the 1930s, then there may well have been a stronger political reaction. There were, however, five main developments of the post-war decades which had taken the edge off the experience of unemployment and rendered unrest less likely. First, the general improvement in living standards over the post-war era meant that most of those out of work started off at a relatively high base in terms of possessions; the homes and consumer durables enjoyed by many of the unemployed in the 1980s would have excited the envy of those in work, let alone those on the dole, half a century ago.

Secondly, changes in the sex and age composition of both the employed and the unemployed meant that being out of work was less likely to deprive entire families of non-benefit income. Whereas the modal unemployed person in the 1930s was a male acting as the sole breadwinner for his family, the expansion of female participation in the workforce over the post-war period meant that there were many two-job families. This reduced the risk that unemployment would leave the family bereft of any job and hence any income from employment. Similarly, one of the new features of unemployment in the 1980s was its disproportionate loading upon the young. The bulge in the numbers of school-leavers coming on to the labour market noted earlier had meant that they had borne the brunt of rising unemployment, which was of course tragic for the young, but at least it left parents with higher incomes in work and as such helped to preserve overall family living standards.

Thirdly, even though benefits were cut in many countries in the 1980s, they still remained generous compared to half a century ago in the sense that those out of work remained above the breadline.

Fourthly, whereas labour market programmes were all but unknown in the 1930s, virtually all Western European countries sooner or later established a range of special employment programmes which absorbed large numbers of those out of work and were of some value in enabling them to obtain jobs.

Fifthly, one of the central reasons why unemployment had been so horrendous in the years between the wars was its geographical concentration within particular regions of countries. While there were still regional differentials in rates of unemployment within countries in the 1980s, these were relatively muted, in part because of the operation over the post-war period of industrial policies designed to correct spatial imbalances in the distribution of employment.

If these factors ameliorated the impact of unemployment in Western Europe in the 1980s and helped to defuse any inclination towards overt protest on the part of those out of work, the issue still remained an object of concern to voters in the high-unemployment countries, although this was insufficient to cost right-wing governments re-election except in France in 1981. This general lack of impact appears to have reflected a combination of, on the one hand, the success of right-wing governments in advancing the case that there was no realistic alternative to monetarist policies, and, on the other, the seeming inability of the left to counter this and pose a convincing alternative employment strategy. In many countries it was left-wing governments which had presided over the initial growth of unemployment amid accelerating inflation and rising debt in the 1970s and neither their record nor their ability to think much beyond discredited Keynesianism helped to change the climate of opinion or open up a party differential on the issue in the 1980s. Many voters came to accept that there were no panaceas for unemployment and remained deeply skeptical of parties which offered one. Only in France, where the left had been out of power for decades and where left-wing policies were untainted by previous failure, was the right made to pay dearly for its record on unemployment. However, the subsequent failure of the Mitterrand experiment rebounded to the disadvantage of the left in France and indeed in other countries where it was used by the right as an example of the chaos which would result from a change in policies.

Turning to the countries in which low unemployment failed to elicit an electoral reward, the most likely explanation would seem to be that voters regarded the achievement as unexceptional and discounted it in their voting calculus in favour of other issues. The reason low unemployment seemed to have been regarded with diffidence was that it was historically embedded as a political goal which all serious contenders for power were expected to achieve as a matter of course. In Sweden, full employment had become the overriding objective of the political system over the forty-four years of Social Democrat hegemony and generated expectations to the extent that, as has been seen, the bourgeois governments of 1976–81 pulled out all the stops to keep the numbers out of work down to the extent of taking the Swedish economy to the brink of collapse before drawing back. The subsequent return of the Social Democrats and the reinstatement of full employment seems to have been regarded by the voters as par for the course, and in 1985 they voted on other issues, including the government's inability to prevent a damaging series of public sector strikes. Norway too had a political culture which was strongly orientated towards full employment, partly because of an all-party commitment to maintain its scattered population structure and partly because the maintenance of low unemployment had been important in the post-war reconstruction of social and political values. For these reasons, as well as the buttress against budget and balance of payments deficits afforded by oil revenues, voters expected their governments to maintain low unemployment. Thus the employment performance of the bougeois coalition of 1981–85 was largely disregarded in the 1985 election when other issues predominated. Finally in Austria, the most socially divided country in Western Europe between the wars, full employment was a potent symbol of national reconciliation and reconstruction after the war as well as a cornerstone of the 'social partnership', and as such accepted by all parties. Low unemployment, then, cut little ice with the voters whereas other issues did, for example the proposed taxation of the secret bank accounts in which 'black economy' earnings were saved, which cost the Social Democrats dear in the 1983 election.

Overall, then, it would seem that in the high-unemployment countries, the absence of party competition stemming from the perceived inability of the opposition parties of the left to offer a viable alternative strategy played a major role in saving governments from punishment at the hands of the voters. In the low-unemployment ones it was again the absence of party competition, but here arising from the in-built expectation that virtually any party would continue to maintain a high level of employment, which denied governments electoral reward. Either way, unemployment was unable to acquire a role as a potentially decisive election issue in Western Europe in the 1980s.

CONCLUSION

In conclusion, the preceding analysis may be summarised as follows.

In the earlier part of the post-war period, full employment in Western Europe was underpinned by a 'long boom' in the world economy, and it was only when the latter collapsed in the wake of the oil price shock of 1973–74 that governments were required to make major efforts to fulfil their post-war pledges to maintain low unemployment via deficit-financed reflation. However, the application of Keynesian policies in 1975–76 produced variable results. Only a handful of countries preserved full employment; the majority experienced both 'stagflation' and a rapid growth of unemployment. This resulted in the widespread discrediting of Keynesianism and lent credence to the alternative strategy of monetarism. When, in the aftermath of the second oil price shock of 1979–80, the world slump of 1981–82, and rapid labour force growth, employment came under severe pressure in the 1980s, the governments of Western Europe followed what has been described as Keynesian, monetarist, or quasi-monetarist strategies. These, mediated by factors identified in the case-studies such as the extent of co-operation between the state, capital, and labour (critical in explaining the different outcomes of Keynesianism in Austria and France) or the imposition of policy constraints through membership of the European Community or the European Monetary System (which allowed Switzerland and Sweden to follow strategies not available to other countries), were associated with high or low unemployment. However, except in France in 1981, the level of unemployment failed to make a major political impact either by triggering social unrest or electoral censure in the high-unemployment countries, or by rewarding governments for their success in the low-unemployment ones.

With regard to the future of unemployment in Western Europe it seems likely that, barring further shocks to the capitalist economies of the kind administered by the stock market collapse of October 1987, the upturn which began in the mid-1980s should continue and this, allied to a sharp decline in demographic pressures on the labour force, should bring the numbers out of work down rapidly in the early 1990s. But this does not mean to say that the problem will simply go away as the mass unemployment of the 1930s vanished after the war. The 'long boom' and full employment of the 1950s and 1960s were products of a conjunction of economic, social, political, and technological factors which was without precedent, and is unlikely to be repeated. Hence work will probably remain in short supply in Western Europe for the foreseeable future. This inevitably raises the contentious question of who should have work and for how long, i.e. it poses a challenge to the traditional expectation that people will work for up to 47 hours a week for 47 weeks of the year for 47 years of their lives. In many countries, this challenge has been far advanced in the 1980s by delayed entry into the labour force for the young, earlier retirement, shorter working hours, and a veritable explosion of part-time working; and these trends can be expected to continue into the twenty-first century. Given the predilection of the right for leaving such matters to the market and that of the left for intervening on grounds of social justice – a division well illustrated by the dispute over working hours in West Germany in 1983–84 – this would seem likely in the course of time to lead to competition between parties based less upon the total amount of work that governments should or could provide, and more upon the best way of allocating the work that is available. In short, the future may see a politics of unemployment based primarily upon distributional issues.

REFERENCES AND FURTHER READING

Bean, C., Layard, R. and Nickell, S. (eds) (1987) *The Rise in Unemployment* (Oxford: Blackwell).

Beaney, M. (1985) *The Rise and Fall of Keynesianism* (London: Macmillian).

Garraty, J. (1978) *Unemployment in History* (New York, Harper and Row).

Goldthorpe, J. (ed.)(1985) *Order and Conflict in Contemporary Capitalism* (Oxford: OUP).

Handy, C. (1984) *The Future of Work* (Blackwell).

Hibbs, D. (1987) *The Political Economy of Industrial Societies* (Cambridge, Mass.:Harvard University Press).

Keynes, J. M. (1967) *The General Theory of Employment, Interest and Money* (London: Macmillan).

Minford, P. (1983) *Unemployment: Its Causes and Cures* (Oxford: Martin Robertson).

OECD (1987) *OECD Economic Outlook*.

Richardson, J. and Henning, R. (eds) (1984) *Unemployment: Policy Responses of Western Democracies* (London: Sage).

Therborn, G. (1986) *Why Some People Are More Unemployed than Others* (London:Verso).

van der Wee, H. (1987) *Prosperity and Unheaval: The World Economy 1940–80* (London: Penguin).

Wattel, H. (ed.) (1987) *The Policy Consequences of John Maynard Keynes* (London: Macmillan).

Webber, D. (1986) 'Social democracy and the re-emergence of mass unemployment in Western Europe', in W. E. Paterson and A. H. Thomas (eds), *The Future of Social Democracy* (Oxford: OUP), pp 19–58.

The above relate mainly to the 1970s and early 1980s. For subsequent developments see the annual OECD reports on countries and the occasional surveys of specific countries in *The Economist*.

CHAPTER 4
Government–industry Relations

Wyn Grant

In this chapter a contrast is drawn between the interventionist character of government–industry relations in Western Europe in the 1970s, and the more market-oriented emphasis of the 1980s. Government–industry relations in the 1970s were characterised by an interventionist paradigm in which national governments attempted to influence the process by which resources were transferred from older and ailing industries to newer and more competitive ones. Such intervention often led to large sums of public money being wasted in futile attempts to rescue failing firms, slowing down the rate at which West European economies responded to changing global demand patterns. The 1970s may be characterised as the era of 'industrial policy', which in practice often amounted to little more than an attempt by national governments to provide a spurious coherence to a series of *ad hoc* programmes of aid to industry. These programmes were often formulated not as part of any planned attempt to influence the evolution of national economic structures, but were more usually reactive, crisis measures influenced by such considerations as the symbolic significance, electoral importance, and regional presence of firms in difficulty. As a consequence of the incoherent and highly politicised nature of industrial policy, it often decelerated rather than accelerated necessary changes in the economies of Western Europe, making the region more vulnerable to competition from Japan and from 'newly industralising countries' such as South Korea and Taiwan.

Industrial policies of the kind pursued in the 1970s are often defended on the grounds that they guaranteed social peace, and an acceptance by a potentially militant workforce of the process of change. Concern about the reaction of the workforce to industrial

59

change is understandable in the wake of the serious labour disturbances which had shaken France and Italy at the end of the 1970s, and persistently poor industrial relations throughout the decade in Britain. In particular, it was argued that 'corporatism' represented a distinctive and workable West European solution to the problem of *negotiating* industrial change. There are many definitions of corporatism but at its core is the notion that government should share the making of economic policy with organised employers and organised labour. In return, the 'social partners' (most importantly the unions) secure the consent of their members to needed changes.

The corporatist paradigm presents two main difficulties, one analytical, the other prescriptive. Effective corporatism requires not only élite co-operation, but, more important, centralised employer and labour organisations which can deliver the compliance of their members. These conditions appear to be met only in some of the smaller European countries, notably Austria. West Germany is sometimes claimed as an example of corporatism, but it would be more accurate to characterise it as a mixture of corporatist and pluralist elements (see Streeck 1983). What was distinctive about West Germany during the 1970s was that its relatively peaceful labour relations were based on what amounted to an implicit collusion between permanent skilled workers and employers (at the expense of the less skilled, guest workers, etc.), underwritten by legal rights given to the workforce to participate in certain decisions in the firm (see Streeck 1984, for a fuller account). If the limited spread of corporatism restricts its value as an analytical paradigm, its prescriptive value is undermined by the fact that the pace of negotiated change can be unacceptably slow in a fast-changing economic environment. Britain's economic performance started to improve (at least on some indicators) only after solutions had been imposed by a government disinclined to pay much attention to either unions or employers.

The corporatist countries at least pursued consistent strategies, even if they ran into problems in the longer run. Austria, for example, attempted to ward off unemployment by retaining labour that was no longer needed in nationalised industries. By the mid-1980s, it was clear that this strategy could no longer be maintained, particularly as a politicised management compounded the inefficiencies resulting from the presence of surplus labour. In countries which were not generally regarded as corporatist, intervention was often based on no clear strategy other than paying off political debts to powerful interests. In Italy in the 1970s state holding companies with politically appointed managements seemed to be more engaged in politics than in commerce, losing large sums of money propping up hopelessly unviable companies which happened to be located in politically sensitive areas, or to have powerful patrons.

By the 1980s, it was clear in most European countries that changes in policy were required. Against a background of budgetary crisis in many countries, the public expenditure costs of supporting loss-making enterprises were becoming intolerable. It was also becoming clear that 'temporary' assistance had a habit of becoming permanent; that once some public money had been committed to an enterprise, there was a temptation to commit more in the hope that the original funding would not have to be written off. Faced with an increasing competitive thrust from Japan, and the apparent success of the American economy (which did have a good track record in creating new jobs), there was increasing talk of 'Eurosclerosis'. It was argued that the institutional density which characterised West European arrangements made effective change very difficult, in particular introducing serious rigidities into the labour market. Against this background, business interests gained a new autonomy. This can be seen most strikingly in Italy. From a situation in the early 1970s where the legitimacy of the business class was at a very low level, with widespread talk of the conventional capitalist economy being supplanted, Italian business leaders won a new freedom by the mid-1980s to pursue commercial solutions to the problems of their enterprises. They stopped being political managers, manoeuvring for position among the various factions of the Christian Democrats, and were able to focus on rationalising the activities of their firms.

Greece has often been seen as an exception to the general trend within Western Europe towards less state intervention. However, even Greece is not immune to changing attitudes. In May 1987 the Economy Minister, Constantine Simitis, warned Greek industry not to count on state protectionism as a safety net for survival in a competitive market. The Socialist government, he explained to the Federation of Greek Industries, was committed to reducing the public sector and minimising intervention: 'We do not seek an expanded state, but a more efficient state.' Improving the quality of state intervention meant reducing the activities of the public sector (*Financial Times*, 29 May 1987).

Although intervention through state ownership, 'bail-outs' of ailing firms, and subsidies for investment have been declining, it should be noted that, if anything, regulation of business activities has tended to increase, despite a prevalent rhetoric of 'deregulation' in countries such as Britain. Although there has been some deregulation, e.g. in relation to air transport, this has been more than offset by pressures for environmental regulation, an area in which the European Community is an increasingly significant actor, and the creation of new regulatory arrangements for financial services. However, regulation and deregulation are not the main focus of this chapter.

As was pointed out earlier, small countries in Western Europe have tended to have somewhat distinctive patterns of government–industry relations, and the main body of the chapter will start with an exploration of these distinctive patterns. Despite the trend towards more market-oriented solutions to economic problems, the state remains a highly significant actor in West European countries, and so we must consider the ability of state bureaucracies to deal with industrial policy issues. Consideration is also given to the role of public enterprise in West European countries. Employers' associations and trade unions also remain significant actors, although the influence of organised labour has weakened in the 1980s. Against a background of international financial instability, the role of the financial sector requires separate consideration; the discussion presented here emphasises the importance of the internationalisation of financial markets. The impact of the European Community (EC) on government–industry relations is also considered, although, for a variety of reasons; it is concluded that its potential has yet to be realised. The chapter concludes with some discussion of likely future developments, with particular emphasis on apparent weaknesses in the West German economy.

THE DISTINCTIVENESS OF SMALLER EUROPEAN COUNTRIES

Both the problems of the industrial economy, and the strategies deployed to cope with those problems, tend to differ between large and small West European countries. There is, of course, considerable variation within the category of large countries (contrast French *dirigisme* with the German attachment to a social market economy) and the category of small countries (Norway's oil-based economy faces very different issues from Denmark's energy-poor economy). Even so, there are some useful generalisations that can be made about the European countries, although for each generalisation it is possible to make a list of exceptions.

First, smaller countries tend to have a rather different industrial structure from larger countries. Not surprisingly, one does not find in the smaller countries all the major industries listed in the Standard Industrial Classification. Rather, 'Light industries are represented disproportionately in the industrial structure of the small European states' (Katzenstein 1985: 83). In general, this means that they have fewer declining sectors that the larger countries. It is these declining sectors, with their substantial workforces, often concentrated in particular communities, that have posed some of the most difficult problems for West European politicians over the last two decades. Admittedly, Austria and Belgium have significant steel industries. The Austrian industry has been relatively successful until recently, but that of Belgium has been a major issue in its own right in the regional tensions that have beset that country. In general, however, the smaller countries do not have problem sectors such as a volume automobile industry. The decision-making burden on their governments is therefore lessened. They are also less likely to have hi-tech industries which require difficult decisions about sustaining research and development. Sweden (the largest of the smaller countries) is admittedly a significant force in telecomunications, and the Netherlands manufactures aircraft. But again, these and other exceptions (such as pharmaceuticals in Switzerland) serve only to underline the general rule. The smaller European states 'rely disproportionately on international research cooperation to compensate for the lack of domestic capacities to gain access to knowledge and technologies developed elsewhere, and to facilitate the process of technology transfer' (Katzenstein 1985: 45).

The smaller countries of Western Europe have succeeded in international competition by specialising in particular tightly defined niches in the market. Examples include specialist branches of food processing (confectionery in Switzerland; cheese in the Netherlands; alcoholic drinks in the Republic of Ireland), and some of the less prominent branches of manufacturing (Lego toys in Denmark; skis and ski equipment in Austria and Switzerland). Katzenstein (1985: 73) describes Switzerland's industrial adjustment strategy as based on 'the production of high-value-added goods (such as luxury consumer goods or investment goods), on the deliberate search for goods with low prize elasticities occupying special market niches, and, most recently, on the transformation of an artisan form of production (e.g. in embroidery or watches) to technical expertise and service (e.g. in machinery)'. Almost all the countries (Finland is perhaps an exception) earn substantial amounts of foreign exchange from tourism. Of course, there are differences in industrial structure and strategy. The Irish Republic, faced with the problems of a geographically marginal economy heavily dependent on agriculture, has successfully attracted inward investment from multinationals producing relatively light, high-value products such as pharmaceuticals and electronics. Switzerland and the Netherlands are more internationally oriented than Austria or Portugal; both the former countries have major multinationals of their own.

All the countries have either followed or experimented with consertationist economic policies, some (Austria) more successfully than others (Irish Republic). It is this propensity to democratic corporatism as a mechanism for handling industrial adjustment that is one of the most distinctive features of the smaller countries. As defined by Katzenstein, this democratic corporatism has three characteristics: 'an ideology of social partnership expressed at the national level; a relatively centralized and concentrated system of interest groups; and a voluntary and informal coordination of conflicting objectives through continuous political bargaining among interest groups, state bureaucracies, and political parties' (Katzenstein 1985: 32). Or, to put it more simply (Katzenstein 1985: 77) government advisory bodies 'assemble, day after day, the same people in different rooms'. In Britain's union state, it has even been possible to claim that Scotland has some of the characteristics (and benefits) of a small country. Explaining the success of the Scottish Development Agency as an industrial policy instrument, its chief executive has argued that much of its success is due to the fact that it is 'a tightly knit organisation operating in a small country with a limited élite of business, financial and political leaders who know each other extremely well'.

The forms which concertation has taken vary from one country to another. Switzerland's 'liberal capitalism' is clearly very different from Austria's 'democratic corporatism' (see Katzenstein 1984). Regional tensions invariably enter into the discussion of economic issues in Belgium, while the Netherlands is less reliant on concertative arrangements than it was in the first couple of decades after the war. Even more important, the industrial policies followed have differed significantly from one country to another. Austria has relied on extensive public ownership as part of its post-war settlement, although by the late 1980s it was beginning to experiment with privatisation. In Switzerland, even modest industrial policy measures have been thrown out in referenda, and the country has dealt with its potential employment problem by expelling its foreign workers.

Sweden only reluctantly became involved in direct intervention in industry in the 1970s. Denmark has tried to adhere to a liberal strategy. As Sidenius (1983: 59) comments, 'Danish industrial policy is conceived of as a liberalistic paradigm, its subsidising measures being general, non-steered and based on profitability.' The Netherlands has used rather extensive industrial subsidies that have sometimes fallen foul of EC rules. The Republic of Ireland has followed a conscious strategy of attracting investors with generous subsidy packages. Because of its status as a deprived region, it is allowed to do more under EC rules, although its most generous tax allowances have had to be phased out.

Katzenstein (1985: 59) argues that 'large and small countries differ considerably in their capacity and willingness to live with the costs of change'. Unlike larger countries such as the United States which have relied increasingly on a variety of non-tariff barriers to protect their industries from intensified international competition, protection has not been a viable option for smaller countries; their reliance on international trade means that the costs imposed by retaliation could be very high. As a consequence, they have not generally sheltered their industries against changes in the international economy. It should be noted, however, that their concentration on specialised products makes them, as a group, less vulnerable to the challenge presented to the larger countries by the newly industrialising nations of the Pacific Rim in such sectors as steel and automobiles.

The variety in the industrial structures of the smaller countries – contrast, for example, Belgium as an early industrialiser with the Irish Republic with a still limited industrial base – means that any analysis of their distinctiveness of a category must focus on their political processes. In the 1970s, it could be claimed that all of the smaller European countries either had established forms of democratic corporatism, or were seeking to do so. In the changed economic climate of the 1980s, however, these arrangements came under increasing strain. Even in the more prosperous smaller countries, there were budgetary limits to the extent to which potential problems could be 'bought off', quite apart from the efficiency consequences of such a strategy. Thus, for example, Luxemburg's industrial structure was based around the steel firm, Arbed, but its debts were such that it was beyond the capacity of the country to solve its financial problems (Mény and Wright 1986: 3).

In the 1970s, then, the smaller countries of Western Europe seemed to offer examples of the enduring virtues of democratic corporatism. The unanswered question was whether corporatism led to

65

prosperity, or whether prosperity made corporatism possible. By the 1980s, the smaller countries found themselves influenced by the new enthusiasm for market-oriented solutions. However, the resistance to the introduction of such solutions was far greater in many of the smaller countries, with countries such as Sweden still successfully pursuing a full-employment strategy in the late 1980s.

STATE ORGANISATION

State bureaucracies, including a variety of paragovernmental agencies, are clearly key actors in government–industry relations. Industrial policies are, in practice, largely devised and implemented by state bureaucracies. A minimal level of competence is required if a state bureaucracy is going to attempt to influence the development of a country's industrial structure. It is open to question whether this criterion is satisfied in some of the countries of southern Europe. Plowden (1985: 19) reports the results of a survey of the extra-mural activities of Italian civil servants in 1980: 19 per cent hardly ever reported for work because no checks were made; 33 per cent were selling goods in ministries during working hours; and 54 per cent had a second job. In practice, the task of modernising the Italian economy was placed in the hands of the state holding companies, although their efficiency and effectiveness were undermined by a persisting tradition of patronage politics.

However, even if the bureaucracy is efficient in the minimal sense that it is in its offices at the appointed times, and engaged in its duties rather than the running of some kind of bazaar, this does not mean that it will be able to develop an effective relationship with industry. In the case of France, it has been argued that the system of élite circulation known as *pantouflage* facilitates mutual understanding between government and industry. The process of industrialisation produced a tradition of acceptable state intervention, while the weaknesses of the political system during the Fourth Republic allowed the bureaucracy to assume a leading role in the development of industrial policy. However, the reality of French planning is that it has not been as effective as is often believed. While intermixing and interlinkages between different élites in the French system are considerable, they may also lead to the industry ministry becoming a lobbyist and spokesman for particular firms. Cawson *et al.* have noted (1987: 33) that, 'The rhetoric surrounding the role of the state in France, and a good deal of academic commentary, *assumes* a level of co-ordination. and a capacity for concerted action within the French state which our research suggests is the exception rather than the rule.'

In Britain, the individualist tradition produced by early industrialisation has persisted, and the state is seen as an outside force threatening the well-being of business. Although the British machinery of government has incorporated the idea of sponsorship divisions to look after the interests of particular sections of industry, this function has been discharged in a rather passive way. Civil servants have resisted attempts to develop a more interventionist relationship with industry.

One generalisation that can be made about state organisation in relation to industry in Western Europe is that it tends to be incoherent and fragmented, characterised by tensions between ministries and fights over 'organizational turf', and with very weak co-ordinating mechanisms to offset these centrifugal tendencies. In part, this could be characterised as a particular manifestation of general tendencies apparent in the organisation of West European governments. However, the problem is exacerbated in the case of industrial policy by the existence in most countries of a number of distinct portfolios which have industrial policy implications distinct from the principal industry ministry, e.g. energy, transport. Some countries also have regional ministries with industrial policy responsibilities (e.g. the Scottish Office). A central line of interministerial conflict that one can find in a number of countries (e.g. Britain and France) is between the central finance ministry and the ministry of industry, with the former trying to restrain public expenditure commitments, and the latter trying to maximise aid for its clients.

The development of an industrial policy by a government has generally been accompanied by the formation of an industry ministry, often split away from an older trade ministry. This was what happened in Norway in 1947 with the establishment of the Ministry of Industry and Handicrafts. This move was seen 'as a major step in developing a concerted policy for industry as a sector' (OECD 1975: 18). However, many ministries of industry tend to be relatively weak in terms of their standing in intra-bureaucratic politics. Hayward (1986b: 33) describes the French ministry of industry as 'fragmented and feeble'. Rather than the ministry being able effectively to control industrial policy, 'the latter tends to disintegrate into a plurality of policies of each of the major firms of the industrial policy community, promoted to the status of national industrial champions'

(Hayward 1986b: 34). Although President Mitterrand undertook to give the ministry 'exceptional powers', in fact these involved servicing and implementing the decisions of a Cabinet committee with the real power centre being the Prime Minister or President (Hayward 1986a: 531).

Apart from their weakness in relation to other centres of power in the government, industry ministries have often faced difficulties in securing adequate internal co-ordination (e.g between divisions responsible for particular policies, and those responsible for particular industries) or effective monitoring of their policies. In the British case, there has been a persistent difficulty in deciding what the goals of policy should be, while resources devoted to monitoring policy implementation have been inadequate. A new internal mechanism for taking a coherent overview of the range of industrial assistance offered was introduced in the 1980s (the Selective Assistance Management Group), but political pressures mean that decisions on new assistance schemes are often taken in the space of a few days. Such failings have not been confined to Britain. In Sweden, there was 'no explicit policy and no adequate administrative apparatus within the Ministry of Industry to cope with industrial crisis' (Lundmark 1983: 241).

The limitations of conventional ministries as industrial policy delivery mechanisms may be one reason why, in a number of countries, paragovernmental agencies play an important role in the development and implementation of industrial policy. The most striking example is in the Republic of Ireland where the Industrial Development Authority (IDA) has acquired *de facto* responsibility for the delivery of industrial policy. A number of countries have used state holding companies as a mechanism for assisting industrial development or to bail out declining industries (e.g. Austria, Italy, Spain, Sweden). Paragovernmental agencies have also been used as mechanisms for the identification and analysis of industrial problems and the building of consensus about possible solutions, a notable example being the National Economic Development Council (NEDC) and its economic development committees in Britain. However, the analytical capabilities of the NEDC have not been matched by an ability to take action to remedy the deficiencies of industrial performance it has identified, and its role was downgraded in 1987.

In a review of industrial policy in its member countries, the OECD emphasised the central importance of policy co-ordination in industrial policy and notes the existence of a variety of co-ordination devices ranging from Cabinet-level co-ordination, through inter-ministerial committees, to various informal arrangements (OECD 1985: 18). These devices have varied in their impact. In the case of France, Green (1983: 175) notes that 'The creation of powerful inter-ministerial committees made it possible to shortcircuit cumbersome administrative procedures and squabbles over competencies . . . they constitute an imaginative and highly appropriate intervention within a tradition of state responsibility for industrial success.' Of course, the need for such committees is a reflection of the multiplicity of agencies involved in French industrial policy, and the need to impose some order on what is, in many respects, a more pluralistic and frag-mented policy-making system than is often acknowledged. At their worst, co-ordination arrangements can add simply another actor to an already confused system. This is what seems to have happened in Italy with CIPI (the Interministerial Committee for the Co-ordina-tion of Industrial Policy) (Eisenhammer and Rhodes 1986: 438). Failing all else, the central finance ministry may take an interest in the co-ordination of industrial policy, if only because of its public expenditure implications. This is what happened under the British Labour government's industrial strategy after 1975.

The record of West European governments in handling industrial policy in the 1960s and 1970s is not generally an impressive one. Even West Germany's high-technology policy was criticised for directing aid to a limited number of firms, not all of them successful. Mény and Wright (1986: 40) conclude that in the management of the steel crisis, governments were hampered 'by their lack of a set of clear objectives and by the administrative fragmentation of the state apparatus'. All too often, industrial policy degenerated into a series of bail-outs of fundamentally inefficient enterprises located in areas which were politically or socially sensitive. The tendency of govern-ment intervention simply to slow down the adjustment process led the OECD to develop a doctrine of 'positive adjustment' in the 1980s which stressed that industrial assistance should be temporary and tapering in character and directed towards the acceleration of in-dustrial change. Even so, there was a recognition that the ability of West European countries to compete with Japan required govern-ment action to provide a framework favourable to industrial innovation. The real issue in the 1980s was whether this could best be provided by a series of national initiatives or through co-operation at the European level, an issue to which I shall return later in the chapter.

PUBLIC ENTERPRISE

Of Europe's ten largest industrial groupings in 1985–86, four were state-owned enterprises (ENI and IRI in Italy, Elf Aquitaine in France and Deutsche Bundespost in West Germany) (*Times 1000* data). However, the *fact* of state ownership does not of itself tell us much about the relationship between the enterprise and government. What is striking about a survey of the relationship between public enterprise and government policy in a number of countries is the extent to which British nationalised industries have been used as instruments to achieve government objectives, with commercial considerations being subordinated to other factors. Even in the country with the most extensive nationalised sector in Western Europe, public enterprises have been used 'for policy purposes only to a limited extent' (Parris et al. 1987: 120).

If the 1970s saw both the extension of public ownership and increased state influence over private companies, a major development in the 1980s has been the large-scale privatisation of nationalised industries in Britain. With some encouragement from the British government, and with considerable assistance from advisory services offered by merchant banks, this policy has been imitated elsewhere, although to varying extents. France passed a privatisation law in the summer of 1986, paving the way for the privatisation of over sixty companies worth an estimated £30bn over a five-year period . Twenty companies with a market capitalisation of over £10bn had already been privatised by the end of 1987. Italy has sold over $5bn worth of assets since 1983. Progress has been slower in West Germany, but then the Federal Republic has fewer industries to privatise.

Changing attitudes towards public enterprise in Italy reflect broader changes in political assessments of the role of state-owned firms in Western Europe. Public enterprise in Italy in the post-war period has gone through three main phases: the optimistic expansion from the 1950s to mid-1970s; the period of serious difficulties in the late 1970s and early 1980s; and the new realism of the mid-1980s. Unfortunately, patronage politics (*lottizzazione*) was often put before considerations of managerial and commercial efficiency. Nevertheless, the state holding companies made an impressive contribution to the conversion of Italy from a relatively backward, agrarian society to a modern industrial state, even if a productionist managerial strategy was often given too much weight. Moreover, plants constructed in the deprived southern portion of the country often had only a limited impact on the local economy. Even so, the Italian emphasis on stimulating the economy of the South was widely admired, and the state holding companies served as a model for the National Enterprise Board in Britain.

However, it was easier to be sanguine about the performance of the industries in the early 1970s than in the late 1970s. In the late 1970s and early 1980s, the state holding companies started to accumulate large losses; it was clear that their intervention in the South had not solved, and had in some respects worsened, its problems; and there was growing criticism of their use as instruments of patronage politics. By 1978 the borrowings of the three leading state holding companies amounted to £16.5bn and they recorded joint losses of £780m. One of the smaller state holding companies, EGAM, responsible for industrial rescues, folded after brief, politically motivated existence with debts of around £800m. Instead of being the most dynamic sector of the Italian economy, the state holding companies provided graphic illustrations of the dangers of encouraging managers to manoeuvre for political advantage rather than seek commercial effectiveness.

Since the early 1980s, there has been a series of major changes in the Italian state holding companies including the closure of some operations, the cautious privatisation of others and, above all else, allowing commercial considerations to override political preferences. A White Paper from the Ministry of State Holding Companies in 1980 placed a new emphasis on productive efficiency and competitiveness, the influence of market forces, joint ventures and risk capital from private shareholders. Professor Romano Prodi, an economist, took charge of IRI (the principal Italian state holding company) in 1982. He insisted that all appointments to IRI companies should be made on the basis of professional qualification, not political affiliation, a major step forward in Italy. Senior managers, including entire boards, were sacked for incompetence. He made it clear that 'he would like to see a revival of the original "IRI formula" in which state participation is not synonymous with total control, as is currently the case in most sectors, but is accompanied by the active involvement of private industry' (Eisenhammer and Rhodes 1986: 451).

The problems resulting from the allocation of managerial appointments on a political basis were not confined to Italy, as scandals in Austrian public enterprises showed. Even Austria, where the public sector accounted for one-third of public output, contemplated cautious steps towards privatisation. However, although there has been a clear trend away from public ownership throughout Western Europe, in almost all countries the railways and the Post Office (which in countries such as West Germany means telecommunications as well) are likely to remain in public ownership. These large, labour-intensive operations with a central role in national economies continued to pose difficult problems for governments, as events in the autumn of 1987 showed. These included a series of strikes on the Italian railways, a narrowly averted strike in the British Post Office, and union opposition to much-needed changes in West Germany's posts and telecommunications. The decision load imposed on government by responsibility for state-owned enterprises may have diminished, but it has not disappeared.

EMPLOYERS' ASSOCIATIONS AND TRADE UNIONS

The literature on West European politics has shown an understandable preoccupation with trade unions. Particularly in the 1970s, they have often seemed to be an invincible force whose co-operation has seemed to be an essential prerequisite of an effective industrial stategy. However, the recessionary conditions of the 1980s have seen a weakening of trade union influence. In any case, it could be argued that the co-operation of employers is as essential to the successful conduct of industrial policy. In countries such as Austria and Sweden, highly centralised employer and union federations are able to reach agreement on the broad outlines of economic policy in a way which considerably lightens the task of government. In Austria, the Parity Commission, which stands at the centre of the process of concertation, is highly informal: it 'has no address or fixed meeting place, no telephone number, no independent finance, no statutes, procedural rules, written agreements or even registered existence' (Marin 1985: 111). It ultimately ends up as an 'intimate face-to-face talk exclusively between two people – the president of the chamber of commerce representing capital and the president of the trade union confederation representing organized labour' (Marin 1983: 209). However, this congenial informality is only possible within the context of a set of highly centralised and integrated employer and labour organisations.

Even if they are not involved in reaching wide-ranging and enforceable agreements with labour about the management of the economy, employers' organisations can act as intermediaries between government and their members in relation to a wide range of other policies – sectoral industrial policies, training policies, health and safety policies, environmental policies, product quality policies, etc. However, the results of an International Institute of Management project on business interest associations showed that most employer associations in Western Europe are not capable of acting as agents for the implementation of public policy. First, in a number of countries (notably Britain), the system of business interest associations is fragmented, characterised by overlapping association domains, and even competition for members and influence. Even in countries such as West Germany, there are variations in the coherence of employer organisation.

Second, business associations may see themselves more as lobbies rather than as potential partners in governance. West Germany is often seen as the large West European country most prone to neo-corporatist tendencies, and it is certainly the case that West German associations are more actively involved than their British counterparts in such areas as training policy, health and safety, and the enforcement of quality standards. They are also capable of showing greater 'employer solidarity' in conflicts with organised labour, leading to greater employer resistance to excessive wage demands. However, one should not push this contrast too far. Streeck notes that German employer associations are characterised by a pluralist self-definition of their task and a lack of any corporate consciousness. He comments that 'the pluralist commitment to interest representation and the resentment against incorporation in the state are genuine and not merely for internal political consumption' (Streeck 1983: 274).

Another, as yet relatively undiscussed issue, is whether big business will rely in future on individual representation as well as working through associations. The American device of the government relations division has been imported into Britain, but there are also indications that in West Germany, with its strong business associations, firms are improving their 'in-house' political capabilities (Grant *et al.*, 1988). At the EC level, the weakness of most European-level business associations has been counterbalanced by firms placing their own representatives in Brussels, or by informal groupings of large firms approaching the European Commission on key issues (e.g. the Group of Twelve on information technology).

If the interests of 'capital' often disintegrate into those of individual industrial sectors or firms, the interests of labour also often lack a unity of expression. Austria, West Germany, Norway and Britain are distinctive in having single national trade union confederations, although Austria's Österreichische Gewerkschaftsbund (ÖGB) is a much more authoritative body than Britain's Trades Union Congress (TUC). In France and Italy, the union movement is divided on political lines; in the Netherlands, religious divisions have been significant; and in Denmark and Sweden, there are relatively strong confederations of white-collar employees alongside those for blue-collar workers. In Sweden, there have been increasing conflicts between the blue-collar and white-collar confederations over membership recruitment and wages policy.

The most striking development in the trade union movement in many West European countries in the 1980s has been a weakening of its influence and/or a willingness to moderate wage demands or accept lay-offs. In Britain, trade union membership (in terms of unions affiliated to the TUC) declined from nearly 12.2 million in 1979 to a little over 9 million by 1987. In addition, there was a sharp decline in closed shop arrangements in private manufacturing. In Britain, there were special political factors at work and therefore Italy presents a more interesting case in terms of general trends.

In the late 1960s and early 1970s, with the Hot Autumn of 1969 as something of a watershed, 'the Italian labour movement was transformed from a weak and divided force with little shop floor strength and limited legitimacy into a cohesive, countervailing power' (Eishenhammer and Rhodes 1986: 426). At the risk of some oversimplification, the Italian model of industrial relations in the 1970s could be said to be characterised by a growing centralisation of industrial relations, shown in the role of labour confederations in relation to labour unions, highly conflictual relationships, high rigidity in facing up to questions of labour market adjustment, and an emphasis by the unions on defending the conquests of the past. The different unions were highly competitive with one another and there was a strong polarisation of those who favoured more confrontational policies and among the employers between those who favoured greater co-operation. The role of the state was largely one of compensating for the effects of unrealistic settlements through public finance. Moreover, through an agreement of January 1975 with Confindustria (the Italian employers' organisation) the *scala mobile* introduced in 1956 was extended to compensate for 100 per cent of annual price rises. This was clearly highly inflationary in its effects and tended to undermine Italian competitiveness in price-sensitive foreign markets.

One sign of a change in attitudes came in 1980 when 40,000 workers (admittedly largely foremen and other higher grades) at Fiat marched through the streets calling for an *end* to a strike. The system of inflation-linked wage increases was set aside following a referendum. A more pragmatic approach by all actors involved in industrial relations was noted. There was less polarisation in employer strategies and less willingness by the unions to take entrenched ideological positions. The trend towards centralization was slowly reversed and there was a new wave of plant-level bargaining. The emergence of more co-operative forms of behaviour at plant level – at least in terms of a willingness to allow joint management of some problems – was perhaps the most significant change. Treu and Martinelli note (1984: 289) that 'The unions have repeatedly declared themselves ready to shift from conflictual toward more cooperative positions both at the enterprise and general economic level, provided they receive a meaningful trade-off from the state and employers.' They also point out that 'The state's attitude towards the unions has moved away from the one-way support of the late 1960s. It is now clearly preoccupied with controlling bargaining results, particularly in the wage area, through a mixture of coercive and consensus-based measures.' It should be noted that, unlike Britain, union membership has stabilised and there is a general acceptance that the unions will continue to play an important role in the conduct of economic policy.

THE ROLE OF THE FINANCIAL SECTOR

The provision of finance for industry is clearly of crucial importance in any discussion of government–industry relations. Even so, it must be recognised that what is often being discussed is a relationship between different parts of capital rather than a relationship in which government is a major actor. Central banks either enjoy constitutional independence (as in West Germany) or considerable autonomy of action even though nationalised (as in Britain). In the case of France, nationalisation of the commercial banking system did not give the government effective control over credit allocation (Hayward 1986b: 23). The rapid internationalisation of the banking system has further undermined the capacity of domestic governments to influence its activities. The build-up of foreign exchange holdings by private sector banks and companies, and the speed with which such holdings can be transferred, has tended to undermine the significance of central bank interventions in the markets. The growth of the Eurocurrency market (originating in US dollars held by residents outside the United States and now embracing European currencies as well), and its importance as a market for short-term funds operating largely outside the control of national authorities, has contributed to a situation in which 'The task of managing the international financial system . . . has become much more complex' (Gilpin 1987: 339).

This pattern of international instability is the backcloth against which domestic developments have to be viewed. What is clear is that there are considerable differences in the modernity of domestic financial systems in Western Europe, with Britain, with two major financial centres (London and Edinburgh), more committed than any other West European country to the provision of financial services as a central economic activity. At the other end of the spectrum, Italy's rapid transformation from an agrarian to an industrial society has left it with an antiquated framework of financial law. The 1913 Stock Market Act and the 1936 Banking Act are badly in need of updating. The increased activity on the Milan Stock Exchange in the 1980s reflects the buoyancy of the Italian economy rather than any fundamental change in the strength of its financial institutions. West Germany also has a stock market system made up of 'highly ineffi-cient institutions, whether efficiency is conceived by narrow reference to the transmission of information about trading condi-tions, or by reference to a more general capacity to deliver service to customers.' (Moran 1987: 15). Moran sees the absence of a finan-cial metropolis as one factor explaining the failure of the Stock Exchange system to adjust to structural change in West Germany.

Much of the debate about financial systems in Western Europe has been centred around a rather misleading comparison between Britain and West Germany. A conventional reformist wisdom has emerged which suggests that the German system is better for industry, in the sense of securing longer-term funding and a better understanding of industry's needs by the financial sector, than in Britain. Many aspects of this debate are of a rather technical character (for example, how one measures loan maturity dates) and cannot be entered into here. However, the broad outlines of the debate can be discussed.

The conventional reformist wisdom argues that the German finan-cial system is organised around 'house banks'. Each firm has a long-term relationship with a particular bank which, as well as providing loans for the companies, also has substantial shareholdings in it (particularly shares held as proxies on behalf of other investors). The bank therefore takes a long-term view of the company's success, and is prepared to back projects which may not show returns in the short run. Because of its commitment to the company, it takes a close interest in the calibre of its management, using the position of bank representatives on supervisory boards to undertake internal reorganisations where necessary.

As stated, this picture is broadly correct, although it may be qualified in two important respects. First, the conventional account pays little attention to the insurance companies who also play an important role in this system both as providers of funds (notably to 'blue chip' companies) and as board members. Second, there has been a neglect of sectoral variations within the West German system. For example, a prosperous sector like chemicals has been able to engage in more self-financing activity than other industries. Because of its expansion plans in the United States, it has also made greater use of American banks operating in West Germany.

At the very least, the house bank model has suffered from overstatement. As Mény and Wright note (1986: 83) 'perhaps the power of the German banks has been exaggerated'. Reporting on research conducted at the University of Sussex, Duchêne comments, 'our research has failed to find much support for active leadership by the banks' (Duchêne 1987: 212). Apart from the fact that the empirical evidence supporting the 'house bank' model is less strong than is sometimes supposed, the model is also open to criticism on the grounds that it has been based on an unstated and unquestioned assumption that an integrated finance–industry relationship is necessarily desirable. Yet one consequence of such an integration is that a financial crisis rapidly becomes an industrial crisis (or vice versa); such an interlocking crisis occurred in Italy in the early 1930s. It could have happened in Britain following the secondary banking crisis of 1973–74 if the banking system and industry had been more closely integrated. Moreover, while the West German system has worked well in times of prosperity, it has faltered when faced with industrial crisis. Dyson and Wilks (1983: 249) admit that the close involvement of banks with industry could be 'a serious economic liability rather than an asset if corporate crises like those of AEG and Korf Industries threaten to drag the banks down with them'. In the steel industry, 'the banks were clearly incapable of dealing alone with the major and multiple corporate crises from the late 1970s' (Mény and Wright 1986: 83).

Discussion of the West German financial system has also failed to take account of recent developments. One of the weaknesses of the British system has always been the extent to which it is centred on the Stock Exchange. This makes companies very sensitive to their share price (because of the risk of a take-over bid) and leads them to pay disproportionate attention to maintaining dividends and short-run profits. However, the West German Stock Exchange has become much more active in the 1980s. Moreover, after being protected by a variety of barriers, the German financial system is becoming more internationalised. West German banks do not have a major presence in the international financial system and it is open to question how well they will stand up to greater competition.

In Britain, the development of the corporate treasurer function by firms and, in some cases, their own 'in-house' banks has increased the sophistication of firms in handling their financial operations. Even so, certain differences between the British and West German systems persist. Investment in Britain is funded largely by retained profits, whereas bank lending is more important in West Germany. There is no equivalent in Britain of the intervention by West German banks in the internal management of firms. Bank shareholdings in firms are on a much more limited scale. London is one of the three great international financial centres along with New York and Tokyo. The British financial system does tend to encourage expansion through take-overs rather than internal growth which may not be good for the health of the economy as a whole. Moreover, although institutional shareholders dominate the stock market, they do not exert systematic pressures on firms of the kind experienced in the United States. Short-term portfolio management is given precedence over seeking to improve company performance.

Although a number of key differences in national financial systems in Western Europe have emerged from this discussion, it must be emphasised that the rapid internationalisation of financial transactions tends to undermine the importance of such differences. Such tasks as securing a measure of exchange-rate stability, which can only be pursued at a global (the Plaza Hotel and Louvre Agreements between the world's leading economic powers) or regional (European Monetary System) level are of greater long-term importance than the character of finance–industry relations in a particular country. In particular, efforts by national governments to regulate their financial systems, although not unimportant (note, for example, the persistence of exchange-control regulations in Italy) are dwarfed by the scope, scale and speed of international financial transactions.

THE EUROPEAN COMMUNITY

Even those European countries which are outside the EC have close links with it (e.g. Switzerland) or are considering whether they should become members (e.g. Norway). All the major economies of Western Europe (unless one counts Sweden in that category) are member states. It is therefore important briefly to consider the impact of the EC on government–industry relations in Western Europe.

The extent of that impact has always been limited by a number of factors: the limited powers in relation to industrial policy in the original treaties (other than the Treaty of Paris which set up the Europe an Coal and Steel Community and has permitted a relatively activist steel policy); the cumbersome decision-making procedures of the Community; the differences of national approach to industrial policy questions (e.g. French *dirigisme* and German 'liberalism'); and the desire of each member state to protect what it perceives as its national interests.

Against this background, it is not surprising that the funding of industry by the Community 'remains extremely limited (less than 1 per cent of national support)' (European Community 1987: 35). Of course, the scope of Community involvement cannot be measured just in financial terms. It is not always realised that the Community has had considerable success in constructing a Common Commercial Policy which limits the autonomy of member states in relation to trade policy (see Hine 1985). However, the most important project on which the Community is engaged is the creation of an internal market by 31 December 1992 – that is, an area without internal frontiers in which the free movement of goods, persons, services, and capital is made possible in accordance with the provisions of the Treaty of Rome. This will be a far-reaching change, although it remains to be seen whether it will be achieved on schedule.

In general, the potential of the Community in the industrial policy field has not yet been realised. However, there are three reasons for believing that this situation may be changing. First, it is becoming increasingly clear (particularly to big business) that the Community countries have problems in common which can only be dealt with on the basis of collaboration. The Community countries face a twin threat from the advanced technology of Japan, and the newly industralising countries of the Pacific Rim 'whose type of industrial specialization has more in common with that of the Community than with that of the USA or Japan' (Europe Community 1987: vi). These challenges cannot be dealt with adequately by single country 'national champions', especially in the area of high technology, hence the importance of Community programmes such as the ESPRIT programme to encourage European co-operation in the area of information technology. Second, the Single European Act ratified in

1987 (effectively a renegotiation and extension of the original treaties) gives new powers to the European Commission; for example, in the area of high technology, thus remedying the 'abstentionist' character of the Treaty of Rome in relation to industrial policy. It also offers the prospect of some speeding up of the decision-making procedure through the wider use of qualified majority voting, reducing the extent to which progress can be hindered by the use of national vetos. Third, there is evidence of greater convergence in the attitudes of member states towards industrial policy. 'Bail-outs' for firms in difficulty or for declining sectors have fallen out of favour, and there has been a greater emphasis on more general measures of industrial development, such as those targeted at industrial innovation.

Often the country which has seemed to be most out of line with the other member states is Britain. In 1987 its objections held up agreement on a new programme of Community expenditure on research and new technologies. Under Mrs Thatcher, Britain has found it difficult to accept the degree of intervention in the workings of the market economy tolerated by continental countries. Particular problems have been caused by the Commission's insistence on working with and through the 'social partners' (organised employers and unions).

One other area in which the Community has had an impact is competition policy, staging dawn raids on firms to uncover cartels. It is also taking an increasing – although controversial –interest in cross-border mergers. A third and important area of Community competition policy activity is in relation to state aid to industry. All too often, member states find themselves in competition for a particular investment project, leading to an auction process of which the main beneficiary is the multinational company seeking aid. There is thus an important role for the Community both in co-ordinating the policies of its individual member states, and in taking initiatives designed to enable the Community countries to withstand Japanese competition better.

CONCLUSION

The 1980s have clearly seen a shift to a more market-oriented approach towards industrial problems across Western Europe, although that does not mean that there is not a significant role for government in setting the framework within which enterprises operate. One unsettled question is whether the pace of change has been sufficiently fast in West Germany. This is an important question because of the centrality of the West German economy to the whole West European economy as its leading manufacturer and exporter with a particularly strong presence in such key industries as cars and chemicals.

For an economy which has long been regarded as the strongest in Western Europe, the performance of the West German economy in the mid-1980s was disappointing. Growth in 1987 was expected to be around 1.5 per cent; only in three years since 1971 (1976, 1979 and 1980) has West Germany performed better than the OECD average. Unemployment at over 8 per cent was above the OECD average, and only a little behind the British level. Labour costs in manufacturing (measured in DM per hour) were higher than those of the other four G-5 countries (Britain, USA, France, Japan), while West Germans worked, on average, fewer hours per year than any of the other four countries. Investment as a percentage of GDP in 1985 was only just above the British level, and below that of France, the United States, and Japan. The one sign of strength was a consistent trade surplus, but this was threatened by the high level of the Deutschmark, and the potential loss of some American markets as a result of that country's difficulties.

This poor performance was seen by many commentators as indicative of a deeper malaise, of a failure to turn a 1970s-style political economy into the more flexible mode required to compete effectively in the 1980s. It was argued that labour markets were unduly rigid, and that the country's dense network of institutions and organisations made change difficult. When the Vice-Governor of the People's Bank of China was taken on a tour of the Bavarian lakes and mountains, the sight of West Germans engaged in hang-gliding, wind-surfing, and other sports led him to remark to his central bank host that young people these days were not afraid to take risks (*Financial Times*, 1 November 1987). In its annual economic report, the European Commission publicly rebuked West Germany for making 'scant progress' in dismantling subsidies in industries with 'no future whatsoever' (*Financial Times*, 16 October 1987). Attempts at the end of 1987 to rationalise the steel industry met with considerable opposition from the affected communities. Efforts to liberalise strict rules on shop-opening hours also ran into difficulties. The relative inefficiency of West German telecommunications services is well known, but attempts at reform have made little progress.

By way of contrast, the liberalised British economy was recording a growth rate of 5 per cent in the year to September 1987. This contrast should not, of course, be overdrawn. The high British growth rates were expected to fall back in 1988, and could not be sustained without encountering capacity constraints (plant and skilled labour), and possibly leading to inflationary pressures. British levels of unemployment remain unacceptably high in terms of the waste of labour resources and social costs involved. Of particular concern is the pronounced north–south divide, with the rapid expansion of 'Roseland' (rest of the South-east, excluding London) not being matched in the geographically peripheral parts of the country. Other West European countries also display north–south divides (e.g. West Germany and, in reverse, Italy), and the reduction of regional imbalances remains a major task for policy-makers in the 1990s.

Will the 1990s see a continuation of the trend towards more market- oriented policies? Much will depend on whether centre–left parties recapture office in such key states as Britain, France, and West Germany. However, if they do come into office, they will face a changed economic and political environment. Many of the mechanisms of control they relied on in the 1970s will no longer be there, e.g. in the case of Britain, exchange controls, sponsorship divisions, an extensive public sector. They could not easily be reinstated, even if there was political support for such a course of action.

It seems possible that in the 1990s, with many of the problems of economic structural adjustment resolved as far as is possible, attention may turn once again to the social agenda, regardless of whether Conservative or Democratic Socialist parties are in office in any country. Issues such as regional imbalances, the problems of single-industry communities, the opportunities open to ethnic minority groups, etc. may reassert themselves on the political agenda. However, they will be seen as social rather than economic issues. One of the great errors of the 1970s was to attempt to pretend that measures that were socially desirable were economically justified. As a consequence, the measures taken were often both wasteful in terms of public expenditure, and misdirected in terms of securing policy objectives, e.g. aid was often concentrated on ailing enterprises rather than on workers displaced by unavoidable economic changes. One lesson that has been learnt from the 1970s, and hopefully will not be unlearnt, is that a clear distinction needs to be made in terms of objectives and mechanisms between industrial policy and social policy.

REFERENCES

Cawson, A., Holmes, M. and Stevens A. (1987) 'The interaction between firms and the state in France', in S. Wilks and M. Wright (eds), *Comparative Government–Industry Relations* (Oxford: Clarendon Press), pp. 10–34.

Duchêne, F. (1987) 'Policies for a wider world', in F. Duchêne and G. Shepherd (eds), *Managing Industrial Change in Western Europe* (London: Frances Pinter), pp. 210–41.

Dyson, K. and Wilks S. (1983) "Conclusions", in K. Dyson and S. Wilks, (eds), *Industrial Crisis* (Oxford: Martin Robertson), pp. 245–72

Eisenhammer, J. and Rhodes, R. (1986) 'The politics of public sector steel in Italy', in Y. Mény and V. Wright (eds), *The Politics of Steel: Western Europe and the Steel industry in the Crisis Years (1974–1984)* (Berlin: de Gruyter), pp. 416–75.

European Community (1987) *Improving Competitiveness and Industrial Structures in the Community* (Luxemburg: Office for Official Publications of the European Community).

Gilpin, R. (1987) *The Political Economy of International Relations* (Princeton: Princeton University Press).

Grant, W., Paterson, W. and Whitston, C. (1988) *Government and the Chemical Industry: A Comparative Study of Britain and West Germany* (Oxford: Oxford University Press).

Green, D. (1983) 'Strategic management and the state: France', in K. Dyson and S. Wilks (eds), *Industrial Crisis* (Oxford: Martin Robertson), pp. 161–92.

Hayward, J. (1986a) 'The nemesis of industrial patriotism: the French response to the steel crisis', in Y. Mény and V. Wright (eds), *The Politics of Steel* (Berlin: de Gruyter), pp. 502–33.

Hayward, J. (1986b) *The State and the Market Economy* (Brighton: Wheatsheaf).

Hine, R. C. (1985) *The Political Economy of European Trade* (Brighton: Wheatsheaf).

Katzenstein, P. J. (1984) *Corporatism and Change: Austria, Switzerland and the Politics of Industry* (Ithaca: Cornell University Press).

Katzenstein, P. J. (1985) *Small States in World Markets* (Ithaca: Cornell University Press).

Lundmark, K. (1983) 'Welfare State and Employment Policy: Sweden', in K. Dyson and S. Wilks (eds), *Industrial Crisis* (Oxford: Martin Robertson), pp. 220–44.

Marin, B. (1983) 'Organising interest by interest organisation. Associational prerequisites of cooperation in Austria', *International Political Science Review*, **4**, 197–216.

Marin, B. (1985) 'Austria – the paradigm case of liberal corporatism?', in W. Grant (ed.), *The Political Economy of Corporatism* (London: Macmillan), pp. 89–125.

Mény, Y. and Wright, V. (1986) 'State and steel in Western Europe', in Y. Mény and V. Wright (eds), *The Politics of Steel* (Berlin: de Gruyter), pp. 1–110.

Moran, M. (1987) 'A state of inaction: the state and stock exchange reform in the Federal Republic of Germany', working paper, Department of Government, University of Manchester.

OECD (1975) *The Aims and Instruments of Industrial Policy* (Paris: Organisation for Economic Co-operation and Development).

Parris, H., Pestieau P. and Saynor, P. (1987) *Public Enterprise in Western Europe* (Beckenham: Croom Helm).

Plowden, W. (1985) 'The culture of Whitehall', in D. Englefield (ed.), *Today's Civil Service* (Harlow: Longman), pp. 19–28.

Sidenius, N. C. (1983) 'Danish industrial policy: persistent liberalism', *Journal of Public Policy*, **3**, 49–61.

Streeck, W. (1983) 'Beyond pluralism and corporatism: German business associations and the state', *Journal of Public Policy*, **3**, 265–84.

Streeck, W. (1984) *Industrial Relations in West Germany* (London: Heinemann).

Treu, T. and Martinelli, A. (1984) 'Employers' associations in Italy', in J. P. Windmuller and A. Gladstone (eds), *Employers' Associations and Industrial Relations* (Oxford: Oxford University Press), pp. 264–93.

CHAPTER FIVE
The Re-emergence of Defence as a Political Issue

Peter J. Byrd

During the 1980s defence re-emerged as a major political controversy in Western Europe after a long period in which there had been a broad consensus on defence between governments and a considerable lack of interest in defence within, domestic politics. This dramatic change was caused by developments outside Europe in the realm of relations between the superpowers and, to a lesser extent, by changes within Western Europe itself. The impact of defence manifested itself in two political arenas: first in foreign and security policy where new and difficult security issues emerged, and second in domestic politics where sharp differences divided publics. Externally and at home defence assumed the highest political salience.

This chapter begins with a brief review of the post-war defence settlement in Europe, founded on the North Atlantic Treaty Organisation (NATO) and, specifically, on the American security guarantee of Europe. It analyses the cracks which appeared in the defence settlement in the 1970s, the proposed solution to which was the so-called double track (or twin track) policy of 1979. The third section of the chapter is concerned with the implementation of the double track policy between 1979 and the American–Soviet Treaty on Intermediate-range Nuclear Forces (INF) in December 1987. Throughout the security crisis of the 1980s the interplay between external and domestic factors made the defence issue an inherently complex one for European governments. Externally, the most important factor for governments was the management of their security relationship with the United States. Domestically, the most important factor was the maintenance of unity. Governments found it increasingly difficult to balance the two: in the early 1980s the management of the relationship with the United States tended to undermine consensus at home. By the late 1980s that consensus had been, in part, rebuilt but at the cost of a new and much less reassuring security relationship with the United States.

THE POST-WAR SECURITY SYSTEM IN EUROPE

After the Second World War security relationships in Western Europe enjoyed unprecedented stability for a number of reasons.

1) Western Europe in 1945 was economically dislocated; recovery from the end of the 1940s and through the 1950s was substantially underwritten by the United States through Marshall Aid (European Recovery Program, 1947). At the same time the United States was anxious to invest abroad to secure its own economic prosperity after the war. Hence there was a high degree of symmetry between European and American needs. The 'open economies' that developed in Western Europe and the United States were underpinned by American-led international institutions, particularly the Bretton Woods system of stable dollar-based currency relationships supported by the International Monetary Fund, the World Bank and the General Agreement of Tariffs and Trade.

2) This economic harmony reinforced a similar harmony of security interests. Western European governments shared increasing security fears. The three interlinked elements in this security crisis were the erosion of domestic stability by Communist-inspired subversion following the crises of May 1947 when Communist parties left the governing coalitions of France and Italy, the failure of the four occupying powers to conclude a settlement on Germany; the increasingly unstable imbalance of power between the Soviet Union and Western Europe which was exacerbated by American disarmament and disengagement from Europe. Gradually the American government developed a broader conception of national security which required support for Western Europe as its own front line in a strategy to contain the Soviet Union. Thus, as Western Europe looked to the United States to guarantee its security, the United States sought to re-establish its military power in Europe. This was the basis of NATO, an alliance of the United States, Canada and ten European states (led by the British and French) concluded in April 1949.

3) The governments of Western Europe concluded, reluctantly, that a new German state would have to be incorporated within this

emerging economic and military system. Economic recovery was impossible without the motor of the German economy, while a military balance of power was impossible if the Soviet Union could dominate Germany. A divided Germany with a strong, but nevertheless controlled, West German state was a satisfactory outcome and between 1946 and 1949 such a state gradually emerged from the American, British and French zones of occupation. From 1949 a major debate continued within and between the European members of the alliance about the rearmament of West Germany, with the Americans strongly in favour. The issue was resolved by the Paris Agreements of October 1954 which provided for German membership of NATO and also for its (non-nuclear) rearmament within a new institution, separate from but operating within NATO, called the Western European Union, consisting of the Benelux countries, Britain, France, West Germany, and Italy.

4) In Germany and Italy, and indeed in the other European states which had suffered the shock of defeat and foreign occupation, domestic societies were rebuilt. The American military and economic presence assisted in what was widely seen as a process of 'Americanisation' of society, which consolidated the growth of the Atlantic Community underlying the political, military and economic arrangements between the NATO members.

In the late 1950s and 1960s this comprehensive set of mutual interests was strained by a number of new developments. Doubts grew about the credibility of the American nuclear commitment to Europe as the Soviet Union developed a long-range nuclear capability which could strike directly at the American heartland and so render American assistance to Europe prohibitively costly. The problem was particularly acute for the Germans who were placed in the front line of European defence and whose territorial integrity remained uncertain as a consequence of the division of Germany into two states with peculiarly unstable arrangements for the divided city of Berlin, lying deep within East Germany. The Christian Democratic-led government of West Germany had not reconciled itself to the permanent division of Germany into two states and looked to NATO for support for eventual reunification. From 1958 onwards the government became increasingly alarmed at the situation in Berlin where Soviet pressure on the Western position culminated in the Berlin Wall crisis in August 1961 in which the three Western occupying powers accepted *de facto* the division of Berlin into two exclusive sectors without movement across the wall. Following the 1961 crisis the governments of Adenauer and Erhard pursued tentative *détente* with the Soviet Union out of frustration with the lack of American support, partly in order to place pressure on the Americans and partly to relieve unilaterally their security problem.

In the period after the successful resolution of the Cuban missile crisis in October 1962, a general *détente* developed between the two superpowers and within Europe. In France de Gaulle pursued an independent policy towards the East, and in West Germany the opening to Moscow was developed first by the Christian Democrat–Social Democrat coalition of 1966 and from 1969, in a more dramatic and comprehensive manner, by Brandt's Social Democrat-led government. The development of *détente* was not unbroken, suffering a major set-back with the Soviet occupation of Prague and forcible removal of the reforming Czech government in 1968. Nevertheless, during the 1960s it became progressively more difficult to sustain NATO on the strength of a perceived Soviet threat, particularly while the projected NATO response to such a threat, massive American nuclear attacks on the Soviet Union, was so manifestly lacking in credibility.

By the end of the 1960s a set of European responses to the new security situation had emerged and been negotiated with the Americans. The outcome constituted a solution of sorts to the threat of disunity and, perhaps surprisingly, carried the alliance through to the late 1970s. The simple, cohesive, framework of the early days of NATO had, however, been lost.

The solutions sought by NATO involved a degree of devolution of nuclear decision-making from the Americans alone to the alliance as a whole. Ultimately a clear-cut answer to the question of sharing nuclear responsibility could not be found, though for several years in the early 1960s the alliance toyed with rather impractical ideas for a multilateral nuclear force made up of contingents from several allies. A second factor in the debates hinged around the extent to which the European states were prepared to increase their own defence expenditures to give a greater conventional, as opposed to nuclear, capability to the alliance and so reduce reliance on the American deterrent. A third factor concerned the alliance's ability to act as an instrument of *détente* with the Soviet Union while still offering security against it. Three sets of responses can be identified.

The French government of de Gaulle concluded that the alliance could no longer guarantee French security. He resented also the pattern of American leadership of the alliance, with Britain enjoying a special status among the European members. Under his presidency the existing French atomic development programme was accelerated and made the focus of French security policy. France remained a member of NATO, but in 1966–67 withdrew from the integrated military structure. De Gaulle's emphasis on national autonomy provided the basis for a domestic consensus on defence which has survived other political vicissitudes. The right wing supported the emphasis on national sovereignty and shared de Gaulle's hostility towards American domination of Western Europe. The Communists supported a defence policy which was less oriented towards the United States and a foreign policy which was markedly independent. The Socialists were less enthusiastic supporters of a nuclear strategy, but in the 1970s, under Mitterrand's leadership and later presidency, they continued the expansion of nuclear capabilities.

The British government was sceptical about devolving nuclear decision-making, and shared the general reluctance of the smaller members of the alliance to give West Germany too prominent a nuclear role. The Conservative governments of Macmillan and Home and the Labour government of Wilson pursued a sort of double track policy. The first track sought new procedures for nuclear consultation in NATO and a more credible military doctrine and strategy. This new doctrine of flexible response, strongly supported by the Americans, was formally adopted by the alliance in 1967. It entailed a continuing American nuclear guarantee, but without the unrealistic reliance on early and automatic use of nuclear weapons. The new military strategy called for greater conventional defences for Europe, largely provided by the Europeans themselves, which would delay the moment at which the Americans would be obliged to 'press the button'. Hence a measure of European rearmament and greater self-help was accepted. At the same time, the American tactical nuclear weapons deployed within Europe were maintained to link ('couple') European defence with the American strategic nuclear forces. This compromise was accepted by the Americans, who favoured European conventional defence, and by the Europeans (France excepted) who favoured the American nuclear deterrent. Alongside this alliance initiative, where they enjoyed a considerable diplomatic success, the British pursued a second track to their defence policy – a development of nuclear weapons under national, rather than NATO, control. This aspect of the policy was defended publicly both as a contribution to the alliance's nuclear capabilities within the new doctrine of flexible response and as a national fall-back insurance in case the alliance should fail. There were thus some similarities between British and French nuclear policies, although the French despised the ambiguities in the British posture while the British claimed that this ambiguity was valuable precisely because it both contributed to the alliance and also offered an insurance if the alliance were to fail.

West Germany and the smaller European members of the alliance had no independent nuclear option and had to rely on flexible response. Each of the European states, with the exception of the two Scandinavian members, Denmark and Norway, who had never allowed nuclear weapons to be held on their territories, hosted American nuclear bases. Ultimate control of these bases rested with the Americans but was regulated by a set of consultative procedures (the Athens guidelines of 1962). West Germany and the smaller members of the alliance also deployed tactical nuclear weapons although the Americans retained a physical control (the 'double key' system) over actual use. The West Germans were given a permanent seat on the alliance's new nuclear consultative councils while the smaller states rotated places. The West German government also insisted that, militarily, flexible response embraced the 'forward defence' of West Germany at the inner-German border, so seeking to spare West Germany the prospect of her defence being secured by war fought throughout her own territory.

Alongside these military changes, introduced in 1967, a further initiative to cement alliance unity was the adoption of the Harmel Report in December 1967. This report coupled existing security policy of the alliance with the goal of relaxation of tensions and improved relations with the Soviet bloc. The coupling of *détente* and defence as complementary goals assisted especially Social Democratic parties and governments in securing support for the alliance.

ECONOMIC, POLITICAL, AND MILITARY CONFLICTS WITHIN NATO IN THE 1970s

The compromises of the 1960s held for about a decade. Relative military stability was enjoyed by NATO and the doctrine of flexible response was unchallenged. However, the alliance was subject to radical economic and political change. In 1971 the international monetary system established at Bretton Woods collapsed; the American economy was no longer strong enough, relative to those of Europe, to underwrite the system of fixed exchange rates against the dollar. The dollar was devalued and, between 1971 and 1973, a system of floating exchange rates replaced Bretton Woods. The relative strength of the West German economy and the role of its central bank, the Bundesbank, became a key factor in European diplomacy. The recovery of the European economies, since the 1940s, and the consolidation of the European Community (EC), undermined the assumption that there was a natural community of economic interests across the Atlantic. By the 1970s the Americans saw the EC as an economic rival and its European military allies as free-riding on the backs of the American taxpayer. The strains to the international economy brought about by the oil shocks of 1973–74 led to pressures for protectionism. The American and European economies have since coexisted uneasily, but there is now a structural conflict of economic interests built into NATO out of which occasional acute crises arise, as for instance over European agricultural protection or over subsidised European steel exports undercutting the American steel industry.

In political terms also the Americans and the Europeans moved apart in the 1970s in three broad areas: a growing divergence of national societies; major differences of policy towards regions outside Europe, especially in the Middle East and Central America; and conflicting attitudes towards the Soviet Union.

Notwithstanding the process of 'Americanisation' referred to earlier, American and European political societies continued to differ and cause problems for alliance management. The Americans accepted European social democracy as a legitimate manifestation of alliance politics, despite deep worries in the 1950s over the neutralist direction of German social democracy. But in the 1970s a new worry developed over the growth in the southern members of the alliance of Communist parties within the framework of 'Euro-Communism'. The Communists appeared as major claimants to political power in the political vacuum in Portugal following the military coup of 1974, and in Spain during the transition to democracy in 1975–77. In both cases, free elections revealed the Communists to be weak. Spain was not a member of NATO but, with strong American support, entry was successfully negotiated by the centrist governments of Adolfo Suarez and Calvo Sotelo. The Americans had long had, and indeed continue to maintain, bilateral defence arrangements including nuclear bases. In Italy the Communist Party appeared throughout the 1960s and 1970s to be on the verge of political control until the election of 1976 which marked, in effect, the conclusion of the 'Historic Compromise' between Christian Democracy and Communism. Italy remained a loyal member of the alliance.

In another sense the community of values cementing and representing Atlanticism came under strain in the 1970s. In the United States political power was moving away from the East Coast liberal élites who had been a dominant force in shaping American foreign policy towards Europe in the immediate post-war period. The dominant forces in American politics were increasingly southern and western, conservative rather than liberal, and oriented westwards towards the Pacific Rim rather than eastwards towards Europe.

In the 1960s the Americans resented the criticism of their policies in South-east Asia by European governments and political parties stretching from left to right. In the 1970s and 1980s differences arose over policy towards Central America and towards what Americans termed the 'Crescent of Conflict' which stretched from Afghanistan through the Gulf and the Arabian Peninsula to the Horn of Africa. Acute differences occurred over Israel where, in the Venice Declaration of 1980, the EC declared itself in favour of a Palestinian state. After disagreeing about the significance of Afghanistan, the European states were nervous about American military deployments in the Gulf in the mid-1980s in response to the Iran–Iraq War. Several European states deployed limited naval forces in the Gulf but did not collaborate with the Americans. A low point of American–European conflict over policy towards the Middle East was the condemnation of the American bombing raid of Tripoli in Libya in April 1986 when only Britain allowed the Americans to make use of air bases and to overfly airspace. So far as Britain was concerned, the low point was reached with the American invasion of the Commonwealth state of Grenada in October 1983.

Relations with the Soviet Union remained a source of potential difficulty for NATO. The Americans and the Europeans rarely succeeded in co-ordinating their policies towards the Soviet Union and the Warsaw Pact. European states regarded the Soviet Union as a neighbour, albeit an uncomfortable and over-large one, and were uncertain about how to respond to the security demands of the Soviet Union. When the Americans, during the Kissinger–Brezhnev 'era of negotiations', appeared to concede Eastern Europe to the Soviet Union as their own backyard, the Europeans were critical. They were equally critical when President Carter pursued a different tack and maximised the human rights issues in Eastern Europe. Above all, European governments were fearful that American arms control agreements with the Soviet Union, and the whole process of improving American–Soviet relations, would be conducted above their heads – in other words, that a 'special relationship' between the superpowers might emerge from which they were excluded.

American acceptance of Soviet strategic nuclear parity in the 1972 and 1979 Strategic Arms Limitation Treaties was potential evidence of such a relationship. Soviet nuclear parity weakened the credibility of the American guarantee of Europe, especially when the treaties did not restrain the Soviet superiority in Europe in INF systems.

THE SECURITY CRISIS OF THE 1980s

Economic, political, and military tensions were developing within NATO during the 1970s, and the 1967 Agreement on Flexible Response was subjected to increasing strain. These tensions remained, however, primarily the concern of governments and barely intruded into the domestic arena. At the end of the 1970s new developments transformed security policy into high politics for governments and for domestic politics. The domestic consensuses on defence, built on NATO's success in resolving the security problems of Western Europe, which had removed defence from the political agendas and thereby allowed governments to make defence policy without major domestic interference, were smashed. Most of the new developments originated outside Europe; each produced complex reactions within Europe.

Détente between the superpowers collapsed at the end of the 1970s, hard on the heels of the conclusion of the second Strategic Arms Limitation Treaty in June 1979. The Soviet occupation of Afghanistan in December 1979 precipitated a sharp cooling of relations and killed any prospect of the treaty receiving American ratification. In December 1980 a political crisis in Poland led to warnings against Soviet military intervention from NATO, which were led by the new hard-line anti-Communist government of President Reagan. The domestic situation in Poland worsened during 1981 as the government's legitimacy faltered before the challenge from the Solidarity movement. In December 1981, paradoxically in a desperate attempt to forestall Soviet intervention, General Jaruzelski led a military coup against the regime and imposed martial law. The banning of Solidarity was condemned by NATO and sanctions were imposed on Poland. The Reagan administration denounced the era of *détente* and arms control, and a new cold war was ushered in. Likewise, the Brezhnev government had clearly abandoned the prospect of co-operation with the West in favour of pursuing its interests in Afghanistan and Poland. Superpower relations became marked by posturing, moral invective and crisis, of which the worst was the shooting down of a Korean airliner in September 1983, and did not improve until the series of conciliatory gestures made by General Secretary Mikhail Gorbachev in early 1985. The cold war between the superpowers ruled out any progress in the arms control talks which actually recommenced in late 1981 and lingered on until broken off by the Soviet Union at the end of 1983.

For NATO, the balance between *détente* and defence was upset as defence displaced *détente*. The alliance tended to divide and its domestic support weakened. Helmut Schmidt, the West German Chancellors, argued that *détente* should be sustained despite set-backs in Afghanistan and Poland. He placed the most positive construction on Jaruzelski's coup and minimised the significance for Europe of Afghanistan. The smaller northern European members of the alliance agreed, while the Conservative governments of the United States and Britain, supported by France, argued the case for rearmament and resolution against the Soviet Union.

During this period, from the end of the Carter presidency onwards, the Americans and NATO sought to develop their deterrent doctrines to meet the situation posed by Soviet nuclear parity. American administrations were concerned about both the general credibility of their deterrent and specifically the credibility of deterrents in Europe. The evolution of policy amounted to an abandonment of mutual assured destruction (MAD), the doctrine adopted in the mid-1960s which emphasised the catastrophic nature of nuclear war to all its participants. In its place was developed deterrence through counter-force or war-fighting capabilities which threatened limited rather than catastrophic or suicidal war. In 1980, after about three years of preparation, a new American doctrine, the countervailing strategy, was announced. In 1982 President Reagan went a stage further with his prevailing strategy which implied the possibility of the United States 'winning' a sustained nuclear war against the Soviet Union.

The deterrent postures of NATO had never been entirely consistent with American doctrines, but governments understood the difficulties of producing credible postures, and public opinion had been kept in ignorance or had shown little interest in the problems. European governments welcomed the attempts by Carter to produce a deterrent doctrine which recognised European worries about coupling, and saw the countervailing policy as sensitive to their needs. However, Reagan's policy appeared to emphasise war-fighting at the expense of deterrence and upset the delicate balance between nuclear deterrence, which the Europeans saw as the basis of their security, and nuclear or indeed conventional war-fighting capabilities as the basis of defence, an idea to which the Americans were more attracted. This was similar to the debates in the 1960s over alliance doctrine which had led to the compromise of flexible response.

Two distinct steps in the implementation of American and NATO doctrines into military practice can be noted. First, in 1977 President Carter decided to deploy in Europe the 'neutron bomb' or enhanced radiation bomb to reinforce the alliance's tactical nuclear capability. Perhaps paradoxically, two Social Democratic leaders, Prime Minister Callaghan and Chancellor Schmidt, gave strongest support, despite opposition from within their own parties. While these governments wanted to increase the American readiness to use nuclear weapons in defence of Europe, large sections of their own parties and of sister Social Democratic parties opposed the policy for this same reason. In 1978 President Carter, alarmed by the European opposition and uncertain about the moral case for deploying the new weapon, changed his mind. Callaghan and Schmidt were unable thereafter to take Carter seriously, but the damage to their own internal standing was clear.

Second, from 1977 to 1979 NATO considered a major expansion of its longer-range nuclear capability (INF) based in Europe. Schmidt was particularly concerned that nuclear parity in very long range, or strategic, weapons had opened up a Soviet 'window of opportunity' to exploit their advantage in INF and conventional forces, decoupling Europe from the American strategic deterrent. In 1977 the alliance adopted a major long-term improvement programme to expand defence expenditures by 3 per cent a year, and in December 1979 announced plans for a modernisation of INF in the double track policy. From 1983 onwards 572 new land-based missiles would be deployed in Western Europe in five member states: 160 Cruise missiles in Britain, 96 in Italy, 48 in Belgium, 48 in the Netherlands and 112 in West Germany along with 108 Pershing 2 ballistic missiles. The decision was justified by reference to the Soviet Union's own growing INF capability based on the SS-20 missile. The NATO declaration held out the possibility that if a major arms control agreement to limit the SS-20 could be negotiated, then the expansion of NATO's INF systems would not be necessary.

In 1979 the double track route to security through arms control or rearmament enabled the alliance to offer a united front. However, the main emphasis was undoubtedly on rearmament in order to re-establish a firmer coupling of the alliance's American deterrents based in Europe with the American strategic deterrent. As the rearmament track came to the fore, Denmark and Greece moved towards an abstentionist line on the whole double track issue, and other alliance members, notably Belgium and the Netherlands, found that domestic opposition delayed acceptance of missile deployments on their territory.

The emphasis on rearmament was reinforced by the general deterioration of relations between Washington and Moscow after 1980, which seemed to rule out the possibility of an arms control deal. The effect of these major changes to nuclear doctrine and military capability carried out by the Americans, acting in partnership with the Europeans, was to focus increasing emphasis on defence as a major political issue in Western Europe. The initiatives stimulated a major development of anti-nuclear peace movements in Europe. The neutron bomb episode began the process, and each stage in the story thereafter – the double track policy, the prevailing doctrine, the general move from *détente* to cold war – assisted the growth of the peace movements. Peace movements also thrived on other concerns of the European left, including opposition to civil nuclear energy, concern for ecology and the environment, and the apparent exhaustion of the classical Social Democratic prescriptions for providing economic growth and social justice. Peace movements developed rapidly in all northern members of the alliance and by 1983 demonstrations of over 1 million people were commonplace. In each country the implementation of the double track policy became the crucial defence issue for governments and peace movements alike. The deployment of the new Cruise and Pershing missiles in the five states assumed enormous symbolic importance. In southern Europe the opposition tended to be more muted. The peace movement was strong in Greece, where the Socialist Papandreou government elected in 1981 maximised its own opposition to NATO policies, and sought (rather ineffectively) to negotiate the removal of all American military bases. In Italy there were demonstrations but the resolve of the government to proceed was not seriously challenged. Only in France was the peace movement hardly represented at all. The governments of President Giscard d'Estaing and, from 1981, François Mitterrand strongly supported the Nato policy but made it clear that there was no question of France allowing the Americans to deploy any of the new weapons on French territory. Above all, perhaps, implementing the double track policy posed major problems for Social Democratic parties in their attempts to reconcile internal unity, consistency with past support for NATO, and short-term electoral support.

IMPLEMENTING THE DOUBLE TRACK POLICY

The implementation of the double track policy in Western Europe passed through four distinct phases:

A first phase, lasting from December 1979 to December 1983, of preparation for the development of the new missiles and negotiation with the Soviet Union.

A second phase, lasting until early 1985, of missile deployments in the wake of the collapse of the arms control negotiations with the Soviet Union.

A third phase, lasting from early 1985 until late 1987, of resumed negotiations with the Soviet Union, culminating in the conclusion of a treaty on 7 December 1987 in Washington.

A fourth phase, commencing with the treaty, of re-evaluation of NATO's security situation.

During the first phase the main commitment required of the allies was financial support for the 'infrastructure' costs of the new missiles – new silos, etc. The financial cost was modest as the Americans were to bear the cost of the new missiles. Politically, however, the new missiles raised difficult problems about control. The Americans would retain military control over the missiles within the alliance's existing arrangements for political consultation. Only Denmark and Greece refused to shoulder their share of the financial cost. One other important element of the implementation of the policy emerged. Schmidt made it clear that missile deployments were necessary on the broad basis of five allied countries. From the start he was concerned at the possibility that domestic opposition or government caution in the other countries might leave West Germany as the sole country deploying such missiles. Such a position, which the Germans termed 'singularity', would leave it dangerously exposed to the Soviet Union. Allied solidarity was, for Schmidt, an important part of deterrence, the risk with the double track policy being that it might expose a lack of solidarity.

After 1979 domestic opposition to the new missiles increased rapidly. Peace movements concerted opposition on a trans-European basis. Hence by the time that talks with the Soviet Union on INF opened in late 1981 the prospect of carrying through the deployments in full appeared uncertain.

In Britain the Campaign for Nuclear Disarmament helped persuade a consistent 2:1 majority of public opinion against the new missiles. The opposition Labour Party opposed deployment unconditionally. However, the Conservative government was unflinching in its support and was able to bypass public opposition to the missiles by articulating public support for NATO in general and opposition to the idea of unilateral or unconditional disarmament with which Labour was identified. In 1980 the government announced its decision to modernise the national nuclear deterrent forces with the American Trident missile. Public opinion was cool towards Trident, but strongly hostile to the total abandonment of the British deterrent favoured by the Labour Party. The government represented both the American Cruise missiles and the renewal of the national deterrent as complementary elements of a resolute defence policy which contrasted with Labour's unilateralism. Labour's standing on defence policy became widely distrusted and contributed to the party's dismal showing in the 1983 general election. Nevertheless, there was consistent public concern both about the new missiles and the absence of a physical veto over their use, and also a broader concern about the reliability and prudence of America as an ally. The American invasion of Grenada highlighted this concern among both the general public and the government itself.

In West Germany Chancellor Schmidt, the originator of the double track policy, lost a vote of confidence in 1982 to the Christian Democrats and saw his own party move decisively against him. In the 1983 extraordinary party congress Schmidt was isolated and humiliated on the defence issue. The Social Democratic Party (SPD) did not unconditionally oppose the double track policy, nor move as far as the British Labour Party in adopting a generally anti-NATO stance, but it argued that the chief obstacle to a resolution of the whole INF imbroglio lay with Washington rather than with Moscow.

The new Chancellor, Helmut Kohl, supported the double track policy against the mass demonstrations of the peace movement. The West German consensus on defence was shaken but not broken. Public support for the double track policy was maintained with a majority of about 2:1 in favour of the deployments in Germany. Nor, despite the efforts of the peace movement, did defence displace the economy as the key political issue. However, there was a greater division on defence than in the 1950s. Supporters of the SPD and to some extent of the Free Democrats, the minority party within the government, reflected the ideas of the peace movement. The new Green Party worked closely with the peace movement, and its electoral impact inevitably shaped the policies of the SPD whose votes it threatened.

The political impact of the peace movements must not be exaggerated in West Germany, nor in Britain. In both countries there were tiny minorities of dedicated opponents and large sections of the public, in Britain a majority, who were opposed to aspects of defence policy. But defence did not become the dominant political issue and in both countries Conservative parties won two striking electoral victories in the 1980s. Politically, another source of support for peace movements by Social Democratic parties was also important. In both Britain and West Germany the Social Democratic model of government had been shaken by the impact of international depression and inflation ('stagflation') following the great economic upheavals of the early 1970s. Party leaderships had contained growing discontent within their own ranks over the orthodoxy of their governments, particularly in Britain following the intervention of the International Monetary Fund in the wake of the 1976 sterling crisis. Following electoral defeat, in 1979 in Britain and in 1983 in West Germany, the parties engaged in a major internal policy debate. Rejection, or partial rejection in the case of the SPD, of the traditional consensual position on defence was therefore part of a much wider programmatic renewal. Moreover, in both countries sections of the left had never been fully reconciled to Atlanticism and NATO. While their parties enjoyed electoral success, leaderships had been able to minimise discontent. In the 1980s leaderships lost this control. Callaghan and Schmidt saw their own parties decisively reject their defence policies within a year of their giving up the leadership. Defence was an important aspect of this search on the left for new policies; it reflected public concern and the strongly mobilised activities of a minority of the public who demonstrated. But the left's revolt on defence must be set in a much broader context of rejection of the old Social Democratic orthodoxy.

In West Germany, as elsewhere in northern Europe, the peace movements found strong support from the Protestant churches who developed an institutional framework of peace councils, but went further in developing a theology of peace that was strongly hostile to nuclear deterrence. In Catholic Europe, including Catholic West Germany, opposition to the double track policy was consistently weaker and less effective. During the 1970s and 1980s the Catholic church developed a position on conditional acceptance of nuclear deterrence, though some national congregations of bishops (the Netherlands and also the American bishops) went further in denouncing specific nuclear policies.

The situation in Belgium and the Netherlands was critical to NATO, since both countries were due to receive forty-eight missiles. In neither country could governments be formed in the early 1980s with a majority for deployment, although, as the first missiles were not due until after the larger countries had begun deployments, the governments of both states concentrated on the arms control track of the policy.

In the Netherlands the peace movement was based around the Dutch Inter-church Peace Council (the IKV), founded in 1966, which included the Catholic church. It had played a prominent role in the campaign against the neutron bomb and in the period after 1979 shaped public opinion against the new missile deployments. In 1981–82 only about 30 per cent of public opinion supported the new missiles. However, there was only minority support for unilateral renunciation of the Dutch nuclear status within the alliance by removing the existing American nuclear bases or giving up the Dutch armed forces' double key nuclear weapons. Within the Netherlands, as in every other country, opposition to the new missiles was higher among women than men and among supporters of left-wing parties. The Dutch Labour Party occupied a critical position within a multi-party system and the governing coalition repeatedly delayed a firm decision on deployment.

A similar situation applied in Belgium where unstable governing majorities found it almost equally difficult to find a parliamentary majority for deployment. The party system was more difficult to manage but the peace movement was less effective than in the Netherlands. There was no equivalent of the IKV and the peace movement suffered from a perception of Communist influence.

In Italy the Christian Democratic (DC) government strongly supported the double track policy, and when in 1983 the leadership of the government passed to the Socialists under Bettino Craxi there was no change of defence policy. The peace movement was strongest regionally in Sicily where the missiles were to be deployed, and politically within the Communist Party (PCI) which was the second largest political party after the DC. Under Enrico Berlinguer the policy of the PCI was ambivalent although the presence of Communists within the peace movement caused conflict with other political parties.

France was not, of course, due to receive any missiles, although the government of Giscard d'Estaing had strongly supported the 1979 policy. Only in France did the peace movement fail to develop strongly. Two reasons seem to account for this. First the defence consensus in France was strong and centred around the national nuclear deterrent force. By the late 1970s the Socialists had come round to support for the deterrent, and in the elections of 1981 for the presidency and the National Assembly the major parties differed on defence only marginally. Second, the peace movement was more handicapped than in Italy by suspicions about the role played by the Communist Party. The French Communist Party was in serious decline, but was much less independent of Moscow than in Italy. In 1981 a non-Communist peace movement, known after its initials as CODENE, was established. It adopted an even-handed attitude towards the nuclear forces of the two superpowers in Europe and challenged the pro-nuclear basis of French defence policy. Herein lay the roots of its failure. The government was deflected not at all from its diplomatic support of the double track policy nor from its expansion of the national nuclear forces.

In Denmark and Norway public opposition to the double track policy was much greater and the non-nuclear tradition an established part of the defence consensus. In these countries the issue became for a time the most important item on the domestic political agenda. In Norway the government sustained its support for the double track policy, but in Denmark the government was rapidly forced into an agnostic position on the whole issue. The left-wing parties in the two systems co-operated quite closely in the Scandilux grouping of parties, which included also the Benelux countries, but in fact the defence traditions of the two countries were quite distinct. In Norway defence expenditure was considerably higher and a military tradition remained unchallenged through the 1980s. In Denmark governments moved against defence spending in general and, even with non-Socialist governing coalitions, adopted a minimalist position within NATO.

Until 1981 the NATO states consolidated their diplomatic unity in preparation for the negotiations with the Soviet Union on INF. In the negotiations, NATO itself was not a party and the Europeans had to rely on consultation with the Americans. When the negotiations began this presented few serious problems, although the British government was nervous that the Soviets would introduce the British national deterrent force into the American–Soviet equation which could easily lead to the continental members of the alliance concluding that the British national force was an impediment to a treaty.

Throughout the first phase of negotiations the two sides remained far apart. Brezhnev and, from November 1982, Andropov refused to countenance any new Western deployments. This intransigence helped unite Western governments, particularly the more sceptical ones, but failed to undermine the self-confidence of the peace movements who adopted a position practically identical with the Soviets of opposing Western policy.

The NATO diplomatic position, developed first by President Reagan, was the 'zero solution'; the Americans offered to forgo all their new missiles in return for the Soviets abandoning their INF systems. The zero option was denounced by the Soviets and the peace movements. Some Western governments, particularly Britain and France, saw it as a negotiation device to gain public support for the double track policy, including the rearmament track, given that the prospect of unilateral Soviet disarmament was remote, when the Western governments might not be able to carry through their deployments because of domestic opposition. The smaller northern allies supported the zero option in the hope that it might remove the need for deployment. The West German government was more sceptical, preferring from the start serious negotiations over a compromise agreement with the Soviet Union, but it too nevertheless supported the zero solution.

In June 1982 an unofficial American compromise offered limited Western deployments in return for limited Soviet disarmament. This was rejected by the Soviets who offered no more than limited Soviet reductions in return for no Western deployments. The Americans then disowned the compromise, the negotiations ground to a halt, and at the end of 1983 the deployments went ahead. The Soviets walked out of both the INF talks, and also of the parallel negotiations on strategic armaments. Soviet intransigence had contributed to the unity of the alliance, even for those governments unable to find parliamentary majorities for their own deployments.

A further success for the alliance was the Spanish entry in May 1982. The Spanish government took no position on the double track policy. Following the Socialist victory in the October 1982 election, the new Prime Minister, Felipe Gonzalez, came under intense pressure to take Spain out of the alliance. Gonzalez agreed only to a referendum on Spanish membership. When this was held in March 1986 he played a crucial role in persuading the electorate to vote for continued membership, overcoming opposition from within parts of his own party, the Communist Party, and from the neutralist tradition of the centre and right parties.

During the second phase of the double track policy, from the first deployments in November 1983 until negotiations with the Soviet Union resumed in early 1985, the European members of the alliance braced themselves against public demonstrations as the deployments of missiles were carried out in Britain, West Germany, and Italy. The peace movements reached a peak with the first deployments and thereafter the governments were able to relax slightly. The demonstrations of the first period were not repeated on the same scale and, though the bases themselves became the targets of permanent protests, it was difficult for the peace movements to sustain momentum. The strategy of the Soviet Union, which had apparently relied on the peace movements to undermine the Western position, failed. By the time negotiations with the Soviet Union resumed in 1985, the Belgium government had agreed to deployment and the Dutch government, in a policy declaration of June 1984, had edged towards a position of conditional support for deployment if the arms negotiations finally failed.

In Greece the Papandreou government elected in October 1981 proved ineffective in implementing its manifesto pledge of a complete removal from Greece of all American military bases. The government proved a permanent thorn in the flesh of the Americans, especially in the Middle East, but this was a nuisance rather than a serious threat to the American position. For Greece and the other southern members of the alliance – Portugal, Spain, Italy, and Turkey – NATO represented not only a security system but also a development and aid system. Each of them looked (or in Italy's case had looked in the past) to the Americans for financial assistance. These poorer members and the Americans were used to complex games of leverage involving financial aid and support for the alliance's policies.

The European governments looked nevertheless to a renewal of arms negotiations with the Soviet Union. The key Conservative governments of Kohl and Mrs Thatcher sought a way out of the confrontation with the Soviet Union. They hoped that the first phase of missile deployments in 1983–84 would persuade the Soviets to return to the negotiating table and open up the possibility of a compromise arms treaty which would produce limited Soviet disarmament in return for a limited Western deployment. Such an outcome would best meet the growing European concern about the SS-20 deployments which had continued throughout the first round of negotiations, while permitting the installation of some new Western missiles as a symbol of the American commitment to Europe. The SS-20, which in 1977 had been a relatively minor part of the security debate, had grown in importance. From about 170 missiles when the double track policy was announced, there had been a relentless increase, with about 220 missiles deployed when the arms talks began in late 1981, 350 when the talks were broken off and a figure by mid-1984 of about 420. At each stage, about two-thirds of the missiles were targeted on Western Europe, a third on East Asia, though the missiles were mobile and of such a range to place them out of reach of NATO's new INF systems. The SS-20 threatened NATO's ability to mobilise and fight, and removal of the weapons became a goal in itself. However, removing all the SS-20s at the expense of the entire Western deployment undermined NATO's concern with coupling. Hence, there was a conflict of objectives and uncertainty about whether NATO's primary objectives were the SS-20 and the INF armaments imbalance or the renewal of the American guarantee, even if achieving this meant at least some of the SS-20s remaining.

During this second phase another European concern had developed. This related to the American Strategic Defence Initiative (SDI) or Star Wars', first announced in March 1983. This was a gigantic research project with the long-term objective of providing strategic defence for the United States against Soviet ballistic missile attack. It was only in 1984 that European governments fully realised the implications of this development – SDI looked distinctly de-stabilising for Europe. First, there was the risk that the vast defensive shield to be erected by the United States would protect only its own territory – the old dream of a Fortress America. Even when European governments persuaded Reagan that the defensive shield be extended to cover Europe, there remained doubts that SDI would reinforce isolationist tendencies and diminish the American interest in Europe as the first line of its own defence. Secondly, SDI implied a move away from deterrence towards defence – an old European fear. Members of NATO led by Britain shifted the Americans towards a more limited conception of strategic defence which would underpin and reinforce nuclear deterrence rather than displace it. In April 1984 the British Foreign Secretary, Sir Geoffrey Howe, spelled out the worries in a series of coded questions, and in November 1984 Mrs Thatcher directly confronted President Reagan with European worries in a summit at Camp David. Thereafter the Americans gradually adopted a more limited version of SDI, though Reagan had not abandoned his dream of a world free from the threats of nuclear deterrence. European governments continued to see SDI as a distraction from the more serious business of reinforcing deterrence and conducting negotiations with the Soviet Union. A further problem was that SDI development and testing, though not laboratory research, would violate the 1972 treaty limiting defence against ballistic missiles. In short, SDI was seen as opening up a whole series of questions to which the answers were at best uncertain and at worst positively damaging.

The third phase of the double track policy was initiated by General Secretary Gorbachev's offer to resume the arms talks in February 1985, within a triple package of strategic arms reduction, INF and SDI. This phase of negotiations was marked by a stronger American lead and by increasing European suspicions that the Americans would conclude a treaty which ignored their security interests. The process of consultation continued, but the Geneva and Reykjavik summits in 1985 and 1986 showed the Europeans that in practice they exercised little effective control over the Americans. At the Geneva summit the idea of the zero solution was resurrected but not finalised; at the Reykjavik summit the zero solution was extended to include a rather imprecise commitment to a nuclear-free world. Both summits floundered over the inability of the two sides to compromise on SDI, but the European governments indicated their worry about the pace of negotiations, and the NATO Supreme Commander, the American General Bernard Rogers, reflected the views of his European 'constituents' in denouncing the proposals. Rogers, a supremely successful commander, was shortly thereafter sacked.

Following Reykjavik the Soviet leader conducted a diplomatic *tour de force* which removed two of the major European objections to an agreement and led in December 1987 to a treaty at the Washington summit. First, he agreed to exclude from an INF Treaty previous Soviet demands on the modernisation of the British and French nuclear forces. Secondly, he dealt with a more substantial British and German objection. The draft INF Treaty outlawed land-based missiles with a range of 1000–5500 kilometres. This left the class of weapons with a range of under 1000 kilometres. On the Western side these were only about 100 ageing missiles with a very short range of under 100 kilometres. On the Soviet side, however, there were almost 400 missiles with a range of only just under 1000 kilometres which had been installed in East Germany and Czechoslovakia since 1983 in a counter-move to the new Western missiles. These missiles constituted a major threat to West Germany. Kohl argued that the removal of the longer-range INF systems would leave Germany dangerously exposed as the only alliance member targeted with these land-based missiles by the Soviet Union – a reversion to the fear of 'singularity' expressed at the beginning of the whole INF process. The British and West German governments argued against the zero solution, despite its acceptance by the Americans until, suddenly, Gorbachev agreed to extend the zero solution into missiles within a range of 500–1000 kilometres – the so-called 'double zero'.

Even this did not fully satisfy the two governments. Mrs Thatcher raised the Soviet superiority in conventional and chemical forces as a barrier, but this argument found no support from the alliance and was dropped. Second, Kohl objected to Gorbachev's insistence that the Pershing 1 missiles deployed by West Germany and armed with American-owned and controlled nuclear warheads be included within the double zero. The missiles had a range of about 700 kilometres and were due for early modernisation. Kohl found no alliance support for his claim that these were really German weapons. His own Foreign Minister, the Free Democrat leader Hans-Dietrich Genscher, opposed him. Confronted by opposition externally from all his allies and internally from his coalition partners, Kohl had no alternative. It was agreed that the missiles would go at the end of the disarmament process rather than being modernised. Third, the British government became concerned about the impact of the superpowers' agreement on Britain. By the summer of 1987 the two superpowers had not only agreed in principle to a comprehensive INF treaty but they were also close to an agreement in principle on a 50 per cent cut in long-range strategic weapons. The British government feared that if such a treaty were concluded the Americans would come under enormous pressure from all sides to cancel the sale of Trident missiles to Britain. The government thus pressed for a general slowing down in the whole disarmament process.

On 7 December 1987 the INF Treaty was signed: INF deployments were frozen and the two superpowers agreed procedures and a timetable for the dismantling and destruction of the existing missiles. The treaty ushered a fourth phase of re-evaluation by the European allies of their security in the post-INF situation. The treaty had, in truth, left the alliance in disarray. It delighted its smaller members, who had always had doubts about its wisdom and had found that support of the double track policy had created grievous and damaging divisions at home. West Germany and Britain in contrast, had never really favoured the zero option and now asked the most searching questions about the reliability of the American guarantee. Whereas the peace movement had charged the Americans of installing the new missiles as part of a strategy for fighting a war limited to Europe, governments saw the missiles as making it impossible for the Americans to fight a war limited to Europe. This had been Callaghan and Schmidt's reasoning a decade earlier. The role of the missiles was political rather than military, coupling the Americans to Europe. Conclusion of the INF Treaty weakened this coupling of the two security systems and left the Americans freer to judge their involvement in any European war. The treaty thus reinforced the security interests of the United States while tending to undermine the Europeans'; it opened up that same potential conflict of strategic interests which flexible response had sought to reconcile in 1967.

In the aftermath of the treaty the alliance sought to find a new common ground. However, this proved extremely difficult to establish. The double track policy had persuaded the smaller members of the alliance to look towards a non-nuclear defence policy. The Dutch government was only able to secure parliamentary agreement to deployment of the missiles on its territory in return for Dutch armed forces giving up their own nuclear functions – a compromise dictated by domestic political considerations rather than military logic. The Danish government found it difficult to define any defence policy. In spring 1988 the government sought a general election to resolve the problem, but the opposition of the Socialists to any involvement in a nuclear defence policy worsened the situation for the non-Socialist government. It is now possible that the opposition of its governments to the deployment of nuclear weapons on Danish territory in time of peace, a condition of NATO membership since entry, may be extended to include NATO ships which might be carrying nuclear weapons. Given that the British and American governments refuse to reveal whether their ships are nuclear-armed, such a ban could in practice, remove allied naval support from Denmark.

In March 1988 the first NATO summit meeting for two decades failed to agree on a clear direction for the alliance in the new situation created by the INF Treaty. The British and the Americans pressed for a speedy modernisation of the alliance's nuclear weapons in the categories not covered by the treaty, particularly air-launched and ground-launched missiles with a range of under 500 kilometres. The key decision sought was the replacement of the old Lance missiles systems with a range of under 100 kilometres by a new system with a range much closer to 500 kilometres. The decisive opposition to modernisation came from Chancellor Kohl. His government had felt the most exposed by the INF negotiations through 1986 and 1987, although NATO deterrent policies had always sought to offer particular reassurance to West Germany as the most vulnerable NATO member. Modernisation of the very short-range INF systems would again single out West Germany. They would be based only on German territory (other countries would be too far from the front line) and Soviet systems similarly would be targeted only on West Germany – in the words of a Christian Democrat foreign policy spokesman, 'the shorter the range, the deader the Germans'. Moreover, very-short-range systems threatened not merely West German territory but also the territory of the Democratic Republic to the east whose sanctuary the West German government was also, so far as it was able, anxious to secure. The West German government sought a much more thorough re-examination of the alliance's deterrent and *détente* strategies than a mere attempt to reinstate flexible response on the old model. Hence, while the communiqué of the NATO summit referred to determination 'to sustain the requisite efforts to ensure the continued viability, credibility and effectiveness of our conventional and nuclear forces', there were wide differences of interpretation of this formula. The Germans held that existing forces were adequate, the Americans and British that further initiatives were necessary.

CONCLUSION

The period of *détente* that characterised the ending of the period of superpower confrontation in the early 1980s has left Europe uncertain about its defence strategies for the 1990s. As in the 1960s and 1970s, the co-ordination of American and European policy towards the Soviet Union has proved extremely elusive. American hawkishness towards the Soviet Union tends to leave European governments feeling insecure and vulnerable to the immediate presence of the Soviet Union: on the other hand, superpower *rapprochement* undermines the reassurance to Europe that deterrence is designed to encourage, and opens up the prospect of an American–Soviet relationship pursued at the expense of European interests.

The report of the American government's commission on long-term strategy, published in early 1988, elaborated a concept of 'discriminate deterrence' which stressed both the global nature of American interests and the unsuitability of general nuclear deterrent threats to sustain those interests. Discriminate deterrence indicated the prospect of a review of flexible response and a possible downgrading of European security interests *vis-a-vis* the growing importance of the Pacific Rim. The INF Treaty thus brought together two distinct sets of fears – *detente* between the superpowers in which the United States would become less responsive to European security fears, and the possibility of changes in American deterrent strategies. In the 1970s INF had begun with a European perception of declining security which could be redressed by a renewed American guarantee; it concluded in the 1980s with that security problem apparently exacerbated by a treaty unforeseen when the INF process began.

The most important European response to the INF issue may therefore be a renewed sense of European identity and self- reliance. This should not be exaggerated. A security system without an American component is unthinkable for the European members of NATO. But a security system in which the American nuclear guarantee plays a less dominant role is now on the political agenda. Such a development would of course increase in significance if pressures for reductions in American troop levels in Europe were to increase.

A number of tendencies pointing towards this Europeanisation of defence can be identified. The most important is probably the revival of the Western European Union (WEU), the defence grouping of the central European core members of NATO established in 1954 as part of the wider agreement on German rearmament. In 1984 WEU began to meet again on a regular basis, at senior ministerial level, offering a European defence forum which includes the French as full members (WEU meets in Paris) and from which the Americans are excluded. In 1988 Spain and Portugal joined. Within this general European framework three bilateral defence relationships are crucial. The first is the Anglo-French axis, unique as a partnership of nuclear states. Since 1986 there have been intensified discussions on nuclear collaboration which may eventually extend to joint procurement of a new air-launched Cruise missile to replace the American INF systems withdrawn under the treaty. The second is the Franco-German axis. Here the defence relationship, existing within the system of regular summits, led in January 1986 to a 'Treaty on Defence Co-operation'. Under the framework of the treaty there have been changes in French nuclear strategy designed to bring the territory of West Germany under the protection of the French nuclear forces. The military role of the French divisions in West Germany, since 1967 outside of the NATO integrated military command structure, has been discussed. A joint Franco-German brigade was established just before the conclusion of the treaty. The military significance of the brigade is minimal but its symbolic and political importance is greater, as the presence of the heads of government at its first exercises indicated. The third axis is the Anglo-German. This has traditionally been the easiest of the three to manage and the practical co-operation has always been the most intensive. Britain retains an army corps permanently deployed in northern West Germany and its commanding officer is, within the NATO military command, the Commander-in-Chief of the Northern Army Group, a multinational group including American, Belgium, Dutch, and German forces. Britain also retains a large tactical air force in West Germany.

The importance of European defence co-operation will have to be judged eventually against three major tests. The first is co-operation on procurement of weapons. The Independent European Programme Group was established in 1976 to discuss European procurement, and revived in 1984. The British involvement in its revival, led by Secretary of Defence Michael Heseltine, was overshadowed by Heseltine's almost immediate resignation over the 'Westland affair' and his failure to persuade the British government that Westland helicopters should develop within a European rather than an American industrial grouping. Nevertheless, there are important procurement projects which do represent an alternative to buying American products. Some of these are relatively small scale, but a number are highly politicised and involve very high technology. The European Fighter Aircraft Programme involving Britain, West Germany, Italy, and Spain (France left the project) is the most im-

Table 6 Defence Expenditures

	1979	1987
Belgium	3.3	3.0
Britain	4.9	4.7
Denmark	2.4	2.1
France	4.0	4.0
West Germany	3.3	3.0
Italy	2.3	2.2
Netherlands	3.3	3.1
Norway	3.2	3.2
United States	5.2	6.6

Source: Based on Ministry of Defence (1980, 1988) *Statement on the Defence Estimates* (London: HMSO).

portant at present. The programme was confirmed only in 1988 after a long period of doubt about its viability.

The second test for European co-operation lies in the trends in defence expenditure. European defence expenditures are relatively low and declining. Comparison can be made between 1979, the year of the double track policy, and 1987 (see Table 6.)

The contrast with the United States is clear. Of course, economies were expanding and, in the case of Britain, this comparison conceals a very rapid increase up to 1983–84 and a similarly rapid fall thereafter. In the long run a European defence identity would depend on a European willingness to pay for defence, just as, after 1967, the credibility of flexible response depended on a greater European commitment to conventional defence. Of the willingness to pay more there remains little evidence.

The third test of a European revival is the extent to which it can unite the European members of the alliance who have hitherto avoided difficult questions by reliance on the United States. The answer here is much more problematic but the evidence available so far is that, following INF, governments in Belgium, Denmark, Greece, and Netherlands are reluctant to place defence again near the top of the political agenda. The three key countries, Britain, France, and West Germany, have not yet completed their reconsideration of defence in the light of the INF Treaty, but if they are unable to concert successfully then the prospect of a European second pillar within a rather looser NATO framework is a non-starter.

At the level of domestic politics the INF Treaty has produced one important consequence, namely a major decline, perhaps amounting to a collapse, of the peace movements. In Britain, France, West Germany, and Italy the peace movements had in fact produced little electoral impact in the sense that Conservative governments (or, in the case of France, pro-nuclear governments) dominated the 1980s. The Greens in Germany had certainly owed much to the nuclear issue. In Spain the Socialist government side-tracked the peace movement. In the small northern members of the alliance the peace movements do appear to have established themselves as permanent forces to the extent that anti-nuclear policies are now firmly entrenched in the political system within the policies of Socialist or Green parties.

The peace movements' achievements are difficult to evaluate. On the one hand they claim credit for pushing alliance governments towards removal of the missiles. The zero option was adopted partly to outmanoeuver the peace movements by governments which did not really favour it. However, the ultimate acceptance of the zero option was forced by the Americans rather than by the peace movements. However, the great weakness of the peace movements is that their strategy would have abandoned the double track policy without securing any reciprocal Soviet concession.

There is more optimistic or benign face to the evaluation of defence policy in Europe in the 1980s. From a conservative perspective the INF produced asymmetrical arms reductions with the Soviets giving up over twice as many missiles as the Americans. This is an important precedent for strategic arms reduction and the new round of conventional arms talks due to begin in Vienna in 1989. From a more radical perspective there are two important implications from INF. One is that arms reductions may cement greater confidence and security in Europe, East and West. The second is the possibility of a reorientation of European defence in the direction of non-nuclear defence. The peace movements stimulated serious consideration of alternative defence policies, the key elements of which would be an emphasis on conventional forces, the defensive deployment of conventional forces (non-provocative defence) and ultimately the development of a non-threatening security relationship with the Soviet Union. NATO itself has given attention to these ideas and is exploring the professed change of direction of Soviet military forces towards a much more defensive military strategy. Whether or not the Americans would support these developments, or whether the Europeans would meet higher defence expenditures, remains uncertain.

With or without the peace movements, defence remains a major policy issue for European governments. The international framework for defence remains uncertain after the INF Treaty and the failure of the NATO summit. It remains to be seen whether European governments have the resources or the will to reconstruct a new set of defence relationships.

REFERENCES AND FURTHER READING

Baylis, J. (1987–88) 'Nato strategy: the case for a new strategic concept'. *International Affairs*. **64**, pp 43–59.

Bertram, C. (ed.) (1983) *Defence and Consensus: The Domestic Aspects of European Security* (London: Macmillan/International Institute for Strategic Studies).

Brauch, H. G. (ed.) (1987) *Star Wars and European Defence* (London: Macmillan).

Calleo, D. (1988) *Beyond American Hegemony: The Future of the Western Alliance*. (Brighton: Wheatsheaf)

Dean, J. (1987–88) 'Alternative defence', *International Affairs*. **64**. pp 61–82.

Flynn, G. and Rattinger, H. (eds) (1985) *The Public and Atlantic Defence* (London: Croom Helm).

Kaltefleiter, W and Pfaltzgraff, R. L. (eds) (1985) *The Peace Movements in Europe and the United States* (London: Croom Helm).

Kirby, S. and Robson, G. (eds) (1987) *The Militarisation of Space* (Brighton: Wheatsheaf).

Laqueur, W. and Hunter, R (eds) (1985) *European Peace Movements and the Future of the Atlantic Alliance* (Oxford: Transaction Books).

Olive, M. M. and Porro, J. D. (eds) (1983) *Nuclear Weapons in Europe: Modernization and Limitation* (Lexington Mass: Lexington Books).

Park, W. (1986) *Defending the West: A History of Nato* (Brighton: Wheatsheaf).

Wyllie, J. H. (1986) *European Security in the Nuclear Age*. (Oxford: Blackwell)

CHALLENGES TO ESTABLISHED POLITICAL PATTERNS

CHAPTER SIX

The Wearing of the Green: Issues, Movements and Parties

Derek W. Urwin

After the initial confusion and worries of the immediate post-war years, the countries of Western Europe settled very quickly into a pattern of sustained economic growth and political stability. The major commitment was to the consolidation of an industrial society as the essential foundation of an effective politics of distribution and a just welfare state. By the 1960s Western Europe, it was being claimed, was on the threshold of post-industrialism, a coming society where economic growth and technological advance would reduce to a minimum the drudgery of labour and satisfy the material needs and aspirations of the population. The symbols of this sanitised picture of material satisfaction were the welfare state and the effective application by governments of Keynesian neo-capitalism; together they provided the base and management that would ensure an equitable distribution of goods and services among all segments of society.

The notion of an expanding economic cake, with larger and larger slices for everyone, had political implications which, it was believed by some, were already apparent. Socio-economic change, an expansion of education, and increasing affluence had launched a process of societal *embourgeoisement*. Economic satisfaction was paralleled by political contentment. The net political effect would be the end of ideological conflict. Very little would distinguish one political party from another; competition between them would be more stylised, concerned primarily with the quality of management than with principles. The coining in Britain of the word 'Butskellism', from the names of Rab Butler, a leading Conservative politician, and Hugh Gaitskell, the Labour leader, was a symbol of what was seen as the general mood and the shape of things to come.

116

Within the space of less than a decade, such prognostications about the course of the future were shaken to the core. Long before the oil crisis of 1973 brought Western Europe face to face with a harsher world of economic stagnation and decline, it was confronted with an escalation of direct action by groups which scorned conventional patterns of political participation and which, with their rejection of the political precepts of two decades of economic and political construction, rocked Western European complacency. The new groups and movements which sprang up after the late 1960s may have had different policy objectives, but taken together they regarded extra-parliamentary methods up to and including mass confrontation as legitimate and normal tactics for achieving the realisation of their goals. More broadly, they were severely critical of the bureaucratic nature of political life and argued for some reorganisation of status and power relationships, for a return to or acceptance of principles and values which they felt had been jettisoned or ignored by governments and political parties in a quest for economic growth that had turned into an auction on unrestrained materialism where élites sought to outbid each other for popular support.

The 1970s ushered in a new era of protest and alienation, of new movements, many of them organisationally inchoate, that expressed new principles and demanded new policies. The first major wave of rejection was a mobilisation of the young, especially students, in the late 1960s. To a greater or lesser extent it affected all Western European countries, most spectacularly so in France where the unrest of May 1968 seemed poised to topple President de Gaulle and his Fifth Republic. This student protest proved to be both a model for future social movements and their forms of action, and a training ground for many of their activists. One of the most enduring and significant forms of new protest has been the so-called green wave, or ecology movement. Its concern for the environment and its vision of an alternative future has, if anything, had a greater impact in the 1980s in terms of its impingement upon the public consciousness and the recognition by governments of its concerns in the content of much public policy.

THE ECOLOGICAL IMPETUS

A political concern about the environment has a long history in Western Europe. Many countries have witnessed organisations dedicated to conservation and other protective measures ever since the emergence of industrial society in the nineteenth century. The modern concern about the environment first surfaced in the United States in the 1960s, with a series of pessimistic forecasts about the consequences of economic growth. More popular books which argued that the environment was under threat from man-made disasters, such as Rachel Carson's *The Silent Spring* (1962) and Charles Reich's *The Greening of America* (1970), had a wide impact. By the early 1970s a host of related issues – air and water pollution, urban encroachment and renewal, harmful substances in food, road construction, noise – were being raised in many Western European countries, though the specific problems debated and the depth of feeling about them varied from country to country. Such differences, rather than any concrete policy programme and agreement, were perhaps the most prominent feature of the ambitious United Nations-sponsored Conference on Man and the Environment, held in Stockholm in 1972.

In the 1970s the ecology movement seemed to gain greater coherence and, through an association of interest with a burgeoning peace movement, greater impetus. The binding force was an anti-nuclear theme. The European economic boom had been fuelled by cheap energy. The quadrupling of oil prices in 1973 and the embargo which the Arab producers levied against some states, such as the Netherlands, drew attention to the political and economic vulnerability of Western Europe in terms of what had become its primary source of energy. In the aftermath of 1973 there was a search for alternative sources and, inevitably perhaps, governments began to consider with rather more urgency the option of nuclear power as an alternative and cost-effective energy source. Britain already had a long-standing nuclear programme, and other countries, notably France, Sweden and West Germany, developed plans for a large-scale nuclear industry. The planned construction of nuclear plants awakened or reinforced fears about the safety of nuclear power, the extent to which effective safeguards against possible accidents or acts of sabotage could be ensured, and about the problems of disposing of nuclear waste.

The nuclear issue gave a radical tinge to environmental concern, adding a further dimension and a new layer of activity to those conservation groups protesting about pollution from man-made activities, and was the inspiration for some of the largest mass demonstrations on the Continent. It was the one issue which, more than any other, served to bring the various pressure groups together under a single umbrella of ecological concern. Again, it was the major factor in the politicisation of the movements. Because demonstrations were necessarily diffuse and often counter-productive in terms of the violence that sometimes occurred at them, there arose a growing acceptance that the cause required a more coherent degree of co-ordination, and ultimately a strengthening belief that the way forward lay in entering electoral politics.

Events conspired to keep the nuclear issue at the front of people's minds. Most dramatic were the major accident at an American nuclear plant at Three Mile Island in 1979 and the massive radiation leak from a Soviet reactor at Chernobyl in 1986. A radiation cloud from the latter passed over much of Western Europe, affecting agriculture and livestock in several countries, including parts of Britain: its consequences were particularly severe in Scandinavia where contaminated vegetation largely destroyed the reindeer–based economy of the Lapps. Other environmental disasters and scandals, such as the several discharges of chemical effluent into the Rhine by both West German and Swiss industries in 1986, provided further sources of extensive media coverage, heightening public awareness and convincing activists of the interrelationship between their various causes. Simultaneously, there was mounting scientific evidence of a causal link between industrial pollution and environmental contamination: dying trees in West Germany, sterile lakes and rivers devoid of life in Scandinavia, lead poisoning from car exhaust fumes everywhere.

Towards the end of the 1970s it seemed that the environmental cause was boosted by another factor: the explosion of peace movements across Western Europe that were protesting against nuclear armaments. The catalyst was the decision by NATO in 1979 to upgrade its nuclear defensive system over the long term to counteract the increasing gap it claimed to detect between its and the Soviet Union's levels of weaponry. To cover the interim period until refurbishment was complete, the United States, at the urging of several Western European governments, agreed to station medium-range nuclear missiles on the Continent. It was the latter decision which unleashed the wave of peace protests, and for a while the anti-nuclear theme became almost an exclusively anti-missile theme. By the mid-1980s, the peace movements seemed to be running out of steam. They had failed in their major target: the intermediate-range missiles were in place in all the countries that had agreed to take them, and the political parties which had become strong advocates of disarmament had not seemingly derived any electoral advantage from doing so.

Thereafter the peace movements failed to find another objective that could help them maintain a momentum. This probably benefited the ecology movement. The missile debate had absorbed much of the energy of the anti-nuclear drive. On the other hand, it was one which failed to make a decisive impact upon national electorates. Many people who may have disliked and feared nuclear weapons nevertheless reluctantly accepted that they were necessary evils, especially in the two European nuclear powers, Britain and France. The exceptions were in countries like West Germany, where radical ecology groups were very strong and able successfully to fuse much of the green and peace protest under a single banner. People did not necessarily draw similar conclusions about nuclear reactors, especially if they were to be located, as it were, on one's doorstep. In the early 1980s, therefore, there began a decoupling of the ecology and peace movements, something which on balance could only be to the advantage of the former.

At the same time, nuclear energy as an issue began to decline in saliency. In some countries, such as Sweden and Austria, public disquiet over a nuclear programme had resulted in referendum majorities against further, or indeed any, development. More broadly, nuclear power was demoted as a priority for governments. In several countries, construction programmes were postponed or abandoned, at first because economic recession had reduced both the demand for energy and the ability of governments to finance the programmes, and later because the feared energy gap had failed to materialise. As the Western European economies began to pick up in the 1980s, it seemed that they could still rely upon abundant and reasonably priced oil supplies. The 1980s, therefore, saw a return of the ecological concern to its original broad focus upon environmental pollution, in all its facets, and the reining back of the excesses of industrial society. But now they were preaching to a greater number of the converted: almost two decades of campaigning had successfully socialised electorates into being more receptive to environmental pleas.

FROM MOVEMENT TO STRUCTURE

The ecology wave of protest and action of the 1970s and 1980s may most appropriately be considered as a social movement, a rather diffuse term which has been used to describe a very wide range of phenomena, all of which at a minimum share a strong element of more or less spontaneous independent action, a limited element of leadership, and minimal hierarchical organisation. The green wave, in fact, has encompassed a heterogeneous variety of groups which have differed, sometimes markedly, from each other in terms of their ideological perspectives, policy objectives, and strategies. One broad group consists of those interest organisations with a long pedigree of service in a particular cause and for which the keyword was conservation: the preservation of the countryside, the protection of wildlife, and so on. While often focused on specific issues and campaigns, some of these groups were sucked into the broader concerns and direct action of the 1970s and 1980s. In party political terms, they could more usually be regarded as non-partisan, or even conservative. Their concerns did not generally lead to demands for sweeping political and socio-economic change, but rather that industrial society take special account of what it was they sought to preserve and protect. Often enjoying high public prestige and reasonable access to governmental circles; these groups were the moderate arm of the ecology movement.

In the 1970s these long-standing organisations were supplemented by new environmental groups, equally devoted to specific issues. Some were concerned with national or even global questions; others arrived at these positions from an original concern with a single limited issue, often of a local character: a proposed nuclear or industrial site, the building of a motorway or dam; the pollution of a local river or lake; the destruction of a local wood. It is surprising how many local activist groups sprang up during the decade, attracting people whose political activity hitherto had been restricted to voting and who probably had never previously dreamed that they would finish up in direct confrontation with legally constituted national or local authorities. Several thousand such local groups were recorded in West Germany alone. More prepared to engage in direct action and mass demonstration than the older groups, they were the potential bulk of a future green movement, and in that way overlapped with the emergence of yet another environmental force, the radical ecologists. It was the latter which provided the ideological motivation for a green movement. Many of these individuals had been schooled in the student protests of earlier years, and tended to regard themselves as part of a broader new left. Their political socialisation had prepared them to accept mass demonstrations and other forms of direct action as a necessary and effective means of protest and pressure. Their objective was not just to secure specific environmental concessions from government, but to implement an alternative vision of society where all policy would be determined by environmental imperatives.

The distinctions that can be made between the various categories of groups are arbitrary, and as time went on blurred even further. Two developments helped to bring groups closer together. One was the nuclear issue; the other was media coverage of local actions, which increased awareness that other people elsewhere shared similar concerns and were waging a similar struggle. Out of the growing acceptance of the interconnections between the several concerns came a desire to establish some form of umbrella organisation, not to provide direction and centralisation, but as something that could assist in the co-ordination of the several strategies and objectives. The multitude of West German groups formed the Federal Association of Environmental Citizens' Initiatives in 1972, at the same time as their Dutch counterparts set up the Environmental Defence Union. The previous year had seen the establishment of a National Association of Environmental Groups in Sweden, and the Friends of the Earth in France. Similar federal associations soon appeared in other countries. While scornful and fearful of any well-developed organisational structure, these fairly loose associations contributed to the socialisation and integration processes. The world was increasingly regarded as one, and for the committed environmentalist one ecological issue could not easily be considered in isolation. The gradual accretion of a composite view was one factor which in most countries eased the decision to found an ecology party as yet another strategy for advancing the cause.

One further binding factor across the groups was the common social background possessed by many of the new activists. The green wave has to a large extent been populated by younger middle-class and well-educated individuals, part of the generation coming of age during and benefiting from the economic prosperity and welfare developments of the previous decades. Comparatively few, however, were in industrial and manufacturing occupations: a disproportionate number of the new activists were drawn from the public sector or from other non-productive fields such as the media and arts. Some writers have pointed to the emergence in the 1970s of a post-materialist generation. As opposed to their parents, whose stress after a life mainly of hardship was on securing satisfaction of material needs, the new generation, growing up in a period of economic plenty, took material satisfaction for granted and instead focused upon a search for the improvement of the quality of life. To argue for such a straightforward causal link may be misleading, but it is a fact that the ecology movement, like much else of the 'new politics' of the 1970s and 1980s, drew its major strength from these segments of the middle classes.

In most countries environmental policy-making is an aspect of both national and local government. Exactly where environmental policy is made, and the extent to which the courts and popular plebiscites can be used as avenues of action, determined the strategy and tactics of the green movement. In Britain, public hearings and inquiries have been a standard procedure within the decision-making process and for long had provided an outlet for the conservationist voice. They continued to offer an avenue of political participation and an opportunity to seek a reasonable compromise, if not outright victory. The opportunity in Britain to resolve 'narrower' issues by this means perhaps contributed to the relative failure in the country of a more radical orientation. Similarly, the Scandinavian countries had developed an extensive pattern of formal and regular consultations between government and important organisations. This structure was also capable of accommodating environmental groups and their interests without undue strain. Of course, it often involved compromise, which the groups could accept or reject. Ultimately, decisions are made by governments: if the latter reject the ecology demands, the groups must seek alternative modes of argument. In Sweden, some ecologists, unhappy with the system, eventually preferred to form their own party. In Norway in 1979 the government insisted upon a hydro-electric scheme in the far north against the wishes of the local Lapp population and most environmentalist groups: the latter were hence forced into mounting mass demonstrations, and even a hunger strike, to try to persuade the government to reverse its decision.

Alternatively, constitutional provisions may allow either a group or a government to test the public mood on a controversial issue through some form of plebiscite. The referendum is an integral part of the political process in Switzerland; three in recent years have dealt with nuclear energy. Similarly, referenda in Austria and Sweden on the development of nuclear energy gave an opportunity to the ecology movement to rally popular support for its views: in both countries the campaign was successful. A later referendum result in Italy in 1987 made politicians pause for thought on their future nuclear plans.

By contrast, the political and administrative structures in France seemed to preclude any effective opportunities for protest movements to effect changes from within the system. Where this was the situation, it led to frustration and it was the more radical elements which often emerged as the dominant force within the ecology movement. In France, however, radicalism came up against the same blank wall: by the 1980s the ecology movement seemed to have been less successful in France than almost everywhere else. Similarly, the feeling that the administrative structures of West Germany were too rigid to accommodate their demands (public hearings are more formalistic and limited in scope than in Britain) was one factor which pushed ecology protesters towards more direct and radical forms of action. West Germany was particularly noted for the sheer number of local action groups and for the huge turn-out at mass demonstrations at nuclear construction sites. Out of these developments there eventually emerged what arguably became in the 1980s the most successful Green Party in Western Europe.

To influence government in a liberal democracy, a protest movement has to win over one or more political parties that have a reasonable chance of participating in government. Environmental issues quite frequently cut across the broad left–right spectrum which has been the most pervasive structuring factor of Western European party systems. Hence it would be possible for all parties to be able to accept some of the environmental demands and accommodate them into their programmes, irrespective of their ideological perspective and electoral clientele. Much of the green movement paid particular attention to Social Democrat and other major left-wing parties, believing that since these parties were inherently more 'anti-establishment', they would be more sympathetic. But few important political parties were willing or able to accept all or most of the ecology package: to do so would mean upsetting the balance of their other multifarious and electorally important concerns. It was generally only small left-wing parties – left Socialists in a few countries or the Radicals in both the Netherlands and Italy – which proved to be willing to wrap themselves in the green panoply (primarily because of the anti-nuclear nexus), but their relative peripherality within the parliamentary and party systems meant that the cause was not advanced very far.

While a commitment to environmental protection and enhancement did gradually enter the agenda of most political parties to the point when, by the late 1980s, virtually all of them were claiming that they were sincere defenders of the environment, the process was too slow and too piecemeal to satisfy many in the green movement. In no way did any party commitment meet the alternative vision of the radical ecologists, while for many single-issue groups there could be no guarantee that their own particular cause would be embraced by a major political party, and even if it was it would be but one of a host of issues and interests that had to be balanced by the party leadership. In particular, to governments wrestling with increasing inflation, high unemployment, mounting debt and a shrinking manufacturing base, and still fundamentally wedded to the precepts of an industrial society, many of the green demands seemed to be economic Luddism. There were, of course, exceptions. One major example was the Swedish Centre (Agrarian) Party which in the mid-1970s attempted to project a green image as a way of securing for itself a new electoral base that would compensate for its contracting agricultural core. Initially successful, by the early 1980s the Centre Party was again in decline. One factor was disillusionment within the party with its decision in 1980 to support an expansion of nuclear energy. Many ecologists deserted the party, to become a nucleus for an independent Ecology Party founded the following year. During the early 1980s the venerable but fading Liberal Party in Norway also adopted a strong green profile to secure a reversal in its political for-tunes: its strong green stance was, it was widely argued, the major factor which contributed to the electoral disaster of 1985, when the party was eliminated from Parliament. In general, however, the ecol-ogy movements failed to win over or colonise established parties; where they did, the outcome was not often to the advantage of the party. This failure was a major impetus in persuading many green activists that the only way forward was to form their own political party.

GREEN PARTIES

The obstacles to any new party seeking a permanent niche in the party system are formidable. Since 1945 Western Europe has wit-nessed the launch of many new parties, but comparatively few have survived over the longer term, let alone been successful. Neverthe-less, within the space of less than a decade, Green or Ecology parties have sprang up almost everywhere and have contested national and local elections. In some countries party formation was the end result of a sequential process. In others a single event served as a catalyst: in Finland, for example, the Green Party was established in 1979 as a reaction to a governmental decision to drain a lake that had served as a bird sanctuary. The first national appearances were in Britain and France. A People's Party was established in Britain in 1973, changing its name to Ecology Party two years later and then to Green Party in 1985. It, however, made very little electoral impact until the 1989 European elections. In France various ecology groups agreed to put forward their own candidate for the 1974 presidential election. Though polling only 1.3 per cent of the vote, they continued to be active, with some limited success. The French ecologists were in many ways typical of the green wave: opposed to traditional patterns of hierarchical political organisation, they clung to the principle of decentralisation, and it was only in 1984 that they eventually agreed to form a single party. Even then, the new party failed to attract all the activists, and in the 1984 elections to the European Parliament it had to face competition from another green group.

The first parliamentary victory came in Switzerland, where a party formed in the canton of Zurich in 1978 won a single seat in the national election the following year. Other parties were subsequently formed in other cantons, and in 1983 most of these agreed to come together in a federation. Again, however, unity was far from complete: radical Greens preferred to offer an alternative list of candidates in the 1983 and 1987 elections. Two years after the Swiss breakthrough, the two parties which had been formed in Belgium's two linguistic regions, Agelev in Flanders and Ecolo in Wallonia, were able collectively to win 4.5 per cent of the national vote and return four deputies to the legislature in Brussels. In the elections of 1985 and 1987 they were able to consolidate their position in the party system, doubling their parliamentary representation.

The Belgian and Swiss Greens, albeit divided in each country between two parties, have arguably been among the most successful of the new ecology parties. Neither, however, has popularly been regarded as a standard-bearer of a new political reality. That honour has gone to the West German Greens. The history of the West German Greens is typical of the ecology movements as a whole. During the 1970s a series of several citizens' action groups emerged. Most were essentially local in character, driven to direct action by what they saw as the inflexible and unsympathetic bureaucratic structures of the political system. Their coming together was aided by the emotive nuclear issue. The government's nuclear programme unleashed some of the largest demonstrations ever seen in the Federal Republic. Green lists had some success throughout the decade in local and regional elections, but it was not until 1979 that a national political alliance was forged, somewhat hastily, to contest the European elections later that year. The alliance won no seats and gained a modest 3.2 per cent of the vote, but the experience and the financial resources gained from the state election subsidies provided to cover campaign costs led to increased pressure for a national party to work for the ecology cause. The following months saw a series of vociferous conferences that illustrated perfectly the heterogeneity of the green movement. Eventually, however, sufficient agreement was reached to form a party in January 1980. Typically, however, it refused to call itself a party, but just the Greens.

Like many other Green parties, its first essay into the national party contest was something of a disappointment: only 1.5 per cent of the 1980 vote. In 1983, however, the Greens advanced to 5.6 per cent of the vote, decisively entering the Bundestag with twenty-seven deputies, a greater proportion of seats than any other Green Party at the time. The West German Greens continued to be in the vanguard throughout the 1980s, and in 1987 increased their vote to 8.3 per cent, and the number of seats to forty-four. The eye-catching qualities of the Greens was not due entirely to the level of electoral success, which was only marginally greater than that of several of their counterparts elsewhere, nor to their eccentric behaviour, which was not particularly distinctive in the green context. The party's newsworthiness was due in the first instance to the fact that the Federal Republic is a large and important European state. In addition, it seemed that the Greens, despite their relatively small size, might well in the near future be in a strong position to influence government policy. With the two major parties, the Christian Democrats and the Social Democrats, being reasonably equally balanced, but with neither having a high probability of reaching, and sustaining itself at, the majority point, and with the persistence of the belief that the small third party, the Free Democrats, could easily and at any time fall below the extinction point in the West German electoral system, there was a widespread assumption that the Greens might well soon hold the balance of power between the two leading parties. All this heightened curiosity about, and a kind of morbid fascination with, the new phenomenon and its aggressive rejection of traditional forms of organisation and espousal of new forms of participatory democracy.

It is undeniable that the overall green electoral record has not been impressive. None has as yet been able to reach 10 per cent of the vote. The Belgian, Swiss and West German parties have been joined in their respective Parliaments by Greens in Austria, Finland, Italy,

Luxemburg and Sweden. On the other hand, some have failed to make any kind of electoral impression: in Britain, Denmark, Ireland, the Netherlands, and Spain, they have failed to get beyond the 1 per cent mark in national elections. In Greece, Norway, and Portugal, Green parties have yet to be formed or to contest an election. Yet electoral performance is not the only or best measure of green success. The 1980s have seen the heightened salience and visibility of environmental issues: the activities of the 1970s' movements and of the parties in the 1980s can claim some of the credit for placing the environment firmly upon the political agenda of government.

The ability of a political party to sustain itself in the political system is to a considerable extent dependent upon gaining parliamentary representation. In that light the variability of green success has been partially dependent upon the electoral system. Countries with a system of proportional representation allow more opportunity for small parties, especially those without a clustered regional base or distinctive and cohesive socio-economic core, to gain a parliamentary foothold. There is less chance of a vote for a small party being regarded as wasted than, for example, in Britain where the simple first past the post system discriminates severely against small parties.

A social movement can content itself with focusing on the narrower issues which lie at the heart of its *raison d'être*; it can ignore the wider ramifications of how one policy will interact with and affect almost all other policies, and rely upon passion and publicity rather than organisation to advance its cause. To be successful, a party needs to adopt a broader policy profile and to ensure a healthy financial base for its activities. It is no longer enough to impress governments with activity, or even just a patina of strength: it needs the hard facts of votes, and they need both organisation and money. To some extent, the Green parties have bit the organisational bullet, though many are inherently anti-organisation. Money is a problem for all small parties. At one extreme is the British situation where parties must rely upon membership subscriptions and voluntary donations for their financial health. But even where state subsidies for parties are available, they tend, as in Scandinavia, to be related to past electoral success and/or present parliamentary strength, a kind of chicken and egg situation for small parties. One special factor in West Germany may have been the high level of subsidies given as election expenses to all parties receiving more than a very minimal number of votes. Since the level of reimbursement is dependent upon votes received rather than actual campaign costs, the Greens were initially able, by receiving expenses that far outweighed the cost of their campaigns and limited organisational infrastructure, to make an 'instant profit' that could be used for other purposes. The electoral system, money, votes, organisation, and policy profile are all factors that must be weighed in the balance by any new party.

THE ECOLOGICAL IMPACT

The success of any social movement will depend not only upon the resources available to it or upon the degree to which its nuisance value, expressed through non-co-operation or disruptive actions, can persuade governments that the political cost of accommodating demands is less than the cost of resistance. It will also depend upon the resolution and resources of its adversaries. The first critical test for the ecology movements was the issue around which they had coalesced: nuclear energy. Success in this area has been rather mixed, depending upon national circumstances such as the structure of government and the extent to which nuclear power had already been developed.

In general, the ecology movements seem to have been more successful in those countries where a nuclear energy programme had not yet left the drawing-board. For example, governments in Denmark, Ireland and Norway shelved their plans more or less indefinitely. However, whether this was due primarily to green pressure or to other factors – for example, the costs involved, the availability and price of other sources of energy – is perhaps a moot point. While nuclear development may ultimately have been ruled out in Norway, for example, in 1979 the government persisted, in the face of massive opposition, with a major hydroelectric scheme in the far north of the country. It is of little consolation to the protesters that, a decade later, the decision is widely regarded as a mistake, costly and not really necessary.

By contrast, the struggle was more bitter in those countries which had already made a commitment to nuclear energy and which had industries dependent upon the nuclear sector for contracts and employment. Here, direct protest more obviously paralleled action in other channels offered by the system for influencing government policy. Referenda on nuclear power were ultimately important in Sweden and Austria as factors contributing towards a reversal of government policy. The relatively weaker position of governments in Italy and the more extensive role in decision-making allocated to regional and local governments provided the movement with more pressure or blocking points. While public attention was caught in West Germany by the mass demonstrations at nuclear sites, the protesters also enjoyed some success in the courts. At the extreme are Britain and France, two states with a major stake in nuclear power and where, especially in France, little headway seemed to be possible.

Given the fact that several environmental themes have been taken up by many major parties, and that many issues and problems have been targeted by governments as priority areas for firm and rapid action, superficially it might seem that the movements have achieved at least some of their objectives. However, it is often difficult to claim a direct link between cause and effect , between social movement and environmental legislation, and even more so in terms of claiming that the green wave has achieved improvements in the environment. Implementation of much legislation is costly and a slow process. Governments, too, in accepting some of the logic of the green argument, have often sought to impose their own interpretations of that logic with modified or partial legislation that both meets the imperatives of the still dominant industrial society and hopefully will defuse some of the green passion and detach it from a broader public opinion. The very fact that since the late 1970s Green parties have emerged more or less everywhere in Western Europe is indicative that, for many supporters of the movements, political parties and governments have not been able to satisfy them. By creating their own parties, they were perhaps admitting the partial failure of the movement structure and phase, and accepting the need to work within the system rather than merely attempting to influence it from the outside.

The Green parties presented a dual challenge to the established political order: not only did they focus upon environmental issues that hitherto had been rather marginal to the established party system; they also placed these issues in a broader spectrum of 'new' political concerns and argued that the way to achieve all these goals would have to involve new forms of political action. The core of what they deemed to be vital social concerns could, they argued, best be achieved within a democratic framework built around a different and broader concept of political participation. In setting up their own political parties, the Greens sought to put into practice these concepts of participatory democracy within the new structures.

The input into the Green parties of the many disparate groups that made up the ecology movement varied from country to country. In general, the combinations produced two broad categories of party. On the one hand were parties – in Belgium, Britain, Finland, France, Ireland, and Sweden – where the dominant element was environmentalist. The major orientation of these parties was reformist within the prevailing neo-capitalist system. Their focus was relatively narrow, and so retained strong vestiges of their pressure-group origins. In terms of strategy, their orientation meant that in a sense they could be regarded as potential partners of existing parties rather than challenges to the party system: in particular, most preferred and hoped for some kind of arrangement with Social Democrat parties rather than settle for an alliance with radical groups that sought a complete restructuring of the political system. By contrast, the second category of Green Party rejected more explicitly the prevailing modes of participation and decision-making. No matter how vaguely, they expressed a broader and alternative world picture that, if implemented, would entail far-reaching social, economic, and political reform. In setting themselves up as radical opponents of the established order, they effectively eliminated the possibility of alliance or co-operation with established major parties, except on their own terms; their natural allies were the other new radical parties of the left that in some countries had appeared in the 1970s and 1980s. The latter view of the Greens is the one which seems to have passed into popular folklore as the quintessential Green Party. That, however, may be due to the fact that the West German party is of this type: other examples can be found in Austria, Italy and Luxemburg.

That the distinction has some significance may be illustrated by the fact that both types of parties can be found in Switzerland. A similar duality developed in Austria, though there the two Green parties did agree to form an electoral alliance in 1986. On the other hand, the dichotomy is somewhat artificial in that both types share some common characteristics that set them apart from the traditional party system. One is the greater commitment to unconventional behaviour: new forms of political protest and direct action tend to be seen as legitimate and essential methods of advancing one's cause and arguments. Another is the conviction that the mode of objectives of industrial production must be modified to incorporate ecological perspectives – indeed, ideally that the latter should determine the future path of the industrial society. Finally, there is the concern with broader and new forms of democratic participation. To a greater or lesser extent, the parties have attempted to introduce participatory democracy into their own organisations. The structure of the parties was to be highly decentralised, with the local branches supreme.

Party officials and elected representatives were to be strictly account-able to the mass membership. Oligarchic and professional leadership was frowned upon: instead there was to be a broader and loosely defined 'leadership', as in West Germany, or merely 'spokespeople' as in Sweden. None of the objectives has, perhaps, been entirely suc-cessful. Too many and too intense an emphasis upon mass demonstrations can be counter-productive in policy terms and costly in the electoral arena.

The West German Greens provide a good example of this new type of party, highlighting the ambiguities and incongruities that occur when it tries to refashion a movement into a political party while still attempting to retain the essential characteristics of the former, especially its organisational style. It was entry into Parlia-ment that brought these problems to the fore. The first Green successes were in regional elections in the early 1980s. In two states, Hamburg and Hessen, these resulted in the Greens holding the balance of power in the regional legislature. The Greens were willing to discuss co-operation with the Social Democrats, but demanded full acceptance of their own programme as a non-negotiable precon-dition of any coalition, a demand that was unacceptable to the larger party and somewhat naive given the pluralistic nature of modern politics. After entry into the national Parliament in 1983, the party insisted that its elected deputies must remain nothing more than the mouthpiece of the grass-roots membership, to which they are always accountable, and that they must resign any party office they held. The Greens reconfirmed the notion of a collective leadership, and further declared that the deputies must resign their seats halfway through the life span of the Parliament in favour of their alternatives or substitutes (there are no by-elections in West Germany, and when a party nominates a candidate, it also indicates an alternative nominee who will occupy the seat when the elected representative dies or resigns). All of this tended to reduce the efficiency of the party as an operating structure within the prevailing political framework.

The extent to which an individual Green Party displays the various components of the new political style has varied from one country to another. They are more visible in those parties, like the West Ger-man Greens, which have had a more radical stance and have specifically argued for a new kind of economic and political democracy. But in so far as the Green parties have all emerged out of a coalescence of various protest groups into a social movement, they do form collectively a distinctive new kind of party in principle, style and organisation. But in these aspects of political life, as opposed to the environmental issues raised, the impact of the parties upon the nature of the political system has been relatively slight.

ASSESSMENT AND FUTURE

In so far as environmental concerns have become accepted as serious local, national and international problems that governments must take on board, the green wave is likely to have an important political effect for some time to come. All political parties and governments have accepted the need to legislate on at least some of the causes espoused by the social movements and Green parties. In addition, action on the environment has been a long-standing commitment of the European Community, with the Commission attempting to strengthen its role in this policy area. Environmental protection was included in the Single European Act, and in the Fourth Environmental Action Programme of 1987 the Commission recognised the need to go beyond seeking more legal compliance towards acquiring stronger powers to ensure compliance and effective implementation of environmental regulations and directives.

The greater salience of the environment for the mass consciousness in the 1980s demonstrates a success for the various reports, press statements and actions of the movements over the past two decades. To some extent, that wider acceptance of the importance of environmental action was aided by its decoupling from the peace movement and its emphasis upon disarmament. By the late 1980s it could be said to have acquired an impetus or inertia of its own which would not require the same degree of goading by ecologists. To say, however, that the environment appears to have established itself as an integral and enduring element of the political agenda is not to say something similar about the future of ecology movements or Green parties.

Ecology movements, and perhaps especially those which focus upon a specific issue, would seem to have a reasonably positive future, given that the current climate suggests that there will be a steady diet of environmental issues and problems that require a political resolution. At the very least, they will be able to act as gadflies to the political parties, pressing the latter to act or to honour earlier pledges of action. Superficially, Green parties also seemed to have been capable of carving out a niche for themselves in the political market. They have introduced new issues on to the agenda in many countries, and in providing a political home for those disgruntled with, or ignored by, the established political system, may have served as a kind of safety-valve. Some writers have argued that the Greens symbolise the emergence of a new kind of political cleavage that is likely to persist for some time. There are, however, two question marks that may be placed against this kind of assertion. First, the cleavage has as yet failed to assert itself as a major determinant of party opposition. The Greens are still but minor parties in the political system, and are likely to remain so. Moreover, a great deal of what they have urged has been accepted and pursued by other parties. Second, and following on from this, one might ask whether all this constitutes a political cleavage or just a nexus of related issues.

In one sense, the formation of Green parties was an admission that the strategies of the 1970s had to some extent failed. Direct action was not guaranteed to produce the desired results, the espousal of the green cause by small radical left parties even less so. Yet in entering the political system, the Green parties sought to do so on their own terms. This is illustrated by their deep distrust of compromise on principles, a dislike of the existing modes of institutional democracy and the emphasis on internally decentralised organisation. To some extent they might even be called 'anti-party' parties that were unwilling to give up many of the essential features of a social movement. The parties could perhaps afford the luxury of this ambiguity and of a singlemindedness as long as they remained negligible political factors. Those that successfully entered the parliamentary system found that the incompatibility between movement and party was simply heightened.

The West German Greens, for example, had to face up to the issue of organisation, to a conflict between the idealists, who wanted to retain the pristine purity of a radical movement, and the realists, who accepted the need to make at least some concessions to the established rules of the game. While it would be misleading to see this difference as being merely between leaders and followers, certainly the party's views on internal democracy made it difficult for it to develop a consistent strategy within the system, and so be able to turn its environmental views into public policy. The parliamentary delegation, not long after taking up their seats, had to face up to the difficulties created by the acceptance of a collective leadership; and when the time came, many showed a marked reluctance to give up their seats according to the principle of rotation. One of the main arguments for reform was that if the party insisted upon rotation in office, it would never be able to acquire the expertise necessary to acquit itself well in, advance its interests through and even perhaps reform the bureaucratic and institutional framework. The case was eventually won in 1987 when the principle of automatic rotation was effectively abandoned.

Whatever the kind of organisational future the Green parties choose for themselves, they will have to face up to the fact that much of their policy has been adopted by major parties, which in the world of harsh political reality, may well be better placed to reap the electoral benefit. On the other hand, the alternative vision held by many green activists is as far away from realisation as ever. In embracing environmental issues, the leading political parties of both the left and the right have nevertheless rejected the radical view of a complete restructuring of political decision-making and policy according to, and the subordination of economics to, ecological priorities. The environment may have become part of the political agenda, but it is not yet the whole agenda nor its major structuring factor. That role is still enjoyed by industrial policy and the politics of distribution, whether one looks at Socialist governments in France or Sweden, or the greater market emphasis and welfare targeting wishes of Mrs Thatcher's Britain. Hence, while environmental problems and issues will continue to be central areas of government policy, it is probable that these will have to be accommodated within a broader commitment to the maintenance of an industrial society. As for the political expressions of the environmental concern that erupted in the 1970s and 1980s, only time will tell whether the green wave will continue to surge or subside to a more gentle ripple.

FURTHER READING

Cotgrove, S. (1982) *Catastrophe or Cornucopia: The Environment, Politics and the Future* (Chichester: Wiley).

Langguth, G. (1986) *The Green Factor in German Politics* (Boulder and London: Westview Press).

Lawson, K. and Merkl, P.H. (eds) (1988) *When Parties Fail: Emerging Alternative Organisations* (Princeton: Princeton University Press).

Müller-Rommel, F. (ed.) *New Politics in Western Europe: The Rise and Success of Green Parties and Alternative Lists* (Boulder and London: Westview Press).

Nelkin, D. and Pollak, M. (1981) *The Atom Besieged: Extra-Parliamentary Dissent in France and Germany* (Cambridge, Mass.: MIT Press).

Papadakis, E. (1984) *The Green Movement in West Germany* (New York and London: St Martin's Press).

Pilot, J.F. (1980) *Democracy or Discontent?: Ecologists in the European Electoral Arena* (London and Beverly Hills: Sage.

Poguntke, T. (1987) 'New politics and party systems: The emergence of a new type of party', *West European Politics*, 10: 76–88.

Rüdig, W. 'Peace and ecology movements in Western Europe', *West European Politics*, 11: 26–39.

CHAPTER SEVEN
Feminism and West European politics: an overview

Joni Lovenduski

By the second half of the 1980s most West European societies had experienced two decades of feminist resurgence, a phenomenon conventionally referred to as the second wave of feminism or the Women's Liberation Movement (WLM). More than a response to important changes in the lives of women in post-war Europe, the WLM was also a powerful impulse for further change. The ideas of feminism demonstrated a power to alter political attitudes, practices and policies, finding their way not only into most households but also the centre of the political arena. Feminist concerns influenced policy-makers during the 1970s, leading to a new range of sex-equality policies, alterations in family and health policies and the establishment of new state organisations in many North European countries. By the middle of the 1980s such initiatives had spread across Europe as many governments, political parties and traditional interest organisations accommodated themselves to women's demands to be included and considered as a political constituency.

However, the dynamism of the 1970s appeared to have faded and many believed that, in Western Europe at least, the WLM was over, that feminism had been removed from the political agenda. Others argue that although one may no longer point to a WLM as such, this is because of its success, because women are now politically integrated. Feminism, it is averred, has been institutionalized, evident not only in the new state bureaucracies established to promote women's rights, but also in the rising presence of women in the formal political arena. In fact, both views are an over-simplification of what is a complex and changing situation. Feminism has had an important influence on West European politics, and women in the 1980s are better politically integrated than they were in the 1960s. But the new women's movement emerged under different circumstances and followed different paths in different countries. Its successes have varied by culture, political climate, political system and policy area. Strong commitments to sex-equality employment or educational policies may be found alongside draconian policies on reproductive rights. Apparently waning movements have been revitalised by new agencies and initiatives. As the movement appeared to falter in some countries, it exhibited a considerable vitality in the new democracies of Southern Europe. Contradictions and paradoxes abound, and the difficulties of analysing feminist politics are legion. Hence the aims of this chapter are modest, limited to a description of the movement's origins and achievements and an assessment of its achievements. After a brief discussion of contemporary feminism, we shall look at women's presence in representative political institutions, their status in the trade unions and the impact of the women's movement on public policy.

THE SECOND WAVE OF FEMINISM IN EUROPE

Following Dahlerup (1986: 5), feminism may be defined as an 'ideology whose basic goal is to remove the discrimination and degradation of women and to break down male dominance of society'. This rather broad definition has the capacity to include the many and divergent strands of feminist thought. Feminists are those individuals who subscribe to feminist ideology. The term 'Women's Liberation Movement' refers to the new feminist movement which appeared in Europe and the United States in the 1960s and early 1970s with the avowed goal of liberating women from male oppression, a demand which went beyond the aim of equality. The WLM was a new social movement, and one which was characterised by a lack of organisational hierarchy, the spontaneous nature of its activities and the introduction of new forms of political action. An outgrowth of the 'New Left', the WLM was also a new manifestation of the traditional women's movement which included all those women organised to defend and expand women's economic, political, social and cultural rights, and describes such established interest organisations as party women's sections, women's institutes and national women's associations of various kinds.

The second wave of feminism began with the WLM. Although the traditional women's movement had taken up issues of women's rights during the postwar years, growing dissatisfaction with slow rates of progress combined with a vision of personal and political liberation to generate a widespread resurgence of feminism. Early recruits to the WLM came directly from the peace, student and anti-Vietnam War movements which were so strong during the late 1960s. However, it soon became apparent that the WLM was mobilising large numbers of previously apolitical women. Despite campaigns of ridicule in the media, and an initial refusal by politicians to entertain its demands, the mobilisation continued across all European liberal democracies throughout the 1970s. The WLM transformed the world of women's politics and with it the traditional women's movement. It brought feminist ideas into the political world, and challenged traditional concepts of politics. The activities of the WLM were directed at influencing women rather than the state. Its success was the success of an idea whose time had come.

In the 1980s second-wave feminism entered its second phase, active in most areas of social and political life and in many cases becoming institutionalised. This change has been accompanied by important developments in feminist theory. Feminist theory has drawn on three traditions in European political thought: liberalism, socialism and theories of society constructed from rereadings of psychoanalytic texts. To this has been added recent philosophical work on language and power which, particularly influential in France and Italy, has generated a proliferation of work on women, language and power by European and American feminists.

Feminist thought, which is not and has never been unified, is regarded as including three distinct theoretical positions, normally typed liberal feminism, Socialist feminism and radical feminism. The first two each emerged from their respective political and philosophical traditions with which they have to some extent developed in tandem: for example, the absorption by Socialist feminism of theories of language and power was accompanied by a similar development among many male Socialist theorists. But radical feminism is an (often uneasy) amalgam of all three traditions. An early coexistence of Socialist and radical feminists soon gave way to tensions, and by the end of the 1970s the movement was split in most countries. Points of disagreement were numerous, but fundamental to the division has been the argument about essentialism and difference. The radical feminist analysis has located women's oppression with men, particularly with male sexuality which is regarded as the site of male power. Male sexuality is seen as a compulsive sexuality innately associated with violence and aggression. In effect, radical feminists argue that there exists essential (superior) female and an essential (inferior) male. Those radical feminists who accept that a degree of male sexuality is socially constructed, find within that social construction a great deal of individual volition. This is because men are advantaged by such behaviour. When men act in male ways they are not just puppets of their childhood socialisation, but are acting in ways which bring them positive advantages in the form of ego, status, authority, and services. Although considerable ambiguities exist, the argument implicitly turns on the notion that there exists an innate female nature (This is often termed the 'nature' argument). Socialist feminists cannot accept the 'nature' argument, pointing out that such theories lead to transhistorical analysis and contain no convincing causality. They argue that (the 'nurture' argument) female nature is socially constructed (see Jaggar 1983; Eisenstein 1984). The debate is a complex one and well beyond the scope of this chapter; what is important for our purposes is that the assumption of innate difference has political consequences. At its most extreme, radical feminism means the political separation of women and men, and while few radical feminists would go that far, many see little point in engaging the political universe as it is, and much of their activity has been structured outside the political arena in the building of alternative institutions.

One important by-product of the feminist nature/nurture dispute has been a recognition that the postulation of an essential or universal female obscures important differences between women. Thus the British movement was criticised for taking insufficient account of its multiracial society, for example by postulating demands for liberalising abortion and for altering the structure of the family which were not in the interests of Black women – a division which became extremely important in the 1980s. Socialist feminists who have understood women's oppression as something which is historically specific have been more aware of differences among women. While they do not deny the importance of men's power, they have sought to understand differences between the sexes without assuming essential or innate capacities to dominate. They seek therefore to transform the political system in such a way that it can act in the (Socialist) interests of both men and women, and are thus closely engaged in the development of relevant political strategy.

At first an American phenomenon, second-wave feminism struck an extremely responsive chord among West European women. Vicky Randall (1987) cites three related explanations for the mobilising capacity of the WLM. These are the aspects of women's situation which predisposed them to recognise their oppression, ideological and institutional factors facilitating a feminist revival, and specific triggering events. Predisposing factors included the increased numbers of educated women in the population, the presence of more divorced and separated women, a tendency to smaller families, an awareness and availability of new contraceptive technology, a greater experience of paid employment outside the home, and a growing sense of relative deprivation. Facilitating factors included, in some countries, the coming of age of the first generation of women to have grown up with the full array of citizen rights and duties. Experience in the New Left politics of the 1960s supplied a significant group of talented and educated women with important political skills. In many countries the New Left was itself a triggering event. Despite its stress on equality, on liberatory goals and on unmasking systemic oppression, the male leadership refused to accept women's initial demands for equality. On the contrary, during the 1960s, many men of the New Left often refused even to listen to the feminist case, believing it at worst to be divisive and at best irrelevant. The result was that angry women began to form groups to discuss their situation. They established journals of their own and devised political activities designed not only to draw attention to their circumstances but also to exhibit the power of their anger.

The WLM focused on grass-roots activities, favouring non-hierarchical small groups as its organisational form. The dimensions of the political world were expanded as the political nature of private relationships between men and women became understood. From the early consciousness-raising groups, self-help and service activities were organised. Women experimented in new ways of living and on trying to establish and develop non-oppressive relationships between men and women both at home and in the wider society. Women's health centres, publishing ventures, bookshops, centres, refuges, theory groups and advisory centres constituted a counter-culture with a huge array of alternative institutions. The commonality of themes of the WLM was one of its most striking features. Although formal international organisations were few and far between, the same preoccupations were apparent throughout Western Europe. Issues of sex equality such as equal pay and equal rights at work, abortion rights, organisations around shelters for battered women, the issue of co-operation with the mainstream political institutions, the challenge of political lesbianism, the meaning of pornography, the political significance of motherhood, and the sexist construction of language were raised everywhere a movement appeared.

When the issue was important enough, the WLM did attempt to engage the traditional political institutions. Often this engagement took the form of amusing and imaginative direct political action. In Denmark the 1970s saw women refusing to pay more than 80 per cent of bus fares because women's pay averaged only 80 per cent of that of men. When arrested and fined they dutifully and cheerfully paid 80 per cent of their fines. Other ways of making the point were more serious. Prominent French, German, Italian, and later Greek women all signed declarations that they had had abortions, challenging the authorities to prosecute them for breaches of restrictive legislation. In what were perhaps the most conspicuous feminist political activities of the 1970s, widespread campaigns were organised to reform abortion statutes in Italy, France, the Netherlands and West Germany. Cultural, institutional, ideological and organisational factors led to variations in and between the WLM and other women's movements. Traditional organisations were very much affected by second-wave feminism. Changes took place in the perspectives and practices of many women's rights organisations and of women's groups within other organisations, becoming highly visible at the end of the 1970s when many European feminists transferred their activities to unions and political parties. By then women's organisations of all kinds had begun to take stands on questions of women's rights. In Britain traditional organisations such as the Women's Institute and the Townswomen's Guild were active on equal pay and opportunity legislation and many associations engaged in lobbying first for the liberalisation and later the maintenance of permissive abortion legislation. The hitherto compliant, Communist-led Union of Italian Women pressured the Italian Communist Party on issues of women's rights and broke ranks with the party over the abortion issue. Women in the Swedish Centre Party demanded and won government action on equal opportunity policy. Thus in a relatively short period of time the WLM had demonstrated that it was a political force to be reckoned with, capable of both influence and mobilisation.

The impact and strength of the WLM varied considerably by country. A number of influences were at work. The decline of the first wave of feminism had been less apparent in the Scandinavian countries which experienced a consistent pressure on women's rights. These countries, which also featured high employment rates for women, had well-developed equal rights policies by the beginning of the 1970s. Where continuity between the first- and second-wave movements was less apparent, the second wave was both more radical and influential. Dahlerup (1986) writes that within the Nordic states the strength of the WLM appears to have varied directly with the strength of the New Left from which it emerged and inversely with the commitment of the political system to equality law. But such generalisations may not safely be extended to the rest of Western Europe. The strong movements in Britain and the Netherlands in the 1970s might also be attributable to the widespread student movements from which they emerged. However, while British rates of women's employment were high, those in the Netherlands were among the lowest in the European Economic Community. Paradoxically, although an influential New Left in Italy generated a concomitantly impressive WLM, neither West Germany nor France – which were also sites of left renaissance in the 1960s – hosted a numerically strong movement in the 1970s. But in France feminist ideas had an enormous political influence and by the end of the decade women were recognised as a distinctive political constituency by nearly all contenders in a competitive bidding for the women's vote (see Mossuz-Lavau and Sineau 1981). In West Germany a dispersed, divided and separatist movement was not mobilised until the Greens took the initiative on matters feminist at the beginning on the 1980s. Such contradictory differences indicate the complexity of the origins and development of the WLM and underline the need for considerable further comparative research.

During the 1980s the great visibility of the WLM gave way to the less spectacular work of consolidation. A considerable effort went into a range of cultural activities, and large numbers of feminists were drawn into the party and union work begun during the 1970s. While important theoretical debates continue, in most countries the split between the radical and Socialist wings of the movement has lost its original heat. Also gone is the elation and spontaneity which was once associated with feminist politics. In the 1980s the WLM has been described as being 'everywhere, but nowhere' a reference to the absence of an organisational centre, a structure, however informal, to which individuals felt they belonged. As the ideas of the movement have developed and spread, the movement has continued to diversify, but there are other reasons for a seeming lack of focus. The absence of any central organisation is part of the explanation, but this was never a feature of the WLM. More important may be a greater pessimism about the speed with which women's lives might be changed, as a result of learning more about the depth and roots of women's subordination. At the same time however, most West European countries have experienced a renaissance of women's culture. Britain, West Germany, and the Nordic countries host women's peace movements, and in Britain a Black women's movement is emerging. If indeed the WLM itself has run its course, then what has survived is a newly energetic women's movement influenced by feminist ideas and a network of feminist structures in the political mainstream.

FEMINISM AND THE POLITICAL SYSTEM

When feminism engages the institutions of state and government, its central problem is the lack of fit between a social movement and a hierarchical political institution. A diverse movement whose ideal form is direct democracy has considerable problems when it is forced to operate according to the principles of representative democracy. During the 1980s the women's movement had to come to terms with this problem, developing strategies aimed at enhancing women's influence while retaining contact with the grass roots. Such strategies are necessarily multi-focused. Experience has shown that the range of political parties must be colonised as well as the unions, the professional associations and the national and local state. In its second phase, second-wave feminism has concentrated on ensuring access to the political agenda via strategies of entrism and networking directed at 'feminising' political élites.

Throughout Western Europe women have either revitalised or organised for the first time groups, sections or caucuses within parties, unions and professional associations which have the dual aims of promoting both women and women's interest. This self-organisation has occurred at the same time as institutional bases have been gained in an enormous array of equality agencies, women's committees and councils. Each country has progressed differently, but important similarities are evident. At first, entry to the political mainstream was gained via parties of the left as Socialist women organised to promote sex equality. But often strategies begun with the left were inhibited by powerful trade unions, mindful of their collective bargaining prerogatives and resistant to any redistribution from men to women. Thus in Sweden, often credited with the most advanced anti-sex discrimination policy in Europe, union resistance to employment policy orientated towards women's rights was only set aside with the formation of a non-Socialist coalition government in the late 1970s. In France, on the other hand, the first Department for the Status of Women was established by a government of the right.

Dahlerup (1986) has written that there were three important signs of interaction between the WLM and the established political system: ideas became absorbed by the system; leaders of the movement were co-opted; and the formerly marginal group gained political access. All three phenomena may be observed in Western Europe today where many feminists are particularly concerned about the problem of co-option. Co-option is not a simple matter of hijacking leaders. It raises important questions about the relationship between the movement and the state, and many feminists fear that a successful 'state feminism' may become a substitute for the women's movement itself. Experience in Spain, Greece, Britain, France and the Netherlands has shown that state equality agencies and women's committees apparently have the capacity to revitalise or even generate feminist movements. But feminist dependence upon state initiatives in the absence of a widespread women's movement means that women's rights will depend on the political fortunes of particular political parties and institutions. When the political fortunes of the sponsoring parties fall, state feminism falls with them. France provides a good example of this. Ducroq (1985) writes that in France during the 1980s activity began to centre around appraisals of past achievements and anniversaries. She describes this transformation of the movement as an ironic result of the accession to power in 1981 of a Socialist government committed to women's rights. It signified its commitment to women by upgrading the Department of the Condition of Women, established by Giscard d'Estaing in 1974, into a full-scale Ministry of Women's Rights led by the able Yvette Roudy who was determined to embark upon a dialogue with the movement. A range of policies were introduced as feminist ideas penetrated many areas of government. But feminists ceased to fight their battles through the grass-roots campaigns and demonstrations that had been typical of the 1970s. Rather, they operated through the actions of large numbers of legally constituted associations or through the work of groups linked to teaching or research institutions. The process of institutionalizing feminism came to a halt when the right returned to power in 1986. Prime Minister Jacques Chirac appointed no Minister for Women's Rights. After a certain amount of press criticism, he established a Delegation for Women's Condition along the old Giscardian lines, but staffing was much reduced, programmes were allowed to lapse, and laws were not enforced. The women's movement has been in disarray, slow to respond, and unable to organise against its expulsion from the state.

In West Germany the relationship between the women's movement and the party system has been particularly interesting. Arguably, the rise of the Greens has mobilised a feminist constituency which otherwise would have confined itself to the politics of social movements and the construction and maintenance of a counter-culture. The West German WLM has always been something of a puzzle and its analysis has been inhibited by the profound split between its radical and Socialist wings and the near absence of a women's studies movement within the social sciences there. But there has been general agreement that after some legal changes mainly accomplished by women in the political parties and legislatures, a weak and ineffectual movement became dispersed into small groups during the 1970s. Despite the fact that the glossy feminist magazine, EMMA, maintained a consistent circulation of around 300,000 and most West German cities featured women's bars, centres, cafes, journals, bookshops, refuges, etc., the organised presence of feminism was minimal. Change was precipitated by the return of the right to power and the entry of the Greens into the Bundestag. The Greens were the first political organisation to give prominence to women's· liberation in their programme. Green women had developed a kind of feminist populism whose influence was soon to be seen in the other parties. A large number of feminists were prepared to work with the Greens, thus highlighting the WLM once again (Haug 1986). Feminist activity at the centre of politics has had important effects on the other parties which have hastened to bid for political support from women. In Ireland too the WLM gathered strength during the 1980s. Within months of the referendum constitutionalising the prohibition of abortion law reform Ireland experienced a feminist renaissance as women's groups formed and organised political, ideological and theological debates, publications and other activities. Weak in numerical terms when facing the organised power of the Catholic Church, its energy suggests that the movement could grow.

The 1980s have also seen the emergence of feminism as a political force in both Greece and Spain. Spanish feminism has an organisational presence in most of the country's provinces. Sensitive to the cultural diversity of Spain, the WLM reflects the aspirations of autonomy expressed by the Basques, Catalans, Galicians and Andalusians. This has added to suspicion of any effort to co-ordinate from the centre. Spanish feminists have a foothold in the state in the Instituto de Mujer, part of the Ministry of Culture created by the Socialist government which came to power in 1982 keen to upgrade the previous bureaucracy for women and to be seen to be giving the issue of sex equality a higher priority and larger budget than its predecessor. Top posts at the Instituto have been filled by committed feminists. Staff appear in a giant photograph of a pre-democracy demonstration which hangs at the entrance and signifies to the visitor that they are not ordinary bureaucrats (Threlfall 1985). The Instituto is a powerful instrument: it is a centre of activity, it funds groups and projects and its grant applications reflect the whole range of feminist activities. But some Spanish feminists fear that it will somehow become a substitute, that it will begin to think of itself as an alternative to the autonomous women's movement. Worrying too is the question of what happens when the government changes.

Spain is a good example of a numerically weak movement able to trade on the power of feminist ideas. Although all parties have spokespersons or committees on women's issues, Spanish feminists have no powerful organisations of their own. But they have been able to compensate for their limitations by skilful management of a favourable political climate. There has been enormous scope for the creation of new institutions, new practices and new laws during the general overhaul of the country's political system. The readiness of the democratising political élite to accept fresh ideas was harnessed so that catching up with women's rights in the rest of Europe came to be officially regarded as part of the general process of modernisation.

Background conditions have also been important for Greek women who have experienced economic marginalisation since 1960. Feminist discussion was stifled by a dictatorship which rested in part on the cult of the family. Only after its fall in 1974 could a women's movement emerge. The character of that movement was affected by its origins, and feminism first appeared within the left led by political women in the Socialist and Communist parties (Stamiris 1986). Once the statutory apparatus of sex equality was established, feminism began to take on the characteristics of the WLM, reopening controversies over abortion and birth-control and focusing on such issues as the media representation of women, violence against women, the law on rape, etc.

The Greek and Spanish experiences underline the importance of democratic forms to the WLM. They also, in their adoption of women's rights as part of modernisation and democratisation processes, demonstrate the importance of a commitment to sex equality to contemporary conceptions of liberal democracy. In Turkey, by contrast, the ban on politics at the end of 1980 under the rule of the new military regime led to an awakening of interest in political problems previously regarded as marginal. The issue of women's oppression gained the attention of those engaged in the struggle for the establishment of democratic rights. Hence feminist ideas gained ground in certain circles, but the democratic preconditions for the emergence of the women's movement did not obtain. Activity is thus confined to a few discussion groups and publishing circles in the large cities.

THE IMPACT OF FEMINISM ON THE POLITICAL SYSTEM

The 1970s pattern of a steady rise in the presence of women in both the electoral and appointive channels of European politics continued in the 1980s. Change took place at both mass and élite level as traditional gender differences in political participation, whereby women were less participatory and more conservative than men, gave way and in some cases were reversed. Often as a result of activities in women's caucuses, political parties began to recognise a constituency of women and to undertake measures both to increase their presence and to represent their interests. Although voting differences had been largely eroded, equality between the sexes in political representation, or even in party membership terms, had nowhere been achieved by the end of the 1970s. Of the four most populous European states in 1983, women were less that 10 per cent of holders of legislative office, less than 6 per cent of senior civil servants, and except in France, less than 5 per cent of holders of government positions. The cycle of elections since that time has produced a considerable improvement in the representation of women in Germany and Italy, a small increase in Britain but a decrease in the presence of women in the French Assembly. A small decline in the representation of Dutch women was also apparent, but elsewhere women consistently gained ground (see Table 1).

The pattern of improved representation is largely a result of changing practices within the political parties. It has been known for some time that European voters do not usually penalise women candidates. Parties, especially where party competition is high, have sought to promote women, introducing, often at the behest of women's caucus or section members, a range of reforms including quotas, special training provisions and other forms of positive action. Change has also been evident at the level of policy. Most party manifestos now include specific pronouncements on policy on

Table 7 The presence of women in West European legislatures (in percentages)

	1983	1987
UK	3.5	6.3
Spain	4.6	5.9
France	5.9	5.6
Italy	7.9	13.0
West Germany	10.0	15.0
Iceland	15.0	21.0
Holland	20.0	18.0
Norway	26.0	34.0
Denmark	27.0	30.0

women's rights, although there remain some notable exceptions to this trend. The results of this activity may be read in two contradictory ways. On the one hand, improvement may be noted and expected to continue. On the other, the very slow pace of the process should also be noted. Why has so much effort yielded such a small improvement? How is it possible that women in some countries are actually losing ground? To answer these questions we need to look much more closely at the progress of women through the parties. Here the examples of Britain, France and West Germany are instructive.

In Britain the rules of the political game do not favour new contenders for power: a high threshold of representation penalises 'third' parties. First-past-the-post elections based on single-member constituencies produce party structures in which jealously guarded local prerogatives have inhibited central party intentions to increase the number of women candidates and MPs. During the 1970s neither the Labour nor the Conservative Party paid much attention to their annual women's conferences, and neither made systematic efforts to promote women candidates. One result was that Britain had, at under 5 per cent, one of the lowest parliamentary representations of women in Europe. At the beginning of the 1980s the pattern changed. Two important developments were responsible. Firstly, party competition increased with the foundation of a fourth national party. Secondly, feminists began a concerted effort to organise within the Labour Party, setting up the Women's Action Committee (WAC) in 1981. The Social Democrats were from their foundation in 1980 concerned to be seen to be promoting women. Thus a process of competitive bidding for women's support was begun. The

WAC launched a major campaign to win political equality for women in the Labour Party with a programme which include upgrading the constitutional status of the Labour Party Women's Conference, the compulsory inclusion of at least one woman on every Labour Party short list, and a reformed parliamentary working day. Although the WAC repeatedly fell foul of the National Executive, some of its demands were met. New short list rules went into effect in 1988, the party committed itself to the establishment of a Ministry of Women with Cabinet status, and women's issues figured prominently in the 1987 election manifesto when more women candidates were nominated than ever before (92 or 15 per cent). But its real accomplishment was to stimulate a higher level of participation and a higher level of awareness of the issues among Labour women.

Within both the Liberals and the Social Democrats a similar, but less formal, process took place. Both parties instituted positive action in the form of quotas of women for parliamentary short lists, with strong policies on women. A considerable overlap between Labour and Alliance policies on women's rights was apparent, with Labour committed earlier to a slightly wider range of policies. The 1987 Alliance election manifesto featured commitments to positive action, contract compliance, and a whole array of equal opportunities policies. Over 16 per cent of Alliance candidates were women. But although party competition and feminist organisation were producing real change on the left and centre of the spectrum, the Conservative Party was doing almost nothing to promote either women's rights or women candidates. Despite some considerable discontent on the part of Conservative women (Campbell 1987), the Tories had no formal policies to promote women and no special appeal to women was made in their election manifesto. The proportion of women candidates at 6.6 per cent was scarcely higher that it had been in 1983, although more women were returned. The British situation illustrates both the need for participatory forms and for specific organisation if women are to make an appreciable impact. The Conservative Party is not democratically structured; the membership has little control over its leadership. Unity and party loyalty are highly valued, hence women have not organised as women within a party which currently dominates the electoral market-place and sees no reason to woo the political constituency of women. This may well be a short-sighted strategy as the Conservative Party can no longer rely on securing a majority of the women's vote in Britain, but so long as it wins elections it has little incentive to change.

In France feminists not only failed to colonise the parties of the right; they were unable to retain their foothold on the left. Although French parties have sometimes led the way in the production of policies of women's rights, they have been extremely reluctant to promote women to positions of party leadership or parliamentary responsibility. When the Socialist Party introduced quotas of women candidates in 1979 other parties failed to follow suit, and in the 1981 general election there were fewer women candidates than in 1978 with only the 'Socialists increasing the proportion of women candidates. The government did make some effort to come to grips with the problem of increasing the number of women candidates, decreeing in 1981 that municipal lists should not contain more than 80 per cent of candidates from either sex. But the Constitutional Court overturned the decree in 1983 and it is unlikely that it will be repeated. Women's organisation within the parties has been limited and an unofficial feminist current within the Socialist Party failed to make any headway during the party's years in office when the very large number of promotions of women which were made went to women who were not members of the feminist *tendance*. By 1986 the *tendance* had left the party and was organising on a cross-party basis in the form of the Feminist Association for an Alternative Policy. The 1986 election showed some limited evidence of dealignment among French women. Although there was no overall swing either to the left or right, younger, better educated, employed women swung markedly to the left. But the left lost the election and the new Chirac government curtailed the powers of the innovative Ministry of Women's Rights. At the time of writing state feminism is on the wane and autonomous feminism is barely politically visible in France.

Electoral volatility and party competition may be the two key components of a successful bid by women for party recognition. In West Germany both the political recruitment of women and the place of sex equality issues on the political agenda were enhanced by the appearance of the Greens and their mobilisation of the feminist constituency. Indeed, by 1987 the restricted access of women to positions of influence in the political parties and legislatures was a national political issue. Volatility among women voters was particularly evident in the marked dealignment of younger women in the 1983 election. In a political environment in which even a small swing may produce a change of government, no party can afford to ignore such a large potential reservoir of votes (Kolinsky 1988). The Greens' record on the political recruitment and promotion of women had always been good, and during the 1980s Green women developed a kind of feminist populism whose influence was soon to be seen at work in the other parties. Schmid (1987) argues that the degree of participatory democracy and grass-roots control achieved by the Greens has been to the advantage of women. The high profile of the Greens on women's issue stems from 1985 when six women took the leadership of the parliamentary party. Such activity is part of a wider green strategy whereby issues from extra-parliamentary politics are taken up and introduced into the legislature in order to mobilise the support of social movements. It has been a very successful approach to political mobilisation. Although women are only one-third of its members, the women's movement is the fourth most important source of green electoral support ranking after the ecological, alternative and peace movements. Thus EMMA, which continues to underline its distance from the Greens, cancelled a call for an electoral boycott when a survey of readers' opinions revealed that some 80 per cent of readers supported them (Kolinsky 1988).

Against such a background the Christian Democratic Party (CDU) used its 1985 party congress in Essen to highlight the situation of women and to engage in discussions of what the role of contemporary women should be. The congress, which was in part an attempt to revive party credibility among younger women, generated progressive legislative measures in family policy, pensions and access to training, and was followed by the appointment of a new Women's Minister to signify achievement for women by the CDU. The CDU now talks of a feminisation of society, a revaluation of housework and a reinstatement of the ethos of family life and a future shaped by motherly values. It has ceased to offer a conservative model of women and has begun to present a neo-conservative hybrid, a caring housewife and mother with part-time work. Haug (1986) points out that the CDU family policies, with their ingratiating feminist language, outflanked the autonomous women's movement which had difficulty in dealing with the use of feminist rhetoric to legitimise cutting the welfare state.

Meanwhile, Social Democrat (SPD) women, radicalised by the appearance of the Green women in the legislatures, moved on from their call for equal treatment to a demand for positive action. In 1985 the Arbeitsgemeinschaft Sozialdemokratischer Frauen (the SPD women's organisation) called for women to fill all the current *land* ministries and at least half the Federal Cabinet. All parties except the Liberals and the Christian Social Union offered proposals designed to increase the number of women parliamentary candidates. The Greens led with a pledge that 50 per cent of its candidates at local, regional and national level would be women, as would 50 per cent of all party office-holders. The CDU promised to nominate women in proportion to their membership in the party and the SPD resolved that by the 1990s 50 per cent of its candidates would be women. Although none of the parties nominated as many women as men for 1987, a record number of women were nominated and a record number were elected (Kolinsky 1988).

Besides colonising existing parties, European women have also occasionally formed parties of their own. The most successful recent example has been the Icelandic Women's Alliance which in 1987 won over 10 per cent of the vote and was surprised to find itself holding the balance of power in the negotiations on forming a new government following the defeat of the centre–right coalition. The Kvennalistinn, which is one of only three European women's parties ever to win parliamentary seats, was formed in 1983 as a result of frustration by Icelandic women who were not benefiting from the promotion of women that was taking place in the other Nordic states. Its effect has been to increase the parliamentary representation of women both by its own efforts and as a result of the pressure its existence placed on other parties. The other Nordic countries feature the highest levels of women's political recruitment of any modern society. Norway, Sweden, Finland, and Denmark are all countries in which strong, continuous women's movements combine with high levels of party competition and in which a sophisticated, mobilised constituency of women has been present since the 1960s. There, political will combines with political organisation to produce parties which have well-developed strategies of promoting women, and politicians are well aware of women as a political constituency. In 1986 the Norwegian Prime Minister, Mrs Gro Harlem Bruntland, brought seven other women into her Cabinet of eighteen. Margaret Thatcher, by contrast, has no other women in her Cabinet. Taken together, what all the above examples show is that politicians rarely promote women or sponsor women's issues out of the goodness of their hearts. They do it when there are good electoral reasons for it, and they have an alarming tendency to stop doing it when those reasons cease to obtain.

Although important, access via the political parties is not the only route to influence. The unions and employers, business and professional associations are major political actors in Western Europe, playing a role in behind-the-scenes negotiations as well as controlling access to important public bodies. Unions have, however, been rather better on the whole than employer and professional associations, and as the 'best case' in the corporate sector it is the unions we will consider here. By the beginning of the 1980s it was apparent that women's membership of trade unions was on the rise in all West European countries, although nowhere were women as unionised as men. During the 1970s trade union support for women's rights became a matter of policy for a number of unions, but only where programmes of positive action in the form of special training, reserved seats for women on union councils and executive committees or expansion in the number of available posts were introduced, or where women had organised within internal caucuses, did women's share of decision-making positions in union movements rise appreciably.

Feminist organisation in the unions has grown in strength since the 1960s. By the 1980s it was a major area of organised feminist activity. Unions have taken up such issues as sexual harassment at work, positive action in training, job-sharing, and parental leave. But willingness to expand the unions' political agenda to accommodate feminist politics has not always been accompanied by union activism on bread-and-butter issues such as equal pay and opportunity at work. Although many white-collar unions have been active in these areas, the powerful industrial unions have been noticeably reluctant to overturn traditional collective bargaining practices and have resisted equal pay and employment equality laws which they regard as state interference (Lovenduski 1986). The gendered segregation of the labour force has meant that these unions organise the industries which are least likely to employ women, but they are also often the unions which have the greatest influence on the parties of the left. They are therefore in a good position to inhibit the equal employment policy plans of Socialist parties. As de-industrialisation proceeds, long-term trends in the labour market indicate a decline in power for the traditional manufacturing unions as employment transfers to the tertiary sector, from full-time to part-time work, and from men to women. Such changes are likely to be accompanied by an overall decline in union power as labour markets are deregulated and union density falls. Thus contradictory trends make it difficult to predict the effect of long-term changes in the union movement on women.

In the short term, however, women's presence and visibility in the unions have continued to increase. Their membership of trade unions rose between 1980 and 1985 as they entered the workforce in increasing numbers. But women's unionisation varies greatly by country. The Nordic trade unions have the highest proportion of women members. In Denmark, Sweden and Finland over 50 per cent

Table 8 Women as a proportion of members, council members and executive members of selected trade union peak organisations in selected European countries in the mid-1980s (percentages)

	Executive members	Council members	Congress delegates	Members
Austria (OGB)	10.0	n/a	n/a	30.8
Belgium (CSC)	8.3	5.2	12.5	33.3
(FGTB)	8.3*	n/a	n/a	23.0
Denmark (LO)	12.0	26.8	18.0	46.0
Finland (SAK)	14.0	30.0	32.0	44.0
France (CFDT)	20.0	n/a	19.0	32.0
Great Britain (TUC)	—	17.6	15.0	34.0
Iceland (ASI)	33.3	25.8	36.0	46.3
Ireland (ITUC)	7.4	—	—	32.0
Italy (CGIL)	3.6	10.2	16.0	32.0
(UIL)	0.0	3.6	n/a	24.0
The Netherlands (FNV)	12.5	12.5	n/a	15.9
Norway (LO)	33.3	18.7	26.3	35.7
Portugal (UGT-P)	0.0	15.0	20.0	46.0
Spain (UGT)	0.0	5.0	7.0	12.0
Sweden (LO)	†	16.0	27.0	43.1
Switzerland (SGB)	7.4	7.5	13.8	12.3

n/a = data not available.
* The FGTB National Bureau has 48 members, 4 of whom are women. But 3 of the women are secretariat members who have no voting rights.
† There is one woman on the LO executive.

Source: Compiled from European Trade Union Congress, (ETUC) (1987) 'Women and trade unions in Western Europe'

of all organised wage-earners are women. In Britain, Italy, Belgium, Austria, and Ireland the proportion is between 30 and 33 per cent. In West Germany 22 per cent of union members are women, while the lowest proportions (between 10 and 15 per cent) are to be found in Switzerland, Luxemburg, and the Netherlands. But the rate of improvement in women's representation on union councils and executives lags behind growth in membership (see Table 8). Despite a general increase in the number of women's committees and specific training courses, women's places at the top are still normally the result of reserved places rather than competitive election, and the commitment of union movements to sex equality appears still to be more formal than substantive.

This is not to say that trade unions have not also promoted women. In Britain the feminist presence in the TUC women's conference has increased year by year since the early 1970s (Coote and

Campbell 1987). Although the political environment for unions worsened as Mrs Thatcher's legislative programme severely curtailed their bargaining power, leading unions to give priority to jobs in a period of rising unemployment and de-unionisation, the momentum of policies to promote women's participation continued to grow. The Union of Shop Distributors and Allied Workers (USDAW), for example, set up a National Women's Working Party in 1982 which recommended a network of divisional women's committees which were established in 1984. Positive action became widely accepted and was promoted by the Women's Advisory Committee of the TUC. When the National Union of Public Employees (NUPE) concluded in 1982 that its system of reserved seats for women on the National Executive Council was not helping women at branch level, it set up a National Women's Advisory Committee, appointed a national women's officer, and instituted women's advisory committees in each of its divisions. These in turn generated far-reaching proposals to enhance women's union participation. Moreover, feminist influence was to be found in the public sector union resistance to the dismantling of the welfare state and to government proposals for changing it. Throughout the 1980s women-centred initiatives continued to be mounted, starting with the unions where women were most numerous, but gradually drawing in more and more unions. By 1987 the largest British union, the Transport and General Workers Union (TGWU) required that each of its regions must send at least one women delegate to the annual TUC. The General, Municipal, Boilermakers and Allied Trades Union (GMBATU) reserved at least 25 per cent of its executive seats for women and the TUC had agreed to establish a special TUC women's department. Other European unions have also responded to feminist pressures. In France the executive committee of the Confederation General du Travail (CGT) was expanded in a move which brought a large number of women into executive posts in 1983. In the same year the Confédération Francaise Democratique du Travail (CFDT) expanded its councils and committees in the same way. In Germany IG Metall, the engineering workers union, launched a scheme in 1986 to promote women officials. Their officer for women's status aims to increase the proportion of women officials from its present level of 12.8 per cent to 21.5 per cent in line with women's membership of the union. Changes in trade unions have been partly a result of organisation by women, but union leaders are also well aware of the need to recruit the growing female workforce. In 1987 three important British unions – TGWU, USDAW and the National and Local Government

Officers' Association (NALGO) – launched major campaigns to recruit part-time workers, 88 per cent of whom are women. In this area too, a combination of organisation and market forces appears to be enhancing the position of women, although ironically women are gaining ground in a movement which is itself weakening.

Considerably less has been done by employer associations. Women are not well represented in negotiations between significant labour market organisations and their needs are often not taken into account in the collective bargaining process. Moreover, the relative absence of women from the decision-making hierarchies has important consequences in other parts of the political system. The success or failure of the drive to increase women's influence in labour market organisations may be measured in the corporate sphere of appointed posts where women continue to be poorly represented on the public bodies, commissions and councils through which the collective bargaining partners often exercise their power.

FEMINISM, PUBLIC POLICY, AND GOVERNMENT

There are two arguments for the inclusion of women in government. First, women have an interest which is best represented by women. Alternatively, the political representation of women is important if it can be shown that policies favouring women have not been pursued where women were not contending successfully for an active political role. The evidence for the first argument is patchy, not because the case cannot be made, but because rarely are sufficient women present in a political élite for an independent gendered effect to be observable. Where women have entered national political élites in significant numbers (for example in the Nordic states and the European Parliament) their influence on women's rights issues, family policy, control over reproduction, and the promotion of women has been more marked (Vallance 1986; Haavio-Mannila *et al.* 1985). Evidence that the active pursuit of political influence generates 'woman-friendly policies' is more extensive. The West German example described above shows what happens when a political constituency of women is mobilised and feminist ideas spread into political organisations; the example of France shows how such policies might be reversed when the grass roots of the women's movement is allowed to lapse.

Yvette Roudy's Ministry for Women's Rights attempted to develop a sustained dialogue with the women's movement, and funding for women's associations was an important part of its activity. Such funding had always been available, but its range was now extended to the whole range of women's groups and projects. In addition, the ministry undertook a substantial legislative programme. Other ministries were also compelled to consider how their policies affected women. Although responses varied, the Ministry for Research and Technology agreed to co-sponsor regional assemblies leading to a national conference on feminist studies which was held in Toulouse in 1982 and attended by over 800 women. A three-year government-funded programme of research on women and politics was inaugurated. The Ministry of National Education agreed the establishment of university posts in women's studies, creating four new posts in January 1984. Thus feminist ideas penetrated government. But the women's movement increasingly came to depend on the state, abandoning its social movement forms in favour of operating through a large number of legally constituted groups linked to teaching or research institutions. A process of institutionalising feminism led to its decline. Although the Chirac government continued to fund women's projects via the delegation within the Ministry for Health and the Family, the governmental feminist project was abandoned when the Socialists lost power in 1986.

Clearly, the simple presence of women is not enough; some sort of feminist commitment must also be present if policies to promote women are to be sustained. The problem is how to maintain the commitment the movement provides, harnessing its ideas to agencies of policy implementation without destroying its autonomous base. Here the example of the British women's committees is instructive. In the absence of a sympathetic party of national government, British feminists have attempted to colonise the local state. During the 1980s the establishment of municipal feminism, as it came to be known, was a major project of Labour Party feminists who were well aware of the need to maintain contact with and nourish the grass roots of the women's movement. The initiative was taken with the Women's Committee of the Greater London Council (GLC) established in 1982 as a result of both GLC commitment to channelling resources to London's disadvantaged communities and in response to organised feminist pressure, which was extremely strong in London. The committee was more than a simple equality agency; it wished to promote the welfare and interests of London women, to advance equal opportunities for women in GLC employment and the London boroughs, and to advocate the abolition of policies which discriminated on the grounds of sex. The committee had its own substantial budget. It established an elaborate consultative framework and evolved a distinctive style of local government based on wide consultation, accessibility, positive action to redress discrimination, and the redistribution of power and resources. As well as funding women's projects and organisations, the committee attempted to ensure that other GLC committees took women fully into account. This meant following detailed plans to consult women in the community, to promote equal opportunity and to meet women's need by considering whether any policy might have differential effects on men and women. Transport planning, for example, was an area in which women had a distinctive interest as they were the majority users of public transport. The GLC Women's Committee was abolished along with the GLC in 1986, by which time women's committees had been established in thirty-three local authorities. It was a short-lived experiment which received backing and support from leading male politicians. Other committees worked under less favourable conditions and their priorities varied accordingly. In 1985 a Standing Conference of Local Government Women's Committees was established with the aim of exchanging ideas and developing common policies (Coote and Campbell 1987). All the committees are in Labour-controlled authorities, hence in danger of dissolution if control passes to the Conservatives.

The 1980s saw local-level initiatives in a number of countries. Most of the German *Länder* now have equal opportunities departments and the Dutch have established women's bureaux in nearly every province. In West Germany feminist groups have come together in local *Weibräte* or women's councils established to pull all currents of feminism together to make demands on the political system.

State feminism has more of a history at national level where – the Chirac example notwithstanding – it is also more likely to have at least formal support from parties of the right. Most European countries had enacted equality legislation and established equality agencies by the end of the 1970s. During the 1980s these were often elaborated and upgraded, and by the middle of the decade a considerable experience of administering equal opportunity and anti-discrimination policy had been gained (Lovenduski 1986). Ironically, the equality agencies are normally structured on corporatist lines, overseen by representatives from government and both sides of industry, a characteristic which may be responsible for their relatively slow rates of progress.

Developments in other areas of interest to women have been more mixed. Often, policies of equal opportunities in employment and education exist side by side with policies which restrict women's domestic and reproductive rights. Ireland is the most extreme example of such state failure to integrate its policies on women. With a good record on employment equality initiatives, Ireland is the country most reluctant to offer women autonomy in matters of reproduction and family life. A general European trend towards the liberalisation of abortion statutes did not prevent a referendum in Ireland in 1983 from inaugurating a constitutional block on any kind of reform. In December 1986 the Dublin High Court ruled against organisations counselling pregnant women, which had been offering referral information for abortions in Britain. A 1986 referendum rejected, by a majority of 63 to 37 per cent, a proposal by the governing Fine Gael and Labour parties to dilute the constitutional prohibition on legislation permitting divorce. Nor does provision for the legal dissolution of marriage exist in Ireland. Divorce is on the statute-books in the rest of Europe, but abortion was still illegal in Belgium and contested elsewhere. The Spanish law of 1983 was blocked by a constitutional tribunal which in 1985 referred it to the government for rewriting. Greece legalised abortion under very tightly defined circumstances in 1986, but by 1987 the relevant enforcing decrees had not been introduced. In France the National Front tabled a bill in 1987 to remove state allowances for the cost of voluntary abortions, and would also like to make abortion illegal once again. In Britain restrictions to the 1967 Act have been placed before Parliament at regular intervals and in 1987 were the subject of a controversial private member's bill. In short, the issue is far from resolved.

In general, however, feminism has had an appreciable influence throughout Western Europe. It is partly, but not completely, politically integrated, organised in many, but not all, of the political parties and unions, able to place its issues on the policy agenda but not always able to secure favourable resolution. The central strategic dilemma for feminists at the end of the decade is how to campaign in the political mainstream while still maintaining the energy and persuasive force of a rising social movement.

REFERENCES AND FURTHER READING

Boston, Sarah (1987) *Women Workers and The Trade Unions* (London: Lawrence and Wishart).

Campbell, Beatrix (1987) *The Iron Ladies* (London: Virago Press).

Coote, Anna and Campbell, Beatrix (1987) *Sweet Freedom* (new updated edn) (Oxford: Basil Blackwell).

Dahlerup, Drude (ed.) (1986) *The New Women's Movement: Feminism and Political Power in Europe and the USA* (London: Sage).

Ducrocq, Françoise (1985) 'The Women's Movement in socialist France: four years later', *m/f*.

Eisenstein, Hester (1984) *Contemporary Feminist Thought* (London: Unwin Paperbacks).

Ellis, Valerie (1981) *The Role of the Trade Unions in the Promotion of Equal Opportunities* (Manchester: Equal Opportunities Commission).

Haavio-Mannila, Elina *et al.* (eds) (1985) *Unfinished Democracy: Women in Nordic Politics* (Oxford: Pergamon).

Haug, Frigga (1986) ' The Women's Movement in West Germany', *New Left Review*, **155**.

Hernes, Helga Maria and Voje, Kirsten (1980) 'Women in the corporate channel: a process of natural exclusion?' *Scandinavian Political Studies*, NS, 3 (2) pp 163–88.

M. Jaggar, Alison (1983) Feminist Politics and Human Nature (Brighton: Harvester).

Kolinsky, Eva (1988) 'The West German Greens – a women's party?', *Parliamentary Affairs*, 41, 129–148.

Lovenduski, Joni (1986) *Women and European Politics* (Brighton: Wheatsheaf Books).

Meehan, Elizabeth (1985) *Women's Rights at Work* (Basingstoke: Macmillan).

Mossuz-Lavau, J. and Sineau, M. (1981) 'France', in J. Lovenduski and J. Hills (eds), *The Politics of the Second Electorate* (London: Routledge and Kegan Paul). pp 112–33

Randall, Vicky (1987) *Women and Politics* (2nd edn) (London and Basingstoke: Macmillan).

Schmid, Carol (1987) 'Women in the West German Green Party: the uneasy alliance of ecology and feminism', Unpublished paper, Guilford Technical Community College, Jamestown, North Carolina.

Segal, Lynn (1987) *Is the Future Female?* (London: Virago).

Stamiris, Eleni (1986) 'The Women's Movement in Greece', *New Left Review*, 158

Tekeli, Sirin (1986) 'Emergence of the feminist movement in Turkey', in Dahlerup (1986), pp 148–59.

Threlfall, Monica (1985) 'The women's movement in Spain', *New Left Review*, 151.

Vallance, Elizabeth (1979) *Women in the House* (London: Athlone Press).

Vallance, Elizabeth (1986) *Women of Europe: Women MEPs and Equality Policy* (Cambridge: Cambridge University Press).

CHAPTER EIGHT
Race and Immigration

Zig Layton-Henry

One of the major challenges confronting the advanced industrial democracies of Western Europe is the acceptance and integration of post-war migrant workers and political refugees and their families, particularly those from the Third World. This challenge is particularly great because it contradicts many of the assumptions and expectations about post-war migration held by political élites and publics in both the receiving and the sending countries.

Before the Second World War immigration to Western Europe had been on a relatively small scale. Migrants came from neighbouring countries with similar cultural and ethnic backgrounds. It was assumed that immigrants would be integrated on the receiving societies' terms and become assimilated into the native population. Although migrants in nineteenth- and twentieth-century Europe, like the Irish in Britain and the Poles in Germany, did face resentment and hostility, they were eventually accepted and assimilated. The major and horrendous exception to this process was, of course, the Holocaust. Jewish communities all over Nazi-occupied Europe were exterminated during the Second World War. The example of the Holocaust is a warning that distinctive minority groups, no matter how well they may appear to be integrated, may be vulnerable to scapegoating and terror by majorities under such conditions as economic recession, invasion, and war.

The intra-European movements of people during and immediately after the war were on a massive scale, but presented European states with economic and social difficulties rather than with a political challenge. The problems were those of feeding, housing and finding work, often for fellow citizens or allies displaced by the war and the subsequent boundary changes and expulsions. Post-war reconstruction and economic recovery in Europe gradually allowed these people to be integrated economically, socially and politically.

In contrast, the migration to Europe of political refugees, often fleeing wars of independence or civil wars in the Third World, and migrant workers attracted by job opportunities created by the post-war economic boom in the late 1950s and 1960s, has been both massive and unprecedented. Some 15 million people, from a wide variety of cultural, linguistic, religious, and ethnic backgrounds, have been added to the populations of West European states. Moreover, although these migrant workers and refugees wish to remain and work in the advanced industrial states of Western Europe for a considerable period of their lives, it is not certain that they wish to give up their national identity, cultural distinctiveness, and citizenship. Nor is it certain that they wish their children to become citizens of their new countries of work and residence and be assimilated into the 'foreign' society which provides them with employment and security.

In many European countries it was assumed that post-war migration was a temporary form of labour migration, albeit on a substantial scale. The decision to migrate was viewed as a form of economic contract between the migrants and the receiving society (Freeman 1979). The migrant workers freely chose to move from their own countries to Britain, West Germany, France, and other West European countries where, in return for employment and wages, they worked in jobs rejected by native workers and so contributed to economic growth. Both sides were believed to gain from this economic bargain. However, it was assumed that if the economic gains to the migrants were reduced or ceased altogether, for example through unemployment, they would return to their home countries. Moreover, the receiving country owed few, if any, debts to the migrants. They chose to come freely and, if their expectations of work and savings failed to materialise, it was assumed that they would, and should, return home. Thus, in times of recession, policies to encourage repatriation would be both justified and successful.

These assumptions have proved to be false, although some countries continue to act as though they were true. In spite of the economic recession after 1973, which caused high levels of unemployment, especially among migrant workers, and despite the efforts of West European governments to halt labour recruitment and encourage repatriation, migrant workers have not only remained but have sent for their wives and children, have bought houses, and are showing every sign of settling as permanent members of their new countries. As the number of foreign residents shows little sign of diminishing, and in some cases continues to rise, despite the ending of labour recruitment, many European countries have attempted to impose much stricter controls. These additional restrictions in turn make it more difficult for immigrants to risk returning to their home countries as the opportunity to re-emigrate to Europe, if they wished to do so, might be lost. In any event, the risks of returning, especially for Third World migrants, is very high as these countries face a combination of economic stagnation and rapid population increase. Migrant workers can often earn more in manual jobs in Europe than they could earn in professional employment in Third World countries. Their chances of finding employment if they return home are poor. Thus the large majority of migrant workers in Europe have little alternative but to remain.

There have been a number of consequences of post-war immigration to Western Europe that have complicated the politics and government of these states. There has been a considerable rise in the foreign populations of West European states. There has been the creation of substantial non-European ethnic minorities. There has been a rise in racism and racial violence and governments have had to wrestle with the problems of controlling immigration and combating racial discrimination. The growth of a second generation, often without citizenship, but with few ties to their parents' home countries, has brought about the realisation that positive policies to encourage integration need to be adopted since repatriation or voluntary return has become impractical. Finally, large-scale labour migration has caused difficulties in the relations between the governments of the sending and receiving countries.

THE FOREIGN PRESENCE

The growth in the foreign population, as a result of post-war migration, has been dramatic. The size of the foreign population in the major receiving countries is shown in Table 9. This table, if anything, underestimates the size of the immigrant population as many migrants to Britain, France, and the Netherlands had the citizenship of the receiving country as colonial or Commonwealth subjects. Also, in countries like Britain, France and Sweden, many foreign migrants have become naturalised citizens of their new country of work and residence. Even so, the size of the foreign population is substantial in all the major receiving countries.

Table 9 The foreign population of the eight major receiving countries of Western Europe (1984)

	Foreign population	% of population
Austria	272,300	3.6
Belgium	897,630	9.1
France	4,485,715	8.2
West Germany	4,378,942	7.2
Great Britain	1,736,000	3.2
Netherlands	558,710	3.9
Sweden	390,565	4.7
Switzerland	839,671	13.0

Sources: European Journal of Political Research, Vol 16, No. 6; Reprinted by permission of Kluwen Academic Publishers; *British Labour Force Surveys*, 1984–86.

The settlement of large numbers of foreign nationals and their families in European countries has had a number of major consequences. There has developed an extensive network of immigrant associations, churches, mosques, temples, schools, and other organisations that foster national consciousness, family ties and cultural links across countries. These tend to encourage the belief that migration is temporary and that return can easily be achieved. The governments of the sending countries often have a strong desire to encourage such beliefs because they gain from the transmission of remittances and savings. They may also not wish to lose substantial numbers of their citizens and future citizens. Labour-exporting countries thus often subsidise immigrant associations and schools in the receiving countries to strengthen national ties and consciousness among their overseas citizens and their children. Yugoslavia is a good example of a sending country which pursues such policies even to the extent of sending teachers abroad so that the children of overseas workers can learn the language, traditions, and culture of their parents' country. Similarly, the Turkish government has opposed proposals in West Germany to amend the citizenship laws to facilitate the naturalisation of foreign nationals born in West Germany, i.e. the children of foreigners (Miller 1986). The West German government dropped the proposals partly because they would have been unpopular at home and partly to maintain good relations with a long-standing ally. This conflict illustrates the problems that the presence of large numbers of foreign nationals can cause between states and also the tension between *de jure* and *de facto* membership of a state.

The settlement of large numbers of foreign nationals in Western Europe has thus raised the question of what constitutes membership of a modern state. In the pre-war period almost all members of a state were citizens with full legal and civil rights, but now many members of Western democracies are not citizens. They are *de facto* members of these societies, participating in the labour market, contributing to the economy, paying taxes, renting or buying houses, bringing up families, sending their children to school, and consuming goods and services. They contribute to and benefit from the welfare state and are involved in the social and cultural life of their local communities. In some local neighbourhoods foreign workers are a high proportion of the population and may even constitute a majority in some inner-city areas. However, they are not *de jure* members of these societies, as they have foreign citizenship, and so are excluded from voting in local and national elections. (Recently, however, Sweden, Norway, Denmark, the Netherlands and Ireland have permitted foreign citizens who fulfil certain residence requirements to vote in local elections). They may also be excluded from public employment and may have lesser rights to social and welfare benefits than citizens.

The long period of residence of most foreign workers in Western Europe – most have been in Europe for over fifteen years – has blurred the distinction between citizen and non-citizen of West European states. All those legally resident in a state enjoy some rights. One could argue that there is a continuum of rights and privileges. Citizens are members with access to all social, civic, and political rights. Legally resident aliens are members with a high degree of security, legal protection, and access to most rights. The process of the blurring of the distinction between citizen and non-citizen has gone furthest in Scandinavia. In Sweden, for example, foreign residents receive equality of treatment with citizens and can even vote in local and regional elections if they have been resident for three years. Only voting in elections for the Swedish Parliament is denied to foreigners. Sweden had also made it easier and cheaper for foreigners to become naturalised Swedish citizens.

In other European countries like Switzerland and Austria the distinction between citizen and non-citizen remains sharp. Austria does not allow foreign citizens a voice at any level of political representation. Foreigners cannot stand for election as shop stewards or elect representatives to local advisory councils, as they can in West Germany, nor do they have the legal security that permanent residents usually have, for example, in Switzerland. The aliens police in

Austria can order a foreigner to leave if his or her presence 'con-stitutes a danger for public peace, order or security or runs counter to the public interest' (Bauboeck and Wimmer 1988). This wide dis-cretion means that unemployment can lead to deportation. In addition, foreigners cannot enter public employment and they have restricted rights to social assistance. Austrian politicians do not regard Austria as an immigration country even though some sectors of the economy are dependent on foreign workers, even in periods of reces-sion, and despite their growing length of residence in Austria. It is also very difficult for foreigners to become naturalised Austrian citizens.

Those people with the most tenuous membership of West European states and the least rights are groups such as seasonal workers, illegal immigrants, illegal workers and asylum seekers awaiting a decision on their applications for refugee status. These groups have few rights and can often be removed or deported arbitrarily or with only limited rights of appeal, because they have not established a legal right to residence. They have few allies in what may be their intended country of residence or refuge. However, in the last decade or so there has been a revival of the medieval concept of sanctuary as illegal immigrants threatened with deportation have sought refuge in churches, mosques, and temples to escape arrest and removal, and in order to mobilise support for clemency or amnesty. They have often been able to obtain support from sympathetic politi-cal groups, churches, local people who know them, and immigrant associations. In 1975, 182 illegal Moroccan workers in the Nether-lands took refuge in Dutch churches after their applications for legalisation were refused. They could not produce documentary proof that they qualified under the terms of an amnesty. Their cam-paign for regularisation of their status was successful. Similar cam-paigns have occurred in other European countries with a high degree of success.

THE CREATION OF MULTIRACIAL STATES

One of the striking features of post-war migration has been the diversity of the areas from which the migrants have come. West Indians, Indians and Pakistanis were the major groups migrating to Britain in the 1950s and 1960s. They were followed by Bangladeshis. Algerians, Moroccans, Portuguese, and West Africans migrated to France. Between 1946 and 1958 the Netherlands received some

300,000 political refugees from Indonesia including some 12,500 South Moluccans who were members of the Royal Netherlands East Indies Army. Most of the refugees were of mixed descent and settled well in the Netherlands, but the South Moluccans, now some 40,000, still dream of returning to an independent republic of the South Moluccas. They have strongly resisted integration into Dutch society. In the 1960s the Netherlands received political refugees from Surinam and migrant workers from Mediterranean countries, especially Morocco and Turkey. In West Germany, Turks have formed the largest group, followed by Yugoslavs, Italians and Greeks. In Sweden the large numbers of Finnish workers have been supplemented by Yugoslavs, Greeks, Moroccans and Turks. Switzerland was the European ·country which relied most heavily on foreign workers, mainly Italians, but did not recruit workers from the Third World.

Post-war migration has thus transformed many West European states from countries with a high degree of ethnic homogeneity to multi-ethnic and multiracial states with large and distinctive non-European minorities. Table 10 gives an indication of the size and age structure of the non-white ethnic minority population in Great Britain. Before the Second World War the non-white population of

Table 10 Estimated population of Great Britain by ethnic group, 1985

Ethnic origin	Population all ages (000s)	Percentage of each population born in Great Britain	Aged 0–15	16–59/64★	60/65†
White	51,222	96	20	61	19
Non-white	2,736	42	34	63	3
West Indian or Guyanese	547	53	26	70	4
Indian	689	35	32	65	3
Pakistani	406	44	43	56	1
Bangladeshi	99	28	51	48	1
Mixed	232	76	55	43	2
Other‡	403	25	25	72	3
All ethnic origins	54,235	94	21	61	18

★ Men 16–64, women 16–59.
† Men 65 and over, women 60 and over.
‡ Includes persons for whom ethnic group was not stated (637,000 in 1985).

Source: Based on *Population Trends, Winter 1986* (London: HMSO), 1986, p. 4.

Britain was only a few thousand, but by 1985 it had grown to 2.4 million or 4.4 per cent of the population. It is composed almost wholly of post-war immigrants and their descendants. It is also an extremely young population and one which will grow at a much faster rate than the population as a whole. This will have the beneficial effect of offsetting to a small extent the growing numbers òf retired people in the population. As most non-white immigrants to Britain were British subjects from colonial or Commonwealth countries, the non-white ethnic minority population in Britain is much larger than the foreign population.

THE RISE OF RACISM

This transformation of European societies largely occurred in the 1960s during a period when economic growth in Europe was proceeding at a very rapid rate. At first there was little popular resistance to immigration and strong support from employers who needed the labour to expand output and meet the great surge in demand for their products. However, immigration is an issue which historically has stimulated xenophobia, racism and the emergence of extreme right-wing groups. Xenophobia can be defined as a dislike of foreigners or outsiders and is an old and familiar phenomenon in human societies. Immigrants, especially when they arrive in large numbers, are often seen as competitors for jobs, housing and other scarce resources. This may stimulate anti-immigrant feeling and campaigns for immigration control. Racism defines people as superior or inferior due to external physical characteristics or according to ancestry. It is used to justify different treatment of a group of people because of these physical or ancestral differences. The racist theories of the Nazis and their attempt to exterminate the Jews for reasons of racial purity have left a legacy of abhorrence of racism and racist ideas in post-war Europe and around the world.

The massive immigration to Western Europe in the post-war period did stimulate considerable popular resentment, though this did not occur until immigration was well advanced. In Britain there was little evidence of hostility to immigration in the early 1950s although there was considerable evidence of racial discrimination in housing and employment against West Indians and Asians. A campaign for immigration control developed, but this had little success until substantial riots against black immigrants in London and Nottingham in 1958 alerted politicians to growing anti-immigrant resentment

(Layton-Henry 1984). In 1962 the first bill to control immigration from the Commonwealth was passed. This legislation did not alleviate public concern as immigration, particularly of dependants, continued throughout the 1960s and 1970s. Further measures to control immigration were taken in 1965, 1968 and 1971. In the 1980s Mrs Thatcher's government has taken additional measures to control immigration, particularly from Third World countries.

In 1967 the National Front, an anti-immigrant far-right party, was formed. This party gained support purely on the basis of its campaign against immigration, and especially against the admittance of the Asians expelled from Uganda in 1972 and Asian immigrants from Malawi in 1976. The publicity given to Enoch Powell's anti-immigrant speeches helped the National Front to gain recruits. Although the National Front failed to win any local government or parliamentary seats, it mobilised sufficient electoral support in the East End of London and in other large cities in the mid-1970s to be taken seriously as a political force (Taylor 1982).

The National Front also engaged in street politics, emulating the Fascists of the 1930s. It organised highly provocative marches in immigrant areas to intimidate residents and generate publicity and support. Violent clashes occurred between supporters and opponents of the National Front, especially in Lewisham in London and Ladywood in Birmingham in August 1977. In 1978 a number of organisations formed the Anti-Nazi League to mobilise support against the National Front. One of the league's supporters was killed in violent clashes between the police and demonstrators, who were trying to prevent the National Front holding an election meeting in Southall, an area of Asian settlement, during the general election campaign in April 1979. (NCCL 1980).

The results of the 1979 general election were a considerable defeat for the National Front. It contested 303 seats but achieved only an average of 633 (1.4 per cent) votes in each seat, after promising an electoral breakthrough to its supporters. The total defeat of the National Front was due largely to Mrs Thatcher's promise that the Conservative Party would respond to popular anxieties over immigration and bring New Commonwealth immigration to an end.

During the 1970s there was evidence that the far right, including members of the National Front, were involved in violent attacks on members of immigrant communities (Layton-Henry 1984). These acts of racial violence and harassment have continued in the 1980s and are a source of great concern, particularly for Asians who are most often the victims of these attacks.

The French tradition of encouraging immigration to augment its labour force and population meant that French political leaders and the public had a more positive view about immigrants than other Europeans, and in particular about their economic contribution to society. They were also confident of their ability to assimilate immigrants. However, the considerable post-war immigration to France and the growing numbers of North Africans and black Africans undermined this positive, self- confident tradition. Opinion polls in the 1970s reported that majorities of respondents felt that there were too many immigrants and that the numbers, especially of non-Europeans, should be controlled (Freeman 1979). In particular, there was very strong hostility to North Africans, which was probably a legacy of the bitter War of Independence in Algeria and of feelings that Muslims would resist assimilation into French society. In the summer of 1973 there was a massive outburst of racial violence directed against Algerian immigrant workers, eleven of whom were murdered between 29 August and 21 September. No one was arrested for the murders, but some immigrant leaders were expelled. Jean-Marie Le Pen and the National Front attempted to exploit this racial tension, but without success.

It was not until the 1980s that Le Pen and the National Front emerged as major political figures in French politics. In 1981 Le Pen was unable to find 500 sponsors for his presidential candidature, but in 1983 the National Front achieved a spectacular success. It gained 17 per cent of the vote in local elections in Dreux and four of its candidates were incorporated in the United Opposition list. Three of these were later appointed assistant mayors. Between 1982 and 1986 the numbers of National Front cantonal candidates rose from 65 to 2000. In 1984 the party achieved 10 per cent of the vote in elections to the European Parliament, and ten of its candidates were returned. In the 1986 General Election to the National Assembly thirty-four National Front deputies were elected. The National Front continued its dramatic impact on French politics in the presidential elections of 1988 when its candidate, Jean-Marie Le Pen, achieved 14.4 per cent of the popular vote.

The 1980s have also witnessed the emergence of racial politics on the left in France. Since the late 1960s Socialist and Communist mayors had protested against the number of immigrants moving into public housing in their areas. However, it was not until 1980 that a major party in France attempted to exploit racial prejudice for electoral gain. Georges Marchais, the Communist presidential candidate, supported Communist Party attacks on North African and black

African immigrants as the cause of social and economic problems. The Communist Party was losing electoral ground and was desperately attempting to mobilise its working-class supporters. The defeat of the Communists, criticism from its trade union allies in the CGT, and the rise of National Front, have caused the Communist Party to reduce its exploitation of anti-immigrant feeling (Schain 1988).

In the 1970s and 1980s the growth of unemployment and the immigration of wives and children has also led to a resurgence of hostility to foreigners, especially Turks, in West Germany. In 1982 opinion polls were reporting that 82 per cent of West Germans thought that there were too many foreigners in the country (Time, 30 August 1982). In the 1980s too, there has been a sharp rise in violence and terrorism against migrants, particularly against Turks (Runnymede Trust 1987). There has also been a sharp rise in asylum applications to West Germany, particularly from Turkey and other Third World countries. Most West Germans feel that these are really economic migrants trying to circumvent immigration controls.

The Conservative-Liberal coalition government, which came to power in 1982 under Chancellor Helmut Kohl, has committed itself to reducing substantially the foreign population of West Germany by maintaining strict immigration controls, encouraging voluntary repatriation and stimulating the naturalisation of foreigners who have worked in the Federal Republic for over ten years. However, the refusal of many West German politicians, including Chancellor Kohl, to accept that West Germany is an immigration country, and the decision not to liberalise the naturalisation laws, suggests that the emphasis will be on encouraging repatriation rather than integration.

Switzerland has been more dependent on foreign labour in the post-war period than any other European country, although the Swiss did not recruit non-Europeans. The Labour Treaty signed with Italy in 1948 began a period of massive labour recruitment so that by 1960 there were 585,000 resident foreigners, representing 16.8 per cent of the workforce and 10.8 per cent of the total population. Family settlement was allowed in the 1960s and the foreign population continued to rise. Concern and opposition to foreign labour recruitment grew in the 1960s and in May 1969 the National Action Against the Over-foreignisation of People and Homeland, led by James Schwarzenbach, submitted an initiative demanding that the percentage of foreigners be reduced to 10 per cent in four years. Despite the opposition of the political parties, employers' organisations, trade unions, and the churches, this initiative was only narrowly defeated

(Heisler 1988). The government responded by introducing stricter controls, which alleviated concern, and five further initiatives to reduce 'over-foreignisation' were defeated. Swiss government policy has been to create two categories of foreign worker – permanent residents who have a secure and privileged position, and seasonal or temporary workers who are subject to strict controls. Two initiatives in the early 1980s to improve the position of foreigners in Switzerland were also defeated. Recently, the rise in applications for political asylum has led to popular approval for tough restrictions on asylum seekers.

RACIAL DISCRIMINATION

Most European countries discriminate in favour of their own nationals and against non-citizens, especially in their labour markets. Foreign nationals are often excluded from public sector employment and nationals are generally given priority in the labour market as a whole. Post-war migration has thus created a substantial class of people confined to the lowest section of the labour market (Castells 1975). However, immigrants may not only be discriminated against because of their foreign nationality but also because of their colour and ethnic origins. In Britain, for example, although colonial and Commonwealth citizens were legally British subjects and were entitled to vote, stand for Parliament and serve in the armed forces, they faced considerable discrimination in the labour and housing markets. This discrimination has been documented in a large number of studies (Daniel 1968; Smith 1977; Brown 1984).

British governments have passed a number of Race Relations Acts in 1965, 1968 and 1976 which outlaw racial discrimination in public places, advertising, housing and employment. However, although the Commission for Racial Equality has had some success in enforcing the law, overall levels of discrimination do not appear to have fallen. Black people are largely confined to manual occupations and to unskilled jobs in particular. In 1982, while the unemployment rate for white men was 13 per cent, for West Indians it was 25 per cent and for Asian men it was 20 per cent. These differences are only partly explained by differences in qualification, work experience and fluency in English. Unemployment rates were particularly high in 1982 for young West Indian men. Those aged 16–19 had unemployment rates of 46 per cent, those aged 20–24 had rates of 42 per cent

173

and then the figure declined sharply to 17 per cent for those aged 25–34 (Brown 1984).

A massive 77 per cent of West Indian men and women say that there are employers who discriminate, compared with 48 per cent of Asian men and 29 per cent of Asian women. The proportions of white men and women agreeing that employers discriminate against non-whites, at 73 and 69 per cent, are similar to the responses of West Indians (Brown 1984).

Research carried out by making test applications for advertised jobs shows that these beliefs in racial discrimination were well founded. In 1973 and 1974 when Political and Economic Planning carried out a study in six different towns, it was found that black applicants were discriminated against in 30 per cent of cases involving non-manual jobs, 20 per cent of cases involving skilled manual jobs and 37 per cent of cases including unskilled and semi-skilled jobs (Smith 1979).

The riots in British inner cities in 1980, 1981 and 1985 occurred within this context of high unemployment and lack of educational attainment by young blacks and the stereotyping of black youth as criminal and anti-authority. The riots reinforced the bad relations between young blacks and the police. The vicious circle in which black youth are seen as suffering from environmental and personal disadvantages which lead to criminality and alienation from the values of society has been reinforced by the failure of the government to devote adequate resources to arresting inner-city decline, combating racial discrimination and promoting equality of opportunity. In the wake of the major recession which began in the early 1970s, governments everywhere in the Western world have sought to cut public expenditure and welfare benefits and reduce personal taxation. It has not therefore been a good period for unpopular, albeit disadvantaged, minorities to lobby for additional resources to remedy bad housing, neglected inner-city environments, and racial discrimination.

THE FUTURE OF THE SECOND GENERATION: CITIZENS OR EXILES?

The attention of policy-makers in West European countries has focused increasingly on the children of post-war immigrants. This is partly because politicians are slowly realising that settlement has taken place, but also because the ending of labour recruitment in 1973 has been followed by a sharp increase in family reunions. In West Germany, for example, in 1973 there were 640,000 foreign children under 16 years. By 1983 this had risen to over 1.1 million (Wilpert 1982). In France it is estimated that between 1946 and 1982 there were 1.4 million children born to parents both of whom were of foreign nationality, and a further 700,000 children who had one foreign parent. In Britain, by 1985 over 1 million children had been born to ethnic minority immigrant parents.

The education of immigrant-descended children raises a number of acute policy dilemmas for decision-makers in the West European receiving countries. Should these children be educated on the assumption that they will remain in the receiving country or on the assumption that they will return to their parents' country? Should their parents be allowed to request that their children are educated in their mother tongue, as is the case in Sweden and France, or should they be forced to receive the normal education provided for all native children? How far can minority cultures, languages, and values be recognised, respected and incorporated into national educational systems which place a high priority on transmitting a common core of beliefs and values such as patriotism and religion? Will national cohesion be undermined if monocultural education gives way to multicultural education?

These dilemmas have been particularly acute in West Germany where the regional Länder governments (which are responsible for education) have adopted three different strategies for teaching foreign children:-

1. The integration of foreign children into the West German educational system which means putting them in normal German classes (Berlin).
2. The establishment of classes or schools based on nationality with the aim of preparing the foreign children for return to their parents' country (Baden-Württemberg).
3. Preparing the children simultaneously for integration into German society or return to their parents' country with the aim of giving them a real choice. This strategy leads to the establishment of long-term preparatory classes (North Rhine-Westphalia).

Whichever strategy is adopted, there is a danger that the children are not adequately prepared for either their country of residence or their parents' country. Moreover, many of these children will have a crisis of identity, not knowing whether to accept their parents' values and national identity or those of the society in which they live (Wilpert 1982). Interestingly, Swiss and West German studies show that foreign parents have high educational and occupational aspirations for their children which the latter accept. A study in West Germany found that 45 per cent of Turkish and 17 per cent of Yugoslav children wanted to become a doctor, teacher or engineer. These aspirations are unrealistic as only a small percentage of working-class children achieve significant upward social mobility. Only 46 per cent of foreign young men between 15 and 24 who had received their education in West Germany left with any kind of graduation certificate. Young male foreigners were concentrated in a few sectors of the labour market such as sanitation and personal services, vehicle manufacture, and construction. Wilpert (1982) found that most young Turks and Yugoslavs wished to return and work in their parents' country. They felt discriminated against in West Germany and felt they would be better off in Turkey or Yugoslavia.

Similar problems exist for young foreigners in France. They are trapped in unskilled and semi-skilled jobs because of poor educational qualifications, poor knowledge of the French language, lack of vocational training and discrimination, and racism, especially in the labour market. French studies suggest that 60 per cent of foreign children enter the same occupation as their parents and 68 per cent claim to have experienced racism (Malewska-Peyre 1982). Among young Algerians 75 per cent claim to have experienced racism. The children of foreign parents in France are members of French society and most (60 per cent) wished to remain in France, but they feel rejected by French society. Only 20 per cent had decided to opt for French nationality. These problems of identity, it is argued, often lead to failure at school, depression, and behavioural problems which result in crime and difficulties with the police and the courts.

Swedish experience suggests that there is strong support among foreign parents for mother-tongue education (Hammar 1985a) but special circumstances may encourage this such as the close proximity of Finland, the major sending country, to Sweden and the absence of travel restrictions between these members of the Nordic Union.

In Britain there is growing concern over the lack of educational attainment of ethnic minority children in British schools and strong pressure among educationalists for the introduction of multicultural curricula and experiments in mother-tongue education. There is also strong pressure from Muslim groups for the introduction of Muslim schools within the national educational systems (Tomlinson 1986).

INTERSTATE RELATIONS

The settlement of large numbers of immigrants in West European states has added a new dimension to relations between the sending and receiving countries. Many European states, notably France and West Germany, signed formal treaties with the labour-exporting countries which laid down conditions for the recruitment and treatment of migrant workers. The government of Yugoslavia, as has already been mentioned, has been particularly concerned to protect the interests of its nationals temporarily abroad, and to maintain contact with them through subsidising Yugoslav immigrant associations and providing teachers for the education of their children.

The large Turkish community in West Germany increases and complicates the relations between these NATO allies. There are strong pressures within Turkey for continued emigration and powerful financial pressures to maintain and encourage the flow of remittances from migrant workers in West Germany to Turkey. The large number of Turkish migrant workers in Western Europe is also a major factor encouraging the Turkish application for membership of the European Community (EC). There are contradictory pressures within West Germany to restrict further immigration from Turkey and to control the increasing number of applications for political asylum from Turks. West Germany and other West European countries are hesitant about Turkey's application to join the EC as this would lead to a massive increase in Turkish emigration to the rest of the Community. On the other hand, West European states are reluctant to antagonise such a strategically important military ally.

A common concern in Europe has been that immigrants will introduce the politics of their homeland into their new countries. Most European countries insist that foreigners should remain politically neutral, but sometimes incidents of violence and terrorism occur. The large Indian community settled in Britain has become a major source of funds for Indian political groups such as the Congress Party, the Communist Party of India, and the Sikh Akali Dal. The Indian government has protested to the British government on a number of occasions that Sikh supporters of an independent Sikh state of Khalistan have been allowed to organise in Britain. The Indian government has also lobbied the British government over the British Nationality Act (1981) and protested about incidents of racial attacks on Asian settlers in Britain. In February 1984 an Indian diplomat was kidnapped and murdered by a group calling itself the Kashmir Liberation Army.

Other European governments have had similar experiences with the governments of the sending countries. In 1973 the Algerian government stopped emigration to France after the murders of several Algerians. The Turkish government in 1985 successfully lobbied West Germany to prevent changes in the latter's nationality laws, and in 1986 Dutch citizens were shocked when the King of Morocco intervened to advise Moroccans not to vote in the Dutch local elections.

CONCLUSION: THE POLITICAL CHALLENGE

Post-war immigration poses a series of major challenges to the political élites of West European states. In every country there are large numbers of immigrants and their descendants from a wide variety of backgrounds who have transformed these countries into multicultural societies. These immigrants are not fully accepted either because they are foreign citizens and are therefore excluded from political participation, or because, although they have citizenship, they are not considered members of the national community and are discriminated against because of their racial or national origins. In Britain Enoch Powell expressed this view when he said: 'The West Indian or Indian does not, by being born in England, become an Englishman. In law he becomes a United Kingdom citizen by birth; in fact he is a West Indian or Asian still' (Powell 1969).

The political élites of the receiving countries are aware that settlement has taken place and that voluntary return or repatriation are unlikely, and impossible on any scale. Some states have taken positive measures to encourage integration such as Sweden which has largely ended discrimination against foreign nationals, eased naturalisation, and extended voting rights at the local and regional level to foreign immigrants who have been resident for three years or more. The British government has passed race relations legislation to outlaw direct and indirect racial discrimination which is enforced by a government-funded body, the Commission for Racial Equality. The French government has liberalised legislation controlling foreign associations and excluding foreign nationals from public sector employment. The Dutch government has adopted a positive 'ethnic minorities' policy and granted local voting rights to foreign nationals.

The extension of social, civic, and political rights, particularly to foreign immigrants, seems, however, to have definite limits. There was considerable resistance in Sweden to allowing foreign nationals to vote in elections for the Swedish Parliament (Hammar 1985b). There is popular opposition in Britain to policies that seem to advocate positive discrimination in favour of non-white citizens. The high levels of unemployment in Europe since 1973 have fostered popular resistance to immigration and encouraged support for tough immigration controls. The relative success of Le Pen in the French presidential elections in April 1988 and the surprising success of the Populist Progress Party in the Danish elections of May 1988 support this view. The Danish Progress Party increased its vote by 50 per cent and its seats from nine to sixteen in the Danish Parliament on a platform that emphasised tighter immigration controls.

Continuing immigration and extension of the rights enjoyed by citizens to foreign immigrants are highly controversial issues in Western European countries. The exclusion of foreign immigrants and their adult children from the political process is justified on the grounds that they are not citizens and can, if they wish, become citizens through the process of naturalisation. On the other hand, naturalisation in some European countries, like Switzerland and West Germany, is both difficult and expensive.

The extension of social and civic rights to foreigners, and particularly voting rights, is seen by many native Europeans as a threat to deeply held preconceptions about membership of a state. The benefits of citizenship—that is, full legal membership of a state, including welfare and political rights—seem to be reserved only for those whose commitment to the state is secure by virtue of community membership by birth or descent, or for those prepared to make a public commitment through the process of naturalisation. Discrimination against foreign nationals is considered justified both by citizens of European states and international conventions on human rights.

European states, however, are faced with a dilemma. There are large numbers of residents in their countries who are taxpayers and members of their democratic societies but who are excluded from decision-making. It offends against the principles of democracy that members of a community are excluded from participating in decisions that affect them and for which they pay. The situation is reminiscent of the slogan in the American War of Independence: 'No taxation without representation'.

However, while the extension of voting rights to foreigners is

179

clearly seen by many Europeans as a threat to their preconceptions about membership of a state, European states must ensure that their new residents are accepted as full and equal members of their new multiracial societies, otherwise the danger exists that the riots which occurred in Britain in 1981 and 1985 will be repeated on a larger scale. Discrimination and racism may create large alienated minorities in many European cities. The slogan 'No representation without naturalisation' should not be allowed to override the more traditional and democratic view of 'No taxation without representation'.

It is urgent that West European countries, and particularly members of the EC, co-operate to adopt common policies on immigration controls, political refugees, and the rights of foreign citizens and ethnic minorities. The implementation of the common European market in 1992 means that there will be much freer movement of nationals and immigrants within the European Community. This could provide an opportunity for guaranteeing and extending the rights of citizens and foreign residents through adopting more liberal policies towards dual nationality and naturalisation. Certainly it can be argued that legal birth within a state should confer an automatic entitlement to citizenship if this is requested. Whether European states will act to combat the reluctance of their citizens to accept immigrants and their descendants, and suppress chauvinistic and racist tendencies, is still an open question, but it is one that needs to be confronted urgently.

ACKNOWLEDGEMENTS

I am grateful to the Economic and Social Research Council for a personal research grant which assisted the research for this chapter.

REFERENCES

Bauboeck, R. and Wimmer, H. (1988) 'Social partnership and "foreigners" policy—on special features of Austria's guest-worker system', *European Journal of Political Research*, 16 (6). pp 659–681.

Brown, C. (1984) *Black and White Britain: The Third PSI Survey* (London: Heinemann).

Castells, M. (1975) 'Immigrant workers and class struggles in advanced capitalism: the Western European experience', *Politics and Society*, 5 (1). pp 33–64.

Daniel, W. W. (1968) *Racial discrimination in England* (Harmondsworth: Penguin Books).

Freeman, G. (1979) *Immigrant Labor and Racial Conflict in Industrial Societies: The French and British Experience, 1945–1975* (Princeton: Princeton University Press).

Frey, M. and Lubinski, V. (1987) *Problem infolge hoher Ausländerkonzentration in ausgewahlken europäischen Staaten* (Wiesbaden: Federal Institute for Population Research).

Hammar, T. (1985a) *European Immigration Policy* (Cambridge: Cambridge University Press).

Hammar, T. (1985b) 'Citizenship, aliens' political rights and politicians' concern for migrants: The case of Sweden', in R. Rogers (ed.), *Guests Come to Stay* (Boulder, Colorado: Westview Press) pp 85–109.

Heisler, B. S. (1988) 'From conflict to accommodation: the "foreigners question" in Switzerland', *European Journal of Political Research*, 16 (6) pp 683–700.

Layton-Henry, Z. (1984) *The Politics of Race in Britain* (London: Allen and Unwin).

Malewska-Peyre, H. (1982) 'Conflictual cultural identity of second generation immigrants', in H. Korte,(ed.), *Culture Identity and Structural Marginalisation of Migrant Workers* (Strasbourg: European Science Foundation) pp 97–108.

Miller, M. J. (1986)'Policy ad-hocracy: the paucity of coordinated perspectives and policies', *Annals of the American Academy of Social Sciences*, 485, May, 64–75.

NCCL (1980) *Southall 23rd April 1979* (London: National Council for Civil Liberties).

Powell, E. (1969) Text of a speech delivered to the annual conference of the Rotary Club of London, Eastbourne 16 Nov. 1968, in B. Smithies and P. Fiddick (eds), *Enoch Powell on Immigration* London. (Sphere Books), pp 63–77.

Runnymede Trust (1987) *Combating Racism in Europe: A report to the European Communities* (London: Runnymede Trust).

Schain, M. A. (1988) 'Immigration and changes in the French party system', *European Journal of Political Research*, 16 (6) pp 597–621.

Smith, D. J. (1977) *Racial Disadvantage in Britain* (Harmondsworth: Peguin Books).

Taylor, S. (1982) *The National Front in English Politics* (London: Macmillan).

Tomlinson, S. (1986) 'Political dilemmas in multi-racial education', in Z. Layton-Henry and P. Rich, (ed.), *Race, Government and Politics in Britain* (London: Macmillan).

Wilpert, C. (1982) 'Structural marginality and the role of cultural identity for migrant youth', in H. Korte (ed.), *Cultural Identity and Structural Marginalisation of Migrant Workers* (Strasbourg: European Science Foundation) pp 117–129.

CHANGING STRUCTURES

CHAPTER NINE

Britain, France, West Germany and the Development of the European community

William E. Paterson

Much of the early writing on the European Community (EC) was preoccupied with the concept of supranationalism. This envisaged the development of central institutions which would be able to overrule states in certain defined circumstances and which would act directly on enterprises and citizens of the member states. This interest in the supranational principle was kindled by the example of the European Coal and Steel Community (ECSC) of 1950 where the High Authority was given very considerable powers of regulation and direction within the coal and steel sectors.

The attempt to extend this principle to the defence field proved to be too ambitious and the proposal for a European Defence Community was rejected by the French National Assembly in 1954. The European Economic Community (EEC) and Euratom, created in 1957, were much less explicitly supranational than the High Authority of the ECSC. There was a much less pronounced stress on the independence of the Commission than had been the case with the High Authority of the ECSC, where the treaty had given the members of the High Authority considerable powers in strictly defined circumstances within the coal and steel sectors.

The Treaty of Rome, setting up the EEC, is of a different character. It is a framework treaty where rather weaker powers are granted over a much wider area. The Council of Ministers was also given a stronger legal role than in the ECSC. It was broadly awarded the right of the decision on most issues while the Commission was given a monopoly on the right of initiative. The idea of supranationality had not, however, been abandoned: it was merely to be achieved by different means. Instead of a grant of power of a once-and-for-all character, the process was to be dynamic. The con-

184

ception involved a parallelism of policy achievement and institutional change. What was envisaged was that, as the EEC achieved negative integration, i.e. the elimination of tariffs between members, and the creation of a common external tariff, the institutional balance would change in the direction of a much more pronounced supranational role for the Commission. The Commission's monopoly of initiative was to be made a much more potent political resource by the intro-duction of majority voting in the Council of Ministers which would mean that the Commission only had to win a qualified majority vote for a proposal.

This transition did not, in fact, take place. Negative integration, or the removal of tariff barriers between member states, was achieved with much less difficulty than some of the Commission's supporters had feared. But the French President, de Gaulle, was implacably op-posed to the introduction of majority voting and withdrew from participation in EC institutions in 1965 in order to persuade the Commission and other member states not to press ahead. The crisis was resolved by the so-called Luxemburg Compromise of 1966 which gave France and, by implication, other members the right to invoke a veto on issues and proposals which it considered affected vital national interests.

The aspirations of the Commission were further constrained by two other developments. The Commission's right of initiative was severely weakened by the interposition between it and the Council of Ministers of the Committee of Permanent Representatives (COREPER). Initially, the Commission had been able to make significant progress towards further integration by presenting the Council of Ministers with package deals which the council then had to accept or reject *en bloc*. The establishment and development of Permanent Representations and COREPER meant that the Council of Ministers no longer considered proposals cold but only after they had been dissected and filtered through the Committee of Permanent Representatives. The Permanent Representations established by each state were microcosms of their own domestic bureaucracies in con-stant contact with their own home ministries. This development practically excluded grand package deals in the manner of the early years and severely compromised the Commission's capacity for initiation.

The second development in the 1970s was the institutionalisation of the summit meetings of heads of government in the form of the European Council. The decision to institutionalise the European Council reflected a perception on the part of member governments that the Community lacked the capacity either to pursue co-ordinated initiatives or to resolve disputes between member states on the question of their financial contributions to the Community. After 1966 the Commission lacked the legitimacy to undertake these tasks. Thereafter, attempts were made to use the presidency of the Council, which is held by each member state in turn, to provide coherence and to resolve disputes. These attempts were bound to fail. The six-monthly period of the presidency is simply too short for one individual government to establish and see through a coherent agenda.

Moreover, the members of the Council of Ministers who were not heads of state or governmental heads were not in a position to commit their governments in the resolution of the strongly zero sum disputes over financial contributions. The solution of involving heads of government , or, in the case of France, the heads of state, in the European Council was calculated to restore some capacity for initiative to the Community and to facilitate the resolution of budgetary disputes. The establishment of the European Council represented a strong trend to intergovernmentalism, i.e. to making the Community a forum for interstate bargaining rather than the supranational model which had dominated the Community's early years.

THE DEVELOPMENT OF THE COMMUNITY: THE ROLE OF THE STATES

France has been far more influential in the institutional development of West European integration than either Britain or the Federal Republic of Germany. It was Jean Monnet who developed the idea of supranationalism and supranational institutions, de Gaulle and succeeding French presidents who have sought to undermine this and to stress intergovernmentalism, and Jacques Delors, a former French Finance Minister, who has presided over a Commission renaissance in the 1980s. The reasons for this pre-eminence in the first decades after the war are reasonably clear-cut. Britain remained aloof from the initial attempts and only attempted to participate in 1962 with its first application to join. By that time the three founding communities, the ECSC, EEC and Euratom, had been established and the main lines of their development had been agreed on – an *acquis communautaire* had been formed, in whose making the British government had played no part.

After a decade of trying, Britain finally became a member in 1972. Its influence on developments did not correspond to its relative size and importance, for a number of reasons. Firstly, the main lines of development had been laid down and the crucial question was that of accommodation between Britain and the EC. After a short transition period the crucial issue for British governments was the question of Britain's budgetary contributions. Most Community spending was on agriculture, and Britain , with its small, relatively efficient agricultural sector oriented towards the domestic market, felt disadvantaged by a system which paid out very large sums of money to encourage efficiency and promote agricultural exports. British hopes that this would be compensated by a massive Regional Fund, from which Britain's decaying industrial regions would benefit disproportionately, were dashed shortly after entry in 1974 because of world economic recession.

A second major constraint on British influence has been the lack of enthusiasm at the level of both government and mass opinion which placed a question mark in the minds of other member states against Britain's commitment. A final difficulty for Britain was the close pattern of co-operation that had been established between France and West Germany in the EC: if these two were able to agree, no matter how difficult the issue, the other member states could usually be persuaded to fall into line. This Franco-German axis was most influential between 1974 and 1981 when Helmut Schmidt was Chancellor of the Federal Republic and Giscard d'Estaing President of France.

The Federal Republic has been more committed to, and arguably centrally concerned with, European integration than the other major European states. This interest is, however, only very imperfectly related to influence on the development of the Community. In the 1950s the Federal Republic was essentially a supplicant. European integration offered it the possibility of access to key markets for its export-oriented economy and a degree of moral respectability after the traumas of the Third Reich. Paradoxically, it also, and perhaps most importantly, offered the Federal Republic a route to the reattainment of sovereignty. For other states integration was at least a potential constraint on sovereignty, but for the infant Federal Republic, still for some purposes an occupied territory, the acceptance of integration represented the only way to escape from the restrictions of occupation, for only then would its neighbours feel safe enough to lift the discriminatory provisions which restricted important areas of German life. A very clear example of this linkage is the establishment of the ECSC in which the Federal Republic was a full member: the ECSC replaced the International Ruhr Authority which had been set up in 1948 to control the production and sales of Germany's coal, coke and steel and in which the Federal Republic had only a minority representation.

The benefits to the Federal Republic of participation in European integration were a central element in the policy programme of the first Chancellor, Konrad Adenauer, who made commitment to European integration a central element in his government's policy. His concept of European integration rested squarely on a Franco-German *entente*. In this entente the Federal Republic was perforce the junior partner: post-war realities and the supplicant position of the Federal Republic excluded West German leadership. Moreover, the much stronger commitment of the Federal government to European integration meant that it was normally in the position of endeavoring to coax a more reluctant France along. This factor gained in importance in the early 1950s as the pro-European forces in France, particularly the Christian Democrats, lost ground electorally. The need to make concessions to win French support became an even higher priority after the failure of the European Defence Community in 1954, after which the French government was able to exploit its weakness to gain a number of concessions for France in the EEC negotiations.

In the early years of the EC, German influence in the development of the EC increased. Adenauer's closest foreign policy confidant, Walter Hallstein, became the first President of the Commission and co-ordination between Brussels and Bonn was extremely close. This influence was generally used in the direction of increasing the powers of the Commission, and the period between 1958 and 1963 can be viewed in some sense as the golden age of the Commission when it was able, with the support of a major member state, significantly to expand its powers.

Adenauer's retirement as Chancellor in 1963 and his replacement by a Chancellor, Ludwig Erhard, who was much less committed to a Franco-German *entente*, did not lead to any perceptible increase in West German influence. Under Adenauer the Federal Republic had developed a notably loose set of arrangements to co-ordinate European policy where responsibility was divided between the Economics and Foreign Ministries. The looseness of these arrangements mattered less under Adenauer since he so clearly dominated in issues in which he was interested. Succeeding Chancellors were both less dominant within their governments and less interested in

European integration. The result was a marked increased in sectorisation in which it was quite difficult to perceive a coherent West German European policy, and West German influence correspondingly waned. The sectorisation/fragmentation of West German policy-making was in strong contrast to the highly centralised European policy-making machinery in France.

THE LARGE STATES AND EUROPEAN POLICY

The best way of examining in some detail the influence of a state on European developments is the role it has played in the policy initiatives which the EC has undertaken since its inception. This section will, however, look at the impact of the major states in only a limited number of key policy areas in the 1980s.

The reform of the Common Agricultural Policy

The EEC was often portrayed as an agreement between West German industry and French agriculture. Such a description highlights the high proportion of the French labour force employed in agriculture in the 1950s and the export-oriented character of the West German industrial economy. It is, however, misleading in an important sense since it suggests that the Federal government was prepared to make concessions on agriculture in order to accommodate French agricultural interests. This was not the central motive. Successive West German governments have been very responsive to their own domestic agricultural sector. The Federal Republic was separated from the traditional agricultural heartlands in the east, a situation which produced extreme hunger in the years after the war, and subsidisation of the farming interest was part of the founding compact of the Federal Republic.

Subsequently, the German Farmers Union, an amazingly cohesive organisation which represents over 90 per cent of those engaged in agriculture, was able to exercise an effective veto on any attempts to reduce the high levels of support for agriculture. Both French and West German governments thus had an interest in maintaining high levels of support for agriculture, with the relatively greater inefficiency of the West German farmers usually influencing the West German government to press for higher levels of support than the French.

The agricultural interest has both been smaller and much less influential in Britain, which had relied until entry on purchasing about half its foodstuffs on world markets, with a bias towards a number of traditional low-cost and efficient producers like Australia and New Zealand. Britain adjusted to the Common Agricultural Policy (CAP) with some difficulty and the arrangements with New Zealand proved to be a particular bone of contention.

By the late 1970s, the CAP absorbed something over two-thirds of the Community budget, and large surpluses appeared in a number of central products like milk, as producers were encouraged to increase their production by relatively high guaranteed prices at the same time as many in industrial societies actually started to cut down on their food intake. Reform was very difficult, however, and an attempt by the Commission to do so in 1975 was a failure. The system of decisions by separate Councils of Ministers meant that the spenders (agriculture ministers) rarely had to confront the revenue raisers (finance ministers). The governments of France and the Federal Republic were not unhappy with the status quo and there was little pressure from their public opinion.

On this issue the French and West German governments were supported by all the other member states with the exception of Britain. British governments were unhappy about almost all aspects of the CAP. They were very unhappy with the budgetary implications, and the problem of agricultural surpluses was one about which there was a great deal of public discontent in Britain. It was very difficult for Britain to get reform of the CAP on to the agenda, however, given the hostility of other member states and the primacy for Britain of the linked budgetary question. The difficulties were dramatically visible when a British veto on higher agricultural prices in May 1982 was overruled by the other members.

The budgetary pressures created by the upward spiralling of the agriculture budget finally put reform of the CAP on the Community agenda in 1984. The greatest surpluses had been in milk production, and at the Council of Ministers in March 1984 it was agreed to introduce quotas on milk production of something under 10 per cent. At the same meeting it was agreed to phase out monetary compensation amounts (MCAs) by which farmers had been cushioned against changes in currency rates. In the West German case the MCA system meant that agricultural prices were not revalued when the Deutschmark gained in value. The effect of this was to keep farm incomes in the Federal Republic higher than would otherwise have been the case. It also meant that West German farmers received a subsidy when they exported produce elsewhere within the EC. This led to a major expansion in West German agriculture and was a major source of annoyance to France which supported Commission moves to reduce MCAs.

During the presidency of the European Council in the second half of 1986 the British government kept pushing reform of the CAP, and in December agreement was reached on reduction of milk production quotas by 9.5 per cent between 1987 and 1989, an average cut in beef prices of 13 per cent and a commitment to a package of structural measures to offer financial support for less intensive farming. Somewhat surprisingly, major reforms of the CAP were made during the West German presidency of the first half of 1988. The Federal government had come under heavy political pressure from its farming union to resist reform of the CAP after 1984, and the Christian Democratic Union/Christian Social Union (CDU/CSU), the main government parties, had suffered electorally as a result of abstention by farmers; moreover, there were two state elections in areas with a large agricultural sector during the German presidency of 1988.

The Minister of Agriculture was a member of the CSU, a party which operates only in Bavaria and which historically has been very sensitive to the agriculture interest. Despite these background conditions, the Federal government presided over an agreement on reform of the CAP at a European Council meeting in Brussels in February 1988. The most important elements of this agreement were a commitment that the annual expenditure on agricultural price support should not increase by more than 74 per cent of Community average GNP growth. This compares with a historical growth of 150 per cent. Production ceilings were to be established (already in force for cereals) and, if production exceeds this ceiling, guaranteed prices will be cut by 3 per cent per annum.

There are several reasons why the French and West German governments accepted some CAP reform after years of successful resistance. The first is budgetary. This applies with special force to West Germany. As the largest net contributor to the Community budget, it has a very strong interest in inhibiting an uncontrolled rise in the EC budget. Although France is a lesser contributor than Britain or West Germany, it was prepared to make concessions on this issue in order to cement an alliance with Britain aimed at restricting the growth in the structural fund which was to help the economically weaker areas of the Community. The reform also contained a major sweetener for the agricultural interest, the so-called 'set aside' policy by which farmers will be paid for taking land out of production. This was expected to make easier the task of the French and West German governments in selling the reform to their own farming constituents. Agreement was also helped by the partial renationalisation of agricultural policy. The Federal government in particular has introduced an ambitious programme of national subsidies, paralleling the reforms, to try to placate their agricultural sector. This has the advantage from the point of view of the Federal government that it will reap the political benefits of these measures, and the new policy of ceilings and stabilisers is calculated to ensure that German contributions do not disappear into the financial black hole of an expanding agricultural sector in southern Europe. The final factor was the continued determination of the British Prime Minister, Margaret Thatcher, who made agreement to a higher rate of contribution dependent on some measure of reform and who, on this occasion, was able to secure the support of the Netherlands.

The budgetary issue

The question of the Community budget has been synonymous since British entry in 1973 with the problem of the British contribution. In 1970 the original six members had replaced a system based on annually negotiated national contributions with one of so-called 'own resources'. These resources were made up of revenues from tariffs on industrial goods entering the EC, levies on imported agricultural products, and 1 per cent of national VAT revenue.

These arrangements imposed a triple burden on Britain. As a major importer of agricultural products from outside the Community, Britain had to pay CAP levies which then had to be surrendered to the Community. There were also problems with VAT. This system was meant to result in a rough parity between a country's wealth and its EC contribution. The problem in the British case was one of a weak economy where the level of consumer spending was out of proportion to the strength of the economy. This effect was increased after 1979 when tax revenues from North Sea oil allowed the British government to keep levels of personal taxation relatively low. The oil effect also buoyed up sterling and rendered imports cheaper.

Not only were British contributions higher because of these factors, but Britain did very badly in terms of receipts from the Community budget. British hopes had been pinned on a very large Regional Fund, but the West German government refused to underwrite this in 1974 when the time came to set up the Regional Fund.

Over two-thirds of the Community's budget was spent on the CAP, but Britain had a very low proportion of farmers. Britain was also not an agricultural exporting country so it failed to benefit from the export subsidies.

The problem had not risen immediately after entry because of transition arrangements. It was seen as a major problem by the Wilson and Callaghan governments and has been the overriding element in British European policy since the advent of the Thatcher government in 1979. Resistance to the British demand for a reduction in its contribution ('I want my money back', Mrs Thatcher said in Dublin in 1979) was very intense. The budget issue was strongly zero sum and, if Britain paid less, others would pay more. The French government was very unsympathetic to any notion of CAP reform and argued that much of the problem would disappear if Britain ceased importing foodstuffs from outside the Community. The West German government was especially unsympathetic to British complaints about VAT payments which were seen to result from a lack of self-control and the absence of the saving propensity so marked in the Federal Republic.

Mrs Thatcher pursued a very aggressive policy on the issue of the budget rebate. It became a standard item in a whole series of very acrimonious European Councils. Tariffs and agricultural import levies proved to be a major sticking-point. They were included by Britain in calculations of the total British contribution. The Commission and other member states insisted that they were instruments of Community rather than national policy and could not therefore be regarded as belonging to any one member.

By 1984 Mrs Thatcher's campaign began to show results. The French government produced a formula based on VAT rather than the contentious agricultural import levies and tariffs. The formula essentially compensated states whose VAT payments in the previous year had been higher than its budget receipts by an initially unspecified amount. This was acceptable to Britain as a starting-point for negotiation, though Britain wanted to have an automatic trigger built into the rebate.

In the final agreement at Fontainebleau in 1984 Mrs Thatcher accepted a rebate of 1 bn. ECUs (the original British demand had been for 1.5bn ECUs) for the current year with future rebates to be calculated on the basis of 66 per cent of the difference between Britain's VAT contributions to the budget and its receipts, with a proviso that they would be looked at again if the VAT rate were raised from 1.4 to 1.6 per cent.

By 1987 the Fontainebleau Agreement was showing signs of strain as the cost of the CAP climbed inexorably upwards and the long prophesied bankruptcy of the EC seemed much nearer. The Commission President, Jacques Delors, suggested that GNP rather than VAT be the basis of natural contribution to the financing of the Community and that expenditure on the CAP be capped. The Delors initiative was shaped by the continued British insistence that agreement to an expanded Community budget had to be linked to enforceable controls on farm spending. The shift from VAT to GNP was also designed to placate Britain and to tilt the burden of financing the EC towards Italy and 'the *petits riches*' of Denmark and the Benelux countries who profited from the existing arrangements (see Table 11).

Table 11 EC budget winners and losers 1987

	Net profit or loss from EC budget (£ m.)	Per capita GDP 1985 figures EC average = 100
Greece	+1100	55.0
Ireland	+ 700	67.6
Italy	+ 490	93.7
Netherlands	+ 490	108.7
Denmark	+ 280	118.6
Spain	+ 280	74.5
Belgium	+ 210	103.9
Luxemburg	+ 210	140.6
Portugal	+ 210	52.5
France	− 280	109.8
Britain	− 770	107.5
(Britain without rebate	−2380)	
W. Germany	−2900	119.3

Source: Based on British government estimates.

There was a great deal of opposition to the Delors proposals by those who rejected the GDP formula and those, like France, who were very unwilling to see restrictions placed on spending on the CAP. However, a compromise was finally worked out at the European Council in Brussels in February 1988. Future spending on the CAP was cut and it was agreed that the annual expenditure on farm price guarantees should not grow by more than 74 per cent of average GDP growth. National contributions were now to be made on the basis of 1.4 per cent of VAT and a proportion of GDP. While spending on the CAP is to grow more slowly than GDP, the resources of the structural fund to aid development in southern Europe are to be doubled by 1993 (an extra 1.3bn ECUs per year). France allied with Britain on this issue to restrict an even larger growth in the structural fund. The British rebate was preserved and the addition of the GDP dimension will increase the British rebate.

The internal market

The abolition of tariff barriers between the member states proved to be much less difficult than many feared and had effectively been completed by 1968. Significant barriers to trade remained, however, in the form of non-tariff barriers, a term which encompasses a whole range of regulations and practices which have the effect of inhibiting trade and protecting national markets. The prospects for their removal appeared slight given the desire of states to protect particular sectors. The Commission attempted to tackle the problem by harmonisation and by introducing 'Euronorms' across a very wide range of products, including a notorious struggle to harmonise the acceptable level of lawnmower noise. Taxes and competition laws were to be harmonised in the same manner. The problem with this approach was that the Luxemburg Compromise and the consequent necessity for unanimity allowed affected states to veto any un-welcome changes. Prospects improved after 1978 when the European Court ruled in the Cassis de Dijon case that the Federal government could not block the import of the French liqueur Cassis de Dijon, on the grounds that it did not contain enough alcohol to conform to German standards. Entry could only be forbidden on grounds of danger to health, fiscal supervision, fair trading or consumer protection.

The effect of the Cassis de Dijon ruling was to make it much more difficult for states to shelter behind discriminatory regulations. But, progress remained limited until 1985. Jacques Delors, the incoming Commission President, had a much more ambitous view of the Commission's role than his recent predecessors, and at the beginning of 1985 he visited the national capitals and probed their reaction to four ideas for progress on Europe: closer collaboration on defence, institutional development, progress on the monetary front, and a sus-tained attempt to create an internal market. Progress was possible on two of these issues, institutional development and the creation of an internal market.

The idea of a much more complete internal market was very enthusiastically supported by the British government which was keen to find an issue on which it would not be the eternal outsider given British objections to institutional development and the difficulties of the budgetary issue. The idea fitted well with the government's attachment to deregulation and market-based ideas, and the British government had long been frustrated about lack of access to financial and insurance markets elsewhere in the Community, a sector in which Britain was held to have a comparative advantage. The Federal government had a slightly more ambivalent reaction. The sheer strength of the West German economy should have indicated strong support for the completion of the internal market, but the sectorised character of policy-making in the Federal Republic meant that the government was still likely to continue to defend the interests of particular sectors like insurance and transport while accepting the general principle. French governments had in the past been notable for dragging their feet on progress towards completion of the internal market, but the long-term effects of the Cassis de Dijon case and the failure of the attempt at reflation in the face of world trends in the opposite direction in 1981/82 meant that France was much less opposed to deregulation than hitherto.

Common to all three governments was a concern about Europe's apparent declining competitiveness with other areas of the world and the persistent failure of intra-Community trade to grow as fast as trade with third countries. This fear of 'Eurosclerosis' was shared by a number of prominent industrialists in all the member states who pressured their governments in the direction of deregulation.

The major states, in agreeing to the idea of completion of the market, had acceded only to a very general policy conception which at the time looked likely to proceed slowly. The portfolio for the internal market was given to Lord Cockfield, a former businessman and member of the Thatcher Cabinet, who acted with considerable decisiveness and acuity in setting out a programme (Completing the Internal Market 1985) that would have to be completed within the life span of two Commission terms. The programme envisaged the adoption of 300 directives by December 1992. The directives were not prioritised, and concentrated on apparently practical measures like the abolition of frontier controls. A great deal of momentum quickly built up behind the general programme and the idea of 1992 as a target, since the holders of the next four presidencies were all in favour of the internal market. However, serious difficulties have emerged in realising the programme, especially in relation to the harmonisation of VAT and standardisation.

Harmonisation of VAT

The abolition of frontier controls would in effect undermine the maintenance of differential rates of indirect taxation since, if there are no controls, consumers would buy where the rates are cheapest. This problem arises in acute form in relation to VAT. Value added tax is the principal form of indirect taxation in EC states and is central to the financing of the Community. At present, rates diverge widely in the EC, from 22 per cent in Denmark down to 12 per cent in Spain and Luxemburg. Britain zero rates books, foodstuffs, and children's clothes. The maintenance of these differential rates, combined with the removal of frontier controls, would give enormous advantages to industries located in states where the VAT rates were low.

The Commission proposed two VAT brackets – a normal rate stretching from 14 to 20 per cent and a reduced rate of 4–9 per cent for basic goods and services, with countries free to choose their rates within those brackets. These proposals have met strong opposition from the British and French governments. Mrs Thatcher was so incensed by the proposals that in 1988 Lord Cockfield was not nominated by the British government to serve a second term on the Commission. Value added tax on food is regarded as politically impossible because the government pledged in the election campaign of 1987 never to impose it. Books and baby clothes are also politically sensitive. It would like to maintain high rates on drink and tobacco for health and revenue reasons. The British preference would be for the maintenance of rate differences and to rely on geography and the difficulties of transport to protect the British position. This is unacceptable to Britain's partners since it would for instance allow British producers of children's clothes to wage a mail-order war on the Continent on the basis of these products continuing to enjoy zero rating in Britain. France is also strongly opposed. It fears that the Commission's tax bands are too wide and wishes to maintain its levels of VAT and public spending at a level higher than that of the Federal Republic. The adoption of the Commission's proposals and the abolition of frontier controls would render this impossible.

Britain and France have both been pushing the idea of greater duty-free allowances to produce market-based convergence. Such suggestions are clearly diametrically opposed to the thrust of the Commission's proposals and would equally clearly not produce the effect ascribed to them. The Federal Republic has supported the Commission proposals.

THE PROBLEM OF STANDARDISATION

All European states have a system of national standards (DIN in the Federal Republic, AFNOR in France and BSI in the Britain), which prescribe product standards to be met if a product is to be offered for sale. The German DIN system is an especially well-developed and complex system which often makes it difficult for products from other Community countries to penetrate the German market. The Commission is attempting to resolve the problem of differing national standards by a strategy of mutual recognition in which representatives of the various national regulatory bodies would agree on a Euro standard. It also envisages that in a post-Single European Act era these decisions will be arrived at by majority vote.

Progress in implementing this aim has been slow and so far agreement has only been reached on toys and pressure vessels though a draft directive exists on machine tools. Even if it proves possible to produce directives at a much faster rate, problems remain. Agreement on the directives would not by itself ensure access for a product since it would also need to comply with national usage regulations. National bodies will remain free to add national requirements to the European directives which set minimum standards, and this is likely to be employed by the German authorities given their commitment to very high standards. Conversely, the smaller countries worry that in practice the system will produce domination by the big three since they produce 85 per cent of the new national standards.

ENVIRONMENTAL POLICY

In the field of environmental policy there has been an accelerating shift away from purely national policy-making to the European level. This shift has been driven by the converging interests of the EC Commission and the Federal Republic of Germany. The establishment of the CAP and the customs union in the 1960s and the Gaullist check on its political impulse left the EC Commission looking for new policy areas. This impulse coincided with a general increase in interest in the environment, dramatised but not created by the Stockholm Conference of 1972. After a protracted series of negotiations between the Commission and the member states, agreement was reached in March 1973 that the Commission should receive prior notification before the introduction of any significant new policy proposals by the member states to protect the environment. The Commission can then block the development of a unilateral national initiative by developing a proposal of its own within five months. In 1978 the Commission's capacity to develop policy in this area was significantly increased by the establishment of a new directorate (DG11) to handle environmental policy.

The other major actor pushing for European-wide regulation is the Federal Republic. Since the late 1970s the environmental movement, fuelled by a high level of prosperity, a new access to mass higher education, the prospect of a rapid expansion of the nuclear industry, and the potent symbol of the dying forest (*Waldsterben*) has been a powerful force in West German politics. The strength of environmentalist pressures has been much reinforced by the entry of the Greens into the Bundestag in 1983. Confronted with these pressures, which constitute a potential threat to the competitiveness of West German industry, the Federal government has a clear interest in creating European regulatory regimes in order that competitors incur the same costs. In recent years West Germany has had to invest a great deal in 'clean technology' and now stands to gain most from the EC-wide adoption of higher standards of environmental protection.

The converging interests of the Federal Republic and the EC Commission were reflected in Article 130 of the Single European Act which is concerned with environmental protection and explicitly endorses the 'polluter pays' principle.

In the Fourth Environmental Action Programme of spring 1987 the Commission recognised that it is important not just to legislate on environmental policy, but also to try to ensure that it is actually implemented. Hitherto, the Commission had looked at implementation almost exclusively from the perspective of legal compliance. This has had two consequences. The Commission often became engaged in protracted negotiations with states that had enacted unsatisfactory legislation, while ignoring countries which introduced no legislation. This problem was seen as likely to increase with the recent entry of Spain and Portugal. Legal compliance is a long way removed in some states from actual practice. To improve the situation the Fourth Action Programme envisages stronger powers to extract compliance. It will now be easier to take intransigent member states to the European Court. Private referrals by individuals or groups to the Commission for non-compliance are also to be encouraged.

Successive British governments have resisted the development of a Community environmental policy. British industry is less convinced of the opportunities in clean technology. Britain, as an island with fast-flowing rivers, is in quite a different geographical situation and is much less convinced of the need for environmental policy. There has been a series of major Anglo-German battles, with a notably long-running conflict over aquatic pollution. Here the Germans and the Commission both favour uniform regulations on controlling the release of waste products into all water systems. Britain with its island situation and fast-flowing rivers, stresses the need for flexible standards to take account of different natural environments.

In opposing the extension of the environmental regulation, Britain often finds itself isolated, since many countries, including France, which do not share the German enthusiasm for environmental regulation, simply rely on the so-called implementation deficit to ensure that they do not in fact need to change their habits. Even with the changed Commission attitude to implementation, it is unlikely that they will be put under pressure unless there are strong environmental movements in the countries concerned since no one will complain to the Commission. Were such movements to develop strongly in France, then it is likely that France would move closer to the British position. France has already demonstrated clear opposition to accepting too stringent standards for products where their interests would be adversely affected, e.g. German proposals for very tight exhaust emission standards for cars under 1.4 litres capacity have been blocked by French and British objections. The French car industry, like other car industries, has a very high volume of small car sales which they fear would be adversely affected by the adoption of these standards since the West German industry is much better equipped to implement the tighter standards than other European manufacturers.

POLITICAL UNION AND EUROPEAN POLITICAL CO-OPERATION

The concept of political union was launched by de Gaulle in 1961 as a rival concept to supranationalism which would build on the Europe of nation-states and decrease the role of the Commission. Its contours remained unclear but certainly involved much closer co-operation on foreign policy, and a stress on European identity since it was conceived in the context of the Gaullist rupture with the United States. Although it attracted some support, notably from Adenauer, there was a great deal of hostility and it was never adopted as EC policy.

Political union re-emerged as a theme in the early 1970s, by which time it had become, if anything, more indistinct and neither Willy Brandt nor Georges Pompidou, the West German and French leaders, was ever able to make clear that it was anything more than a rhetorical flourish on intergovernmentalism. The task of giving it a more concrete shape was given to Leo Tindemans, the Prime Minister of Belgium, in 1975. In the event his report on political union and a greater coherence for the Community was quietly filed: Helmut Schmidt and Giscard d'Estaing had other priorities in the wake of the 1973 oil price rise and the British Labour government was resolutely opposed.

Political union remained on the back burner for the French and West German governments, a theme to be tacked on to the end of a summit communiqué, probably mainly as merely a rhetorical statement but not intended to be acted on until the governments were prodded into action by the European Parliament. The one exception to this situation was in the notion of European Political Co-operation (EPC), the extension of the procedures for co-ordination of the foreign policies of EC member states, where the West German government had been very active.

The reappearance of the theme of political union on the agenda with the adoption of the Draft Treaty on European Union in 1984 was not a development that had been fostered by the major states, but rather one to which they had to respond. The British government was resolutely hostile to the extension of the European Parliament envisaged in the draft treaty and to extensive institutional innovation. The French government was opposed to a major extension of the powers of the European Parliament but was, rhetorically at least, prepared to accept some institutional development. The Federal government's views were ambivalent. Rhetorically in favour of the extension of the powers of the European Parliament and institutional development, it lost its enthusiasm if there was any real prospect of these changes being achieved.

The key decisions on the response of the major states were taken at summit meetings in Milan in June 1985 and Luxemburg in December 1985. At the Milan summit a Franco-German proposal for a 'Draft Treaty on European Union' was presented. Despite its title, it was a fairly modest document concentrating on the extension of EPC. Its force had in any case been weakened by the use by Ignaz

Kiechle, the West German Agriculture Minister, of a veto in the Agricultural Council only a month earlier. Given that the paper envisaged the extension of majority voting in the council, the use by the West Germans of a veto in the council for the first time did much to undermine the German position at the summit. British reservations on the paper were shared by Denmark and Greece while the Italian government felt the commitment to majority voting was too modest.

No agreement was possible at Milan and an intergovernmental conference was established which provided the basis of agreement at Luxemburg in December 1985. The final version of the Single European Act clearly bears the imprint of British objections. Majority voting was extended only in limited areas mainly to do with the internal market. Majority voting was not to apply on some aspects of taxation, free movement of individuals, environmental policy, health controls and the rights of employees. These were all areas where the British government had important interests to defend. In the case of taxation and free movement of individuals they enjoyed the firm support of West Germany. The British and French governments were able to ensure that there was no major increase in the power of the European Parliament despite heavy pressure from Italy. The Single European Act in its final form was a disappointment to the maximalists of the European Parliament, but reflected in its commitment to the completion of the internal market and the extension of EPC the aspirations of the major states, especially Britain and the Federal Republic.

All three major states have had a strong interest in EPC. Successive French governments have seen in EPC a forum for demonstrating a European as distinct from an Atlantic identity. It has also been viewed positively by British governments which have perceived it as facilitating the maintenance of an important British role in world affairs. It offends no significant domestic interest group, and the responsible ministry, the Foreign Office, is by far the most pro-European of all Whitehall ministries and support for EPC is seen as an important way of establishing British bona fides, particularly when Britain is engaged in a dispute with other member states.

The major state which invests most political capital in EPC is the Federal Republic. In the view of successive West German governments the excesses of the Third Reich excluded a too explicit leadership role for the Federal Republic, and the EPC has acted as a proxy in which the Federal Republic can play a role more commensurate with its economic power than when it acts unilaterally. The

West German Foreign Minister, Hans-Dietrich Genscher, launched a joint initiative with the Italian Foreign Minister, Emilio Colombo, for the extension of the EPC procedure in 1981. Because of the objections of some other member states, this was finally accepted only in a weakened form in the 1983 Solemn Declaration on European Union. The Federal government again pushed, together with the French government, in 1985 for a further strengthening of EPC and this became the EPC element in the Single European Act.

The EPC procedure is vital to the formulation of the foreign policy of the Federal Republic. It serves most importantly as the connecting-rod between the Federal Republic's *Ost-* and *Westpolitik*. The Federal government has a more intense relationship with one East European state, the German Democratic Republic, than is enjoyed by any of its Community partners with any East European state. At times this relationship is perceived as too intimate, especially in France, and the EPC is the forum in which the conflicting pulls of the two relationships are balanced out and other states are able to point out to the Federal Republic when they think the relationship with the German Democratic Republic is too close. This consideration would become even more important if the Soviet leader, Mikhail Gorbachev, really were to accord more autonomy to the foreign policies of the East European states.

The economy of the Federal Republic is highly dependent on imported sources of energy, especially oil, and the use of the EPC as a proxy greatly facilitates its relationship with the Middle East. The shadow of the Holocaust imposes singular obligations on the Federal Republic towards Israel, yet it is dependent on Arab oil. This dilemma is resolved by formulating the West German position in the context of EPC. Similar considerations apply in policy towards Southern Africa where West German industry has been notably keen to export but where the Federal government is reluctant to incur the opprobrium of a too close identification with the South African government.

CONCLUSION

This survey of the interaction between the major states and the Community suggests that some pieces of conventional wisdom need revision. The Commission, for so long a bent reed, has, under Jacques Delors, staged a comeback in the 1980s and has been a major force in most of the issues examined here. Britain, for long considered to be much less influential than France or West Germany, especially when the latter were acting together, proved to be very influential in all the issues examined except environmental policy where it seems appropriate to talk of policy failure on the part of the British government. In a sense Mrs Thatcher's project for curing the British disease has made some headway as an antidote to Eurosclerosis.

France, which clearly made the running in the 1950s and 1960s, appears to have become much less influential. One explanation here is the divided nature of the French executive with a Socialist president and a Gaullist prime minister between 1986 and 1988. Both incumbents are now Socialists but the government has a very weak parliamentary base. The West German government is very influential in relation to environmental policy and, if a European Central Bank were ever to be established, it would be dominated by the Bundesbank as the European Monetary System is now. It is much more difficult to discern an overall influence of the Federal Republic that is commensurate with its economic strength. This is partly a function of its fragmented mode of decision-making. This has been further complicated by the desire of the West German states (*Länder*) for a much greater say in the wake of the Single European Act. More importantly, there is an incoherence of objectives: budgetary discipline versus agricultural support, freemarket rhetoric and a practice of subventions.

Although all three states continue to exert a disproportionate influence on the evolution of the Community, none of the three, or even any two acting in concert, is able to manage Community policy in any overall or co-ordinated way. The Commission has not recaptured the capacity for co-ordinated leadership it enjoyed under Hallstein, but it has made some recovery and the provisions of the Single European Act allow it more scope. Jacques Delors may have been vainglorious in claiming that within ten years 80 per cent of all decisions would be taken at the European level, but he is surely correct in pointing the trend that will emerge.

REFERENCE AND FURTHER READING

Bulmer, S. and Paterson, W. (1987) *The Federal Republic of Germany and the European Community* (London: Allen and Unwin).

Ceccini, P. (1988) *1992: The Benefits of a Single Market* (Aldershot: Wildwood House).

George, S. (1987) *The British Government and The European Community* (London: University Association for Contemporary European Studies).

Morgan, R. and Bray, C. (1986) *Partners and Rivals in Western Europe: Britain, France and Germany* (Aldershot: Gower).

Pelkmans, J. and Winters, A. (1988) *Europe's Domestic Market* (London: Routledge).

Pryce, R. (ed.) (1987) *The Dynamics of European Union* (London: Croom Helm).

Simonian, H. (1985) *The Privileged Partnership: Franco-German Relations in the European Community 1969–84* (Oxford: Oxford University Press).

CHAPTER TEN

European Community Decision-making: towards the Single European Market.

Juliet Lodge

The entry into force of the Single European Act (SEA) on 1 July 1987 added a further tier of complexity to a decision-making process which is commonly derided as monolithic, ossified, and Byzantine. It is true that the European Community (EC) exhibits marked weaknesses of bargaining at all its levels and across policy sectors. Even so, EC decision-making is relatively adaptable. The criticisms levelled against it reflect unrealistic expectations of what the EC should be able to deliver and of who is responsible for its failings, as well as a lack of appreciation of what the EC's goals are. This mismatch between expectations and capacity to deliver continues to grow. It is further compounded by assumptions that the EC's policy processes are supposed to yield rational and optimal results.

The context within which EC decision-making unfurls inevitably detracts from rational and optimal outcomes, no matter the ideal. There are numerous reasons for this: the lack of consensus among the twelve member states over the EC's *raison d'être* ; the scope of its policy competence; its institutional system; and the role of member states within a supranational polity. Organisational problems seriously inhibit the distillation of a consensus over even primary goals and the pursuit of optimal policy outcomes. These problems are not new: they have existed since the creation of the European Communities in the 1950s. However, the magnitude of the problems has grown as a result of successive enlargements of the Community, major and rapid shifts in the international political economy, and the challenge this poses to the EC's position in, and expectations of, it. The member governments posture and engage in political rhetoric with the aim of maximising their own self-interest or minimising its erosion. Sometimes, coalitions of member governments form with the intention of ensuring that the EC develop along lines that they favour. The injection of political impetus into the EC in the 1980s simply underlines the fact that the essential element of development is the political consent of its members. All member governments use the EC instrumentally and see it as the most important vehicle for the pursuit of an increasingly wide variety of goals.

THE EC'S RAISON D'ÊTRE

Individual member governments attach their own meaning to terms like 'ever closer union', 'European union', 'European co-operation', and 'European integration'. It is not just a matter of nuance that separates the different ideas of union or co-operation. Rather, there is a sharp division between those who advocate an accretion of the EC's policy competence and those who favour no more than loose intergovernmental co-operation on an *ad hoc* basis when it is clear that national action alone will not satisfy the interests of member states. As a result, a crude divide separates the advocates of the EC as a federal European union and those fighting a rearguard action against the ceding of more national sovereignty to a supranational body whose authority has vastly increased since its establishment.

The lack of consensus over the EC's *raison d'être* and the meaning of European union has been accentuated as the EC's jurisdiction has expanded, with its intrinsically federal institutions becoming more active in a system once subject to a more or less discrete executive process. The absence of consensus is exemplified in the current tensions over co-operation and the renewed debate on the lack of democratic control within Community institutions. Governments which felt that the EC's democratic deficit had been overcome with the introduction of direct elections to the European Parliament have been disabused. It is epitomised by the efforts to distil, institutionally at least, a set of democratically accountable political institutions capable of acting efficiently, responsively, and effectively. Underlying this continuing effort lies a shared conviction that the existing institutions are in some important ways inappropriate and deficient. That their functioning and relationships could be improved is not denied. But the lack of consensus over a *raison d'être* makes it very hard to determine what institutional arrangements would be appropriate. Consequently, the relative strength or dominance of certain institutions is seen as an indicator of the type of system towards which the EC is moving: hence the battle over more or less federalism and the concomitant problems over sectoral policy goals and their implementation.

More recently, efforts have been made to reform the EC to make its activities and policy-making processes more transparent and to clarify the relationship between the member states and the supranational bodies. The 1984 Draft Treaty establishing the European Union (EUT) outlined a constitution for union and defined the principle of subsidiarity for dividing authority between supranational institutions and national authorities. It advocated allocating only as much competence to the union's authorities as was necessary to enable them to meet policy demands that individual states alone were unable to handle. This was coupled with the notion of devolving to the lowest possible authority policy areas not subject to exclusive or shared union competence (see Lodge 1986). Either way, national governments would lose. The idea of national governments losing power on a zero-sum basis to the EC underlies the disagreements over the *raison d'être*. As a result, even from its inception, the EC's ultimate goal has always been loosely defined. Tension has persisted between the ideas of a federal Community and an association of states co-operating with each other to mutual advantage. This tension is expressed daily through institutional confrontation and through the allocation of more or less restricted competences to the EC under the terms of the Rome Treaty and the SEA which amended it.

Thirty years after the EC's establishment, however, it is clear that integration has an inherently expansive logic. What distinguishes the EC of the 1990s from that of the 1950s is the more extensive conception of those policy sectors that are its proper concern. We shall consider only two policy areas that illustrate the need for institutional adaptation: trade and agriculture.

THE SCOPE OF POLICY COMPETENCE

In the 1950s a sector-by-sector approach to integration was pursued, not in response to a conscious theoretical model, but rather as a result of pragmatic political and economic considerations. Underpinning the approach was an intention to make war between France and West Germany unthinkable, and so build an enduring peace in Europe. This was to be achieved by promoting co-operation on a constructive basis, by a linkage of economic fortunes, rather than by keeping potential antagonists apart.

208

Out of these concerns a consensus emerged over the necessity of co-operation. It found institutional expression in the creation of the European Communities by six countries – France, Belgium, the Netherlands, Italy, Luxemburg and West Germany – which found that intergovernmental co-operation, the dominant characteristic of the other European bodies set up after 1945, was not useful for practical purposes, since without unanimity on a course of action nothing happened. This did not mean, however, that the Six were ready to embrace a federal European Union, as attempts in the 1950s to create a European Political Community and a European Defence Community revealed.

Instead, in line with the emphasis on gradualism and the building of indissoluble and constructive economic links between countries committed to a form of binding European co-operation, a supranational organisation was created in 1951 based on a pooling of Franco-German coal and steel production, the European Coal and Steel Community (ECSC). Britain, wary of its pre federal structures, declined to join. The ECSC served as a model, in terms of a sector-by-sector approach to European integration and in terms of its institutional arrangements, for the subsequent European Economic Communities, established by the Treaty of Rome in 1957.

Its major innovations concerned the creation of an independent body, the High Authority (later the Commission in the EC), entrusted with formulating policy in terms of a 'common good'; a Common Assembly with the power to censure the High Authority, an arrangement which paid lip-service to the idea of executive accountability to Parliament; a Court of Justice to ensure compliance with the treaty; and a Council of Ministers to represent the six member states acting by unanimity or qualified majority vote. The latter was not designed or expected to become the omnipotent body that it evolved into during the 1960s and 1970s within the EC. Equally importantly, the ECSC was given the power to make its decisions binding upon its members.

The sector-by-sector approach was consolidated with the creation of the EEC, but the idea of European union remained as imprecise as ever. Under the ECSC the members had been committed to 'substitute for historic rivalries a fusion of their essential interests'. The Preamble of the Rome Treaty records the determination 'to establish the foundations of an ever closer union among the European peoples'. This phrase stresses the evolutionary character of the EC and signals the possibility of reforms leading to even closer links. The name 'European Economic Community' is also telling. It was deliberately chosen over 'Common Market' because the Six expected integration to develop well beyond the trade area implied by the latter. The EEC was intended to be much more than a customs union. It was designed to facilitate the adoption of common economic and social policies, common arrangements for investments within states, a common external tariff, and a common commercial policy towards third countries. However attaining the EC sectoral goals was fraught with difficulties. Although committed to the elimination of customs duties and other restrictions on intra-EC trade, the member states have been adept at maintaining a vast array of technical barriers to trade which have prevented the operation of a common market (but which have been successfully challenged in the Court of Justice). As for external trade, numerous derogations have been agreed for the states' former colonies and dependent territories, which rely heavily on relatively unrestricted access to the EC market for their exports.

Each enlargement of the EC has aggravated these arrangements and brought problems for other states whose exports (notably of primary products) to the EC compete with those of the more favoured scales. The Mediterranean enlargements of 1981 and 1986, which brought Greece, Spain and Portugal into the EC, corroborate this. Each EC enlargement has been accompanied by trade diversification, and has accentuated trade problems and competition with the United States. The latter has had to adapt to a trading bloc which has moved from a position of economic dependence (and an outlet for US exports) to an independent competitor in the world market.

All these developments pose a major burden on the EC's institutions. The Commission was given jurisdiction over external trade and has negotiated a host of bilateral and multilateral trade agreements with Third World states. The member states, with Commission help, adopt a shared position in several international economic and political organisations. But external trade is not a self-contained policy. External relations of the EC interface with bilateral trade accords of its members. The EC may be responsible for tariff policy, but it has little control over the range of non-tariff barriers and voluntary export restraint agreements operated by the member states towards imports (Beuter and Tsakaloyannis 1987: 154). In addition, the EC's development policy rests on three main pillars: the Common Commercial Policy, the Common Agricultural Policy (CAP), and the partially Common Aid Policy.

Equally problematically, external trade matters cannot be segregated from high politics and diplomacy. The logic of the sectoral approach has been repeatedly challenged as political considerations have come to the fore, whether these have taken the shape of demands for economic sanctions against other states (for example, Argentina during the Falklands War of 1982, or South Africa) or for a less restrictive interpretation of external trade. The last decade has seen increased dissatisfaction over the compartmentalisation between trade and politics, between industrial policy and security issues. Not until the SEA was any formal recognition given to the interlinkage between the economic and defence aspects of security. Indeed, defence issues were deliberately omitted from the Rome Treaty, and member states have been exceedingly wary of discussing defence and security within the framework of European Political Co-operation (EPC).

The establishment and refinement of EPC since the 1970s marks both a step forward in European integration, even though its goal is simply to promote information exchange and the co-ordination of members' interests where possible, and a reassertion of intergovernmentalism in that it is not formally part of the supranational system. Also EPC represents recognition of the willingness of member states to co-operate and to work towards common positions on sensitive matters. Its achievements and working methods are a good deal more sophisticated than is often supposed (see De Vree *et al.* 1987). One of the strengths of this 'Community method' is that it can foster the coexistence of parallel operations without undermining the essence of supranationalism. Parallel endeavours form a testing ground for subsequent integrative operations that may be switched to the EC arena proper.

The contradictions highlighted by the sectoral approach to external relations testify to its success in achieving some results in the first place. Whatever the problems that have arisen since, there can be little doubt that the institutions charged with administering the relevant EC measures did so with some success (see Hine 1985). Difficulties in this area have inevitably been compounded by another sectoral policy, the CAP. The latter is an integral part of many EC policies: it frustrates a rational budgetary policy and affects internal policies as well as external relations.

It is not really surprising that EC sectoral policies are not as self-contained as the picture painted of them suggests. Indeed, it is doubtful that policy sectors anywhere can be said to be self-contained entities. The illusion that they are in the EC has arisen from the approach of 'selling the idea of binding co-operation' on a sectoral basis in order to allay member states' fears about the impact upon national sovereignty. These fears are accentuated in the case of the

CAP because agricultural policy touches upon so many facets of economic and social policies. The denial of such an intermeshing underlines many of of the problems that commonly are ascribed solely to the CAP.

The CAP is certainly flawed in its conception, and protectionist in its operation and effect, yet despite all the criticisms levelled against it from both within and outside the Community, the CAP has proved very difficult to reform. There are several political and economic interests which are resistant to change. In addition, the CAP is seen as perhaps the EC's only common policy. Nevertheless some attempt has been made to advance supranational ideals through supranational methods. The idea that farmers should receive the same price for a given commodity irrespective of where in the EC it is produced has a certain logic and attraction. To achieve this, however, many other non-agricultural conditions have to be met. Even so, the institutional arrangements for managing and implementing the CAP have been, in many respects, appropriate to the task. On a day-to-day basis the Commission is responsible for managing the CAP, with the assistance of a complex bureaucratic machine. The Council of Ministers, too, has a Special Committee on Agriculture to service it instead of COREPER, the body of national government officials which usually prepares Council business. The bureaucratic nature of CAP management is reinforced by expert inputs from the farming lobbies at both the national and European levels.

At the technical level, the administrative machinery and extensive regulatory arrangements for the CAP seem relatively appropriate, although the Commission's staff is too tiny to allow it to counter fraud effectively. However, technical appropriateness does not imply that the instruments of the CAP are appropriate or that its share of the EC budget (over 70 per cent of EC expenditure) reflects an appropriate distribution of available resources to individual policy sectors. While the reform measures of 1988 were designed to rectify the imbalance to some degree, there are systemic problems with the CAP that cannot be solved on this basis, not least because they are inherent to the redistributive design and reflect the disproportionate power of agriculture in national politics, which undoes the 'common' intent of the agricultural policy.

The problem for the CAP itself derives from the fact that redistribution can undermine the notion of a unitary, single common policy when national agricultural interests, backed by national government, seek to maximise their gains come what may. The costs of redistribution are unevenly and irrationally spread both among the member states (a 'rich' state like Denmark gaining far more from the CAP than a 'poor' net contributor like Britain) and within the states ('rich' farmers deploying technical knowledge, earning more than 'poor' farmers), while the poorest sections of states' populations, who outnumber EC farmers, are unable to organise themselves to alter the CAP's priorities. The arguments over agriculture between the northern and southern members of the EC are but a recent manifestation of the redistributive pröblem. All this occurs because policy instruments are inappropriate and divorced from supply–demand market mechanisms (see Wallace *et al.* 1983: 143–76; Jenkins 1983).

The CAP's priorities were as much a product of their time as are today's new goals in the technology and environment sectors. Indeed, there is a striking similarity between the announcement of sectoral policy ideals or goals in the SEA and Rome Treaty which it amends. Both make general references to rather broad objectives, but omit the definition of implementing measures. The SEA, for example, refers to 'economic and social cohesion', just as the Rome Treaty announced broad rules and objectives that were not entirely compatible. This deliberate vagueness is no doubt necessary to secure the initial political commitment upon which to base further action that will inevitably arouse member states' opposition.

The Rome Treaty sets five goals for the CAP: increased productivity; a fair standard of living for farm populations; stable markets; security of supplies; and reasonable prices to consumers. Its main elements were markets and prices, external relations, and structural policy. Price guarantees for farmers have been the most important element (taking up 75 per cent of the available funds), based upon the principle of redistributing income from the non-farm sector to farmers, and upon a unified internal market with common prices for agricultural products to permit the free circulation of goods. Not only has the guarantee scheme, in consuming so much of the funds, left little scope for structural support, the system of common prices is undermined by a wide variety of national financial aids to agriculture and by currency fluctuations. Key CAP goals, like self-sufficiency and reasonable prices to consumers, are undermined by a system which supports a production that is not related to demand and associated price levels, but instead supports surpluses through export subsidies and intervention practices.

The overall effect is an attempt to pursue a common policy in a sector that cannot be neatly segregated from adjacent sectors, especially fiscal, industrial, regional, and social policy. In addition, the absence of a common EC currency used by everyone in the member states from the outset upset the common price policy the moment that monetary instability became a feature of international trade after the early 1970s.

Clearly, the type of machinery necessary to deal with the vast array of issues and policies that interface with the agricultural sector and overlap with one another demands a degree of convergence on macroeconomic policy that hitherto has been missing. Indeed, since political integration is seen as the goal of the sector-by-sector approach, political and economic convergence must be linked. Given the primacy allotted to setting up the CAP and the common commercial policy, it is not surprising that many other EC goals took second place; only now is pressure for real progress on them beginning to emerge. This change in economic and political priorities is related both to the Mediterranean enlargement of the 1980s, to recurring budgetary crises precipitated by the cost of the CAP, and to a recognition by the member states of the need to promote their industrial competitiveness in the world market through collective action and the realisation of the internal market. More attention, therefore, is being paid to barriers that inhibit the free movement of individuals and capital; the role of the structural funds, notably the European Social Fund and the Regional Development Fund; investment, competition and company policy; transport; education and training; and technology. Technical and other barriers to trade, standards, and consumer issues have all been considered, and EC involvement can be justified in terms of a more appropriate distribution of available resources to facilitate the realisation of the internal market (or the Single European Market), a phrase that has superseded the Rome Treaty's commitment to a progressive establishment of the Common Market.

The redistribution of available resources to different, or to a more balanced set of, policy sectors presupposes that the Commission's contemporary interest in medium- to long-term sectorally linked programmes can be implemented, and that both within and between key institutions – notably the Commission, the Council and the European Parliament (EP) – policy priorities can be defined and consensus reached on their implementation. The internal organisation of these institutions as well as the competence bestowed upon them render this difficult.

INTERNAL INSTITUTIONAL BLOCKS

There can be little doubt that one of the major deterrents to more rational decision-taking resides in the composition and role of the EC's *de facto* legislature, the Council of Ministers. The Council performs a contradictory role in the EC. Comprised of national government representatives, its members seek to protect national interests. In most areas except budgetary matters and those covered by the SEA, the Council exercises supreme legislative authority, acting with little or no regard to the views of other institutions. It was the ability of the Council to determine whether and at what pace legislation should progress which led many observers to see the Commission, originally regarded as the 'motor of integration' because of its unique and independent status and right to initiate legislation, being demoted to being an appendix of the Council, serving merely as the latter's secretariat. This view has been challenged by contemporary developments and by the way in which increases in the power of the EP have reinforced the Commission's position and authority. This was one of the key elements of the EUT and is a much-overlooked facet of the SEA.

The discontinuous and sectorally determined composition of the Council means that there is no mechanism for ensuring that individual sectoral objectives are compatible with each other. An all-embracing Council and the more comprehensive joint Councils of Finance and Agricultural Ministers are exceptions rather than the norm. As a result, contradictory decisions can be made depending upon the sectoral composition of the Councils. Since the Commission has to draft proposals with a view to securing their adoption by the separate sectoral versions of the Council, and since it will adapt them according to what it understands (following on wide discussions with national officials) will be acceptable to a particular Council, any initial coherence that a proposal may have in terms of its relation to other policy areas may be sacrificed. The result is that compartmentalised policy-making reinforces sectoral segregation.

Furthermore, the nature of the policy formulation process within the Commission itself does not lend itself easily to the promotion of intersectoral coherence. Some member states have systematically colonized a Commission directorate in order to ensure that a particular conception of policy developments should prevail. There is, despite the Commission's formal independence from member governments, great competition among the latter to ensure that their nationals assume responsibility for important portfolios. Various measures do exist for seeking coherence or minimising major discrepancies. The Commissioners each have influential 'cabinets' that are not part of the Commission's formal establishment and that engage in a wide variety of information and communities activities. Recently, reforms have been made within the Commission in an attempt to overcome these severe organisational problems.

If it is difficult for Commissioners responsible for drafting policy proposals to discern the linkages between different policy sectors and to anticipate how the implementation of proposals may affect other policy sectors, it is almost impossible for national civil servants. The reasons for this lie not only in the nature of bureaucratic politics, interdepartmental rivalries, and inadequate means of ensuring co-ordination across policy sectors, but also in the fact that ultimately the proposal goes to the Council where a national minister can, if need be, veto it. However, the extension of qualified majority voting under the SEA will place a far greater premium on Council members seeking to accommodate their views within a proposal that has the support of the majority. Failure to aggregate interests in either the Commission or the Council would complicate matters; more importantly, the Council may be tempted to see a proposal fade away rather than struggle for agreement on difficult and technical measures. This puts pressure on the Commission to ensure that its 'cabinets' adopt a more pro-active role and not just act as filters between the various departments. In that sense, the Commission's politicisation is inevitable both internally and in its relations both with the national governments and the other Community institutions. The 'co-operation procedure' represents the latest attempt to ease the situation without simultaneously increasing the power of the supranational bodies (Commission and EP), and so raising the spectre of federalism.

Any assessment of the co-operation procedure must recognise the fact that the EP played a major role in the 1980s in promoting and engineering institutional reforms and the expansion of the EC's policy competence. The EUT gave impetus to an intergovernmental dialogue that essentially sought to resolve two incompatible goals. Many governments wanted to avoid altering the institutional balance, lest this presage a step towards federalism; and all governments wanted to increase the EC's capacity to respond effectively to the pressures, challenges, and dilemmas posed by its deteriorating international competitiveness. Institutional change was the precondition of the latter.

The reforms that the SEA introduced into the Rome Treaty in

terms of interinstitutional relations confront the problem of the EC's *raison d'être*. The national governments rejected the EUT's neo-federal option of using the *acquis Communautaire* as the basis of a new constitution for a European union. Instead, they favoured the minimalist approach of amending the Rome Treaty, a difficult approach since amendments required unanimous approval and ratification by all member states in accordance with their own constitutional practices. Major, even rational, reforms could not be part of such a package. Any internal institutional reforms necessitated by the implementation of the co-operation procedure perforce developed on an *ad hoc* basis and depended on good personal relations between key actors.

There can, however, be little doubt that the co-operation procedure does increase the influence and political clout of both the Commission and the EP. The latter's role is particularly sensitive because it is seen as the villain of the piece in the states' battle to maintain national sovereignty. It is often argued that because it is now elected by direct, universal suffrage, the EP has become the repository of popular sovereignty. The argument about gains in supranational sovereignty being obtained at the expense of national states is part of this debate. More generally, the more legitimate the EP can make itself, the greater its claims for more power to initiate and determine legislative outputs, and the more its demand that the Council, the embodiment of national sovereignty and interests, be held democratically accountable for its actions seem justified. Hence the tension between the two institutions. The co-operation procedure tries to steer a mid-course between the two 'antagonists' by making daily co-operation between them essential. This, too, is a consequence of the SEA.

The SEA deals with EPC in the same document as treaty amendments. This may seem no more than a small matter of detail, but its political significance should not be underestimated. It is important to stress that the areas subject to SEA rules are interpreted expansively. The notion of realising the internal market has consequences for a wide variety of policy areas, including many not mentioned by the EC treaties or the SEA. How then does the SEA alter decision-making?

The SEA consists of four 'Titles' and a 'Final Act' that includes numerous reservations entered by the member states. Most importantly from our perspective, Title II covers provisions amending the original Community treaties and 'Provisions relating to the foundations and the policy of the Community', central to which is the

217

realisation of the internal market, which is also linked to the EC's monetary capacity, social policy, regional economic and social disparities, research and technological development, and the environment. Equally significantly, Title III deals with European cooperation in foreign policy, which now explicitly includes political and economic aspects of security. While much controversy has centred on the treaty amendments (especially in respect of the internal market) designed to ensure majority voting in the Council, the significance of other aspects of the SEA has been underestimated.

Central to realising many SEA goals, especially the internal market, is the idea of improving the EC's decision-making capacity and efficiency. This is a necessary but not sufficient precondition of success. However, it is a highly contentious area. It remains to be seen whether the new 'co-operation procedure' will actually help to make EC decision-making more democratic and efficient. However, unless budgetary discipline is restored and the EC disposes of sufficient financial resources, new policies will remain merely aspirational rather than operational possibilities.

THE CO-OPERATION PROCEDURE

The co-operation procedure is designed to enable the EP to play an effective, albeit still restricted, role in the EC's legislative process. Its powers are formally increased in that it has a right to assent to enlargement and association agreements. Financial protocols attached to such agreements offer scope for EP influence. More important, however, is the provision that makes the EP part of a 'co-legislature' with the Council. If its members, the MEPs, are to realise their legislative ambitions, they must strike alliances with both Council and the Commission, because the EP's powers to amend draft legislation depend primarily on the Commission's willingness to comply with the EP's wishes, and secondarily on Council openness.

The new procedure offers the illusion of a balanced system of co-equal chambers without vesting them with equal opportunities and powers to affect the outcome. Even so, MEPs have seen the new arrangements as an improvement on the traditional decision-making procedure. Consequently, they wish to ensure that as much draft legislation as possible comes under the terms of the treaty articles to which the co-operation procedure applies. This means that the legal base of draft legislation assumes critical importance: both MEPs and the Council may challenge it in order to ensure the EP's participation or exclusion. Problems will arise because redistributive policy goals cannot be implemented without reference both to the structural funds (which are subject to the budget procedure) and to the more focused aims of the convergence programmes of the SEA (subject to the co-operation procedure). These problems will compound the usual altercations over the classification of expenditure as compulsory or non-compulsory. The latter concerns the EP inasmuch as it seeks to increase spending on these items at the expense of the former (mainly the CAP).

The co-operation procedure establishes a system of two readings tied to deadlines designed to expedite legislation and avoid the protracted deliberations and non-decisions that characterised the past. Under the old procedure, the EP gave its formal 'Opinion' on draft proposals being deliberated by the Council, but the latter could amend them without further reference to the EP. Now the Council cannot act (though it may begin its deliberations) until after the EP has acted on a Commission proposal.

The EP may reject, amend, withhold, or issue its opinion during the first reading. It may even persuade the Commission to amend or withdraw a proposal. If the Commission refuses, the EP can still delay things by referring the proposal back to its own committee. And even if the Council has its own 'common position' ready, it cannot announce it until the EP's opinion has been issued. Only then does the proposal go, along with the Commission's view on the Opinion, to the Council. Only a qualified majority is necessary for the Council to adopt a 'common position', which is then sent back to the EP.

The EP then has three months in which to approve the 'common position'. If it does so or if it fails to express a view, the Council adopts the proposal. Alternatively, the EP may reject the common position by an absolute majority. The proposal may nevertheless still be adopted by the Council providing the latter is unanimous. The need for Council unanimity at this point may give MEPs an opportunity to influence the outcome by seeking to persuade a member government to thwart the attainment of unanimity without necessarily employing a veto. More constructively, the EP can also amend the common position by an absolute majority. If it does so, the proposal reverts to the Commission which, within one month, has an opportunity for revision before sending it back to the Council for a second reading.

The Council then has three months within which to take a number of courses of action. If unanimous, it may adopt EP amendments which the Commission has not incorporated into the proposal. It may, by qualified majority, adopt the Commission proposal, or amend it if unanimous. It may delay a decision for a further month with EP agreement to allow more time for the proposal to be considered. Or it may fail to act, in which case the proposal lapses.

The new procedure thus demands co-operation between the three main institutions. It obliges the Council and EP to collaborate in a manner almost alien to them. It will be much more difficult for the Council (and the Commission) to ignore EP views. As a result, informal but politically significant contacts have developed between the three institutions as a way of seeking to smooth the passage of legislation. The EP has been clearly inserted into the decision-making process and given a right of influence, if not a power of veto.

During the first reading, EP–Commission links are crucial: before then, contacts can be usefully exploited by both bodies. The Commission is ready to discuss legislative priorities with the EP. Inevitably, MEPs of all parties will jockey for position and try to determine these. But useful as these discussions may be, they cannot guarantee subsequent parliamentary approval of a Commission proposal. The EP has the chance to flex its new muscles during the first reading: it is only at this stage that MEPs can amend and significantly influence the parameters of a proposal. At the second reading they can merely reject a proposal, so laying themselves open to the charge of negative action. Hence, in order to point to a record of achievement, the EP has a vested interest in acting constructively. Denied a formal right of legislative initiative, it has had to rely on the Commission both to take up its 'own initiative' proposals or to collude with it at the various stages of the cooperation procedure.

By contrast, the Council appears to retain the upper hand. It can overrule EP amendments or delay action so that time makes them obsolete. However, the EP has already proved able to find some weak points in the Council's armoury. The Council may at times have little incentive to act constructively unless it is anxious to deter MEPs from rejecting a proposal at second reading, or wants to see legislation passed quickly. Even if it stresses urgency, success may not be guaranteed. Early experiences of the new system suggest that the Council may have to be more accommodating towards EP amendments and involvement, especially when under pressure of time.

Member governments can, of course, easily hinder a piece of legislation's progress during the first reading. Irrespective of deadlines, a government unhappy with either the principle or the content of a proposal could simply reject the setting of a deadline for the first reading. This is of critical importance since deadlines only become operative after the Council has adopted its common position. Theoretically, the EP could refer the lack of action to the Court of Justice, but this is not a remedy that can be used on a daily basis. A threat of legal action with the attendant implications of delay could, however, prove powerful if carefully used.

All this highlights the importance of effective follow-up action by the EP at all stages. Close scrutiny of the Council and better organisation and management of the EP's own business, a keener selection of political priorities, and a more important role for its own committees are essential. The EP will have to prioritise issues and be able to muster the requisite majorities behind them to ensure the credibility of its positions which in turn must be internally consistent. Its new rules facilitate this.

The co-operation procedure therefore provides the mechanism through which the EP can exercise a greater degree of co-respon-sibility in legislation with the Council than hitherto. Whether it will want to claim co-responsibility will depend on the extent to which it is able to influence the content of legislation. And that in turn depends upon the willingness of the Commission to co-operate with the EP. The Commission is not obliged in the second reading to accept EP amendments. Morever, the member states retain ample opportunities to halt progress on the problematic area of the com-pletion of the internal market, either by seeking or unilaterally invoking derogations or 'safeguard clauses' in harmonisation measures. Moreover, the 1992 deadline lacks automatic legal effect. Even so, MEPs have acted as if genuine co-operation is the name of the game: Opinions emitted before 1987 on issues that become sub-ject to the co-operation procedure have been put forward for processing as part of a first reading. The outcome is still awaited, but provides a testing ground for interinstitutional collaboration.

Effective EP action demands good information exchange between it and the Commission and Council, both of whom have privately agreed to provide EP committees with relevant documentation. The onus for allowing the EP to act as a co-equal in the co-operation procedure falls on the Council and the Commission. Both will need to reconsult the EP if changed circumstances or the passage of time alter the nature of proposal, or if the Commission wishes to withdraw the initial proposal upon which the EP has delivered its Opinion and replace it with another text. While the new procedures do not demand such additional consultation, it must become the norm for the system to be effective.

The EP can, of course, use a range of negative sanctions to exact compliance, especially during the second reading and follow-up stages: the censure motion remains a possibility; a conciliation procedure could be convened; a budget veto could be threatened. All would be contrary to the spirit of the co-operation procedure, whereas a threat to reject a proposal at second reading unless the Commission and Council accommodate the EP's views could be productive. Council members broadly in favour of a Commission proposal enjoying EP support might be inclined to lobby waverers in order to obtain the necessary majority for its approval. Informally, MEPs may pressurise national parties and Parliaments for the same end. Collusion between Council and EP could also be useful in persuading a waverer to change sides and so prevent the attainment of unanimity or a qualified majority in the Council.

Informal knowledge of governmental positions could clearly be useful to the EP. However, care would be needed to ensure that a government did not use the argument that, for instance, it could not back the proposal before the Council unless the EP's views were accommodated as a ruse to disguise a national veto. Governments could be tempted to employ such covert vetos, especially if they were reasonably sure that they could use this façade in situations where at least one other government was more forthright in its opposition to the measure. Less damage might be done to the public image of a government keen on vetoing or frustrating a proposal if it could credibly pretend that its action was inspired by the laudable democratic aim of ensuring that the views of the elected parliamentary majority be given due weight. The danger is that rhetorical Europeans could multiply. Only if a government committed itself from the outset to backing only those proposals enjoying EP support could it escape the accusation of invoking a disguised veto.

A further disguised veto for the Council lies in another procedural device which could have the effect of emasculating EP inputs. If enough governments refuse to indicate a position on a proposal incorporating some of the EP's amendments, and so deter the proposal being put to the vote in the Council, or prevent the attainment of the required majorities, the proposal will lapse: the EP's efforts will have been nullified, and MEPs denied any redress.

On paper, the EP's ability to influence a proposal during the second reading seems negligible. Its incentive for seeking compromise with the Council is correspondingly heightened. A less than optimal solution may result, but that may be better than nothing, especially as it may be more to the liking of some member governments which otherwise might have found themselves in a losing minority in the Council. It is not inconceivable that on occasions there may be a Council–EP alliance that could oblige the Commission to redraft its proposal. Follow up by the EC is critical.

There are other areas where there is scope for tension between institutions. These relate to foreign affairs, where the EP has a strong interest but limited powers. The EP will surely insist on its voice being heard and its views accommodated whenever new financial measures are envisaged and in respect of the annual review of the financial protocols that form part of the agreements with third countries. The EP's interest and high profile in external relations may encourage it to try to exert more overt and effective influence over foreign affairs, loosely construed, than in the past. This means that there is further room for inter-institutional conflict, not least because of the high regard many countries have for the EP: MEPs can make political capital out of this regard.

If the co-operation procedure is to be successful, informal links between EP, Commission, and Council will also be critical. With a view to promoting effective liaison, the three institutions are to provide each other with lists of the officials responsible for each proposal under the co-operation procedure. This practice is bound to lead to pressure for it becoming a routine part of all Community decision-making, as is the pressure for fixing a monthly legislative timetable.

The SEA and the co-operation procedure must be seen as a step forward in the longer process of reforming EC decision-making. The co-operation procedure politicises decision-making and affects the prevailing inter-institutional balance. The EP will continue the strategies that it has pursued since 1979 to advance its legislative ambitions in order to realise co-equal bicameral status with a constrained Council, and a more federal Union. The longer term demands the exercise of effective supranational parliamentary controls over the initiation and passage of legislation, given the virtual exclusion of national Parliaments from EC decision-making and their weakness over governments whose ambition and authority in the EC have not been (by their own design) sufficiently controlled at the supranational level.

The SEA's seemingly narrow perspectives and goals raise major institutional and policy issues that require urgent attention by the EC's main institutions and by national governments and administrations. The Commission is keen to promote progress on six major targets set by the SEA: the internal market, economic and social cohesion, research and technology, the European Monetary System, the social area, and the environment (see Cecchini 1988; Pelkmans and Winters 1988). These objectives are to be obtained by adapting the CAP to the new world agricultural trade context, developing both policies with real economic impact and sufficient, stable and guaranteed own resources, and imposing effective budgetary discipline. None can be achieved by the SEA alone.

However, the co-operation procedure does not tackle intrinsic institutional problems in the Community. It attempts to improve relations between the supranational institutions by engineering situations in which accommodation is essential. This rather crude instrument is typical in many respects of the approach to problem-solving in the Community: a goal is established, in rather broad terms, and those responsible for its attainment are left to work out how and when it should be implemented, often on an *ad hoc* or trial and error basis. This has the advantage of flexibility, but also the concomitant disadvantage of being expensive in terms of time and optimal or rational decision-making. So far, new technologies coupled with the desire of the most supranational institutions to develop an effective working relationship have expedited the necessary interaction among the Community institutions. Even so, traditional difficulties in these multinational administrations will not disappear overnight. Rather, those charged with managing the co-operation procedure have had to respond in a way that can help the institution to which they are attached maximise its role.

There is little indication that this has been replicated at the national and regional levels of government where intra-organisational communication is not as effective as it must be if responses within the member states to the policy challenges and opportunities are to be met promptly and effectively. This would require reform both of vertical and horizontal responses and of the psychological predispositions of those involved. At all levels of government, it is clear that the lack of precision that attends the prescription of EC policy goals makes for confusion in policy execution and implementation. While it is possible to develop appropriate institutional mechanisms to deal with technical issues over the longer term, anything that is seen to be novel is interpreted differently according to the particularistic interests of those involved. The lack of apparent accord over the Community's *raison d'être* also means that in the national setting the true extent of integration implied by new or redefined goals is often exaggerated, misinterpreted, or underestimated. The implications of the realisation of the single European market for law and order issues, invironmental protection, health, welfare, education and training have eluded the comprehension of many governments. The lack of some broader vision of how the member states and the EC 'fit' together inhibits and compounds the problems of rational policy-making.

Consequently, it may be suggested that the EC institutions are only appropriate to certain tasks. The ways in which policy is initiated and formulated may be far from ideal. Definition of the ideal depends on the institutional perspective adopted. Policy implementation and execution occur with varying degrees of speed, and governments will continue to prefer directives over regulations since the former unintentionally permit delay and wide deviations in interpreting and implementing the policy goals. Moreover, haphazard decision-taking within the national and regional administrative machines means that effective policy co-ordination remains elusive, with potentially unintended and 'irrational' costly roll-on effects. Information gathering can be equally haphazard and poor, with similar results. Not only can this increase the room for private sector interests to fill the deficit with biased information; one result could well be a very muddy picture of what a given region's or state's interest is. This in turn has implications for effective inter-state as well as intra-state bargaining.

Furthermore, as yet, public participation in EC policy areas has been minimal. It may not, and perhaps must not, be so in the future. The signs are that EC decision-making will become increasingly politicised and public. Council secretiveness will be attacked and the issue of which institution should perform what role will be evaluated not simply in terms of institutional effectiveness and appropriateness but in terms of democratic precepts traditionally associated with ideas of representative government.

Transformation and adaptation may be leitmotifs in the policy-making environment. However, from the point of view of European integration, the SEA confirms the symbiotic nature of the relationship between the member states and the EC itself. The EC is founded on a dual legitimacy, of the states and the EC. Consultation, co-operation, and collaboration are imperative if the EC is to realise its goals and to withstand the economic and technological challenges from without. Inter-institutional co-operation will be needed across a wide range of policies, both those subject to the co-operation procedure and those falling under the old procedure, to avoid being hamstrung by nervous or wary governments and scarce financial resources. However, it is clear that unless inter-institutional under-standing permits a constructive operation of the co-operation procedure, progress towards the Grand Rendezvous, making the EC a common economic area, and genuine co-decision in all EC decision-making will prove elusive. In that case, the SEA would be a very small step rather than a qualitative advance in European integration. The imperatives of realising the Single European market, with all that means for expanding policy competence, highlight the need for reform of the institutions and their relationships at all levels.

REFERENCES AND FURTHER READING

Beuter, R. and Tsakaloyannis, P. (eds). (1987) *Experiences in Regional Cooperation* (Maastricht: European Institute of Public Administration).

Butler, Sir M. (1986) *Europe: More Than A Continent* (London: Heinemann).

Cecchini, P. (1988) 1992: *The Benefits of a Single Market* (Aldershot: Wildwood House).

De Vree, J. K., Coffey, P. and Lauwaars, R. H. (eds.) (1987) *Towards a European Foreign Policy* (Dordrecht: Nijhoff).

Hine, R. (1985) *The Political Economy of European Trade* (Brighton: Wheatsheaf).

Ifestos, P (1987) *European Political Cooperation: towards a framework of international diplomacy* (Aldershot: Avebury)

Jenkins, R. (ed.) (1983) *Britain and the EEC* (London: Macmillan).

Leonard, D. (1988) *Pocket Guide to the European Community* (Oxford: Blackwell).

Lodge, J. (ed.) (1986) *European Union: The European Community in Search of a Future* (London: Macmillan).

Lodge, J. (ed.) (1989) *The European Community and the Challenge of the Future* (London: Pinter).

Pelkmans, J. and Winters, A. (1988) *Europe's Domestic Market* (London: Routledge).

Pryce, R. (ed.) (1987) *The Dynamics of European Union* (London: Croom Helm).

Tugendhat, C. (1986) *Making Sense of Europe* (London: Macmillan).

Wallace, H. Wallace, W. Webb, C. (eds.) (1983) *Policy-making in the European Community* (London: Wiley).

CHAPTER ELEVEN
The Consolidation of New Democracies

Richard Gillespie

Following a decade that saw the demise of dictatorships and transitions to democracy in southern Europe, the 1980s witnessed less spectacular but equally momentous developments as the new regimes became more consolidated. A process that brought greater political homogeneity to Western Europe was bound to draw more attention to the countries of the northern Mediterranean, and interest in the region also grew as a result of economic and geostrategic trends. Increasing economic integration brought southern and northern Europe closer together, their interdependence consolidated by the entry of Greece (in 1981) and Spain and Portugal (in 1986) into the European Community. Meanwhile, the southern countries acquired a greater strategic significance too with the rise of militant Islam in neighbouring regions and tentative moves by some Mediterranean Socialist governments to break with established pro-Western foreign and defence policies.

The transitions to democracy during the 1970s were varied, though they possessed some common features. Military behaviour was the main variable affecting the patterns of democratic transition. This is hardly surprising given that the Iberian regimes headed by Franco, Salazar and Caetano, like the Colonels' regime in Greece, had been principally based upon the armed forces, even though the military's presence in government varied from country to country.[1] Portugal's transition differed through being initiated by a military rebellion that opened the way for a powerful revolutionary process. Unwinnable colonial wars in Mozambique, Angola, and Guinea-Bissau provided the catalyst that helped produce the military coup of 25 April 1974. Though the subsequent advance of the civilian left was checked after the turbulent events of mid-1975, the military were to play an important and direct role in Portuguese politics until the 1980s, acting as guardians of the 'conquests of the revolution'. Only gradually did the political parties manage to become dominant: institutionalised military influence persisted until the Council of the Revolution was abolished in 1982, and another four years were to elapse before the new polity gained its first civilian President in the form of Mario Soares.

The story was rather different in Greece and Spain. After a far shorter period of authoritarian rule than the other countries experienced, Greece became democratic by way of a reaction against the domestic and foreign policy failures of a military junta installed only in 1967. So isolated from society had that junta become as a result of these failures, and so humiliated was it by the Turkish invasion of Cyprus in 1974, that the military was left in no position to influence greatly the subsequent course of events. Political party élites were thus dominant in shaping the features of the Greek transition to democracy right from the start.

The same could not be said of Spain, where the military had suffered no defeat; indeed it still celebrated its victory in the Civil War. There an army which was hostile to change had to be persuaded to accept democracy, for the anti-Franco forces were never strong or united enough to impose a decisive *ruptura democrática* of the kind that sectors of the left had hoped for. To gain the upper hand in Spain, civilian forces had to rely upon the military's sense of hierarchy and discipline (in particular, its loyalty to King Juan Carlos), repeated demonstrations of moderation by the political parties, and the promise and allocation of more resources to the armed forces. Even so, there were several military conspiracies against the new regime, and the threat that these posed was a major constraint on policy-making for several years.

The political party picture was rather more unified than the military situation. While it is true that dissimilar party systems have evolved in Greece, Portugal, and Spain, it is the common features rather than the differences that are the most striking: the dominant roles played by centre–right and centre–left parties competing for a mass of votes clustered around the centre of the political spectrum; the move away from radicalism by the Socialist parties; the decline of the Communist parties from their earlier position as pre-eminent resistance forces; the difficulties encountered by Conservative parties seeking to modernise themselves; the failure of the far right to survive in the electoral arena; the adoption by most successful parties of 'catch-all' tactics, designed to win the support of a broad range of voters; and the strong flavour of personalised politics, with success going to charismatic leaders (Constantine Karamanlis, Andreas Papandreou, Adolfo Suárez, Felipe González) or at least to popular figures known for their patriotism or industry (Ramalho Eanes, Anibal Cavaco e Silva).

In all three countries the political parties played an important and often crucial part in the process of democratisation. However, it would be unjust to attribute solely to the parties the achievement of a high degree of political stability during the transition. In the Iberian countries the head of state intervened decisively at moments of crisis, and in Spain, particularly, interest groups also helped to in-stitutionalise potentially conflictual relationships. Thus when the second Suárez government, elected in 1979, began to experience in-ternal dissension and to lose direction and authority, the Socialist union confederation (UGT) and the main employers' association, the Spanish Confederation of Employers' Organisations (CEOE), contributed to the stabilisation of the new order by negotiating an agreed framework for industrial relations. And when part of the army threatened to seize power on 23 February 1981, King Juan Carlos's repudiation of the attempted coup helped rally the more professional officers to the defence of the constitution.

An important reason for the considerable stability surrounding the transitions is that the early political arrangements gave a measure of protection to interests that had been accommodated under the pre-vious regime and which now felt vulnerable. Clearly this is less true of the Portuguese case, where a real revolution led to the departure of landowners, industrial barons, and senior military personnel. Yet even there the old *political* class managed to survive right through the democratic transition. The substantial powers enjoyed initially by the Spanish king and the Greek and Portuguese presidents provided some guarantee against excessive radicalism, as did the initial setting of a high minimum voting age in Greece and Spain, which left young workers and students without influence. In Spain and Greece purges of those involved in the previous authoritarian regimes were either absent or extremely restricted, and most politicians tainted by an authoritarian past were given every opportunity to adapt to the democratic system. The right-of-centre complexions of the transition governments provided further reassurance to elements of the old regime. So too, in a sense, did the military in Portugal, for although part of the armed forces had become left-wing and populist, most officers remained committed to authority and public order: they reacted against the insurgent disorder of mid-1975 and any hint of a return to it.

However, the involvement of conservative old-regime elements during the transitions did not simply facilitate the process of democratisation: it also influenced its outcome, and in the process created problems for democratic consolidation in the 1980s. For although the new regimes have become more stable, they possess certain characteristics that are inimical to democratic values, such as a high concentration of power in the executive — as opposed to a clear separation of the executive, legislative, and judicial powers — and fairly authoritarian political establishments, remote from civil society. These characteristics may well be allowed to persist in the name of maintaining stability.

TRANSITION AND CONSOLIDATION

Analytically it is not difficult to differentiate between transition and consolidation as stages in the evolution from authoritarian regimes to democracies. During the former, the 'basic institutions of the new political order are organized and begin to work and interact according to new rules of the game'. Consolidation, which tends to take longer, requires the 'institutionalization of the new regime's norms and structures, the extension of its legitimacy, and the removal of the obstacles that, in its initial phases, make its establishment difficult'. More specifically, it has been described as embracing four processes: the emergent regime's elimination, reduction to a minimum or incorporation of its initial ideological and institutional inconsistencies; the establishment of its autonomy *vis-à-vis* the old established powers, especially the armed forces; its mobilisation of civil society into political forms of expression; and its development of a relatively stable party system, capable of guaranteeing popularly accountable government (O'Donnell *et al.* 1986: 73, 89).

Of course, in real life these processes lack clearly demarcated boundaries and it is particularly difficult to state with any great confidence precisely when each of them ends. The fact that in practice there is a degree of temporal overlap between the processes makes the picture rather confused. None the less, it is possible to isolate the most significant shifts within the democratisation processes of southern Europe and to see the 1980s very much as a decade of consolidation. Greece's transition commenced in 1974 with the fall of the Colonels, and a new constitution was in place as early as 1975. The late 1970s, though, were still very much part of the period of transition, for the military command was not reorganised and placed completely under civilian authority until 1977, and it could be argued that in a historical and symbolic sense either the election of Karamanlis as president in 1980 or the country's accession to the European Community (EC) a year later marked the real end of the transition. Karamanlis in 1974 had appeared as something of a providential leader who would steer Greece back towards democracy: 'Karamanlis or the tanks' had been the dominant election theme of that year, and his New Democracy (ND) party in government had later relied heavily upon him for popular support. Moreover, the whole debate about the kind of post-authoritarian system that Greece was to have was intimately bound up with differing attitudes to EC membership; especially for ND, the idea of 'belonging to Europe' involved having a liberal society and capitalist economy at home.

Portugal's transition began in the same year and a new constitution was promulgated in 1976. However, there is a case for taking 1982, the year of the first constitutional revision, as the end of the transitional phase. Parts of the original document had been deliberately provisional, and in particular it had been understood that the military would possess an institutionalised political role only during the early uncertain years. Spain's transition only moved into forward drive in mid-1976 when the new king appointed Suárez as prime minister. To regard 1979 as the end of the Spanish transition, following the promulgation of the constitution the previous December and the first general election under it the following March, would be to ignore the importance of the regional question in Spain. Technically speaking, the new institutional arrangements were not completed until 1983, when mainland Spain's map of 'autonomous communities' was finalised, although there is a case for taking 1980, the year of the first regional elections in the Basque country and Catalonia (where historical claims to autonomy are most solidly based), as the real turning-point.

The consolidation of the new Mediterranean regimes did not simply occur after these events: rather it began to get under way during the transitional phase, at least as early as the first elections under the new constitutional arrangements. It was not a progressively cumulative process. Some extremely hazardous situations had to be negotiated, such as in Portugal in 1978–79, when President Eanes appointed three successive non-party governments because of the inability of the political parties to form a viable government. Above all, there was the Spanish drama of 23 February 1981, when tanks rolled in the streets and shots were fired in the Cortes. The abortive military coup, eventually frustrated by the king, was more than a hazard for the new regime to surmount: it actually persuaded the democrats to retreat. Shaken by the extent of military involvement in the coup attempt, an elected government and the main opposition party felt obliged to try to claw back some of the autonomy recently granted to the Basque and Catalan regions, presenting this as a 'harmonisation' of the devolution process, and they also made concessions to military hard-liners in the field of counter-insurgency measures.

Democratic consolidation advanced greatly when the new regimes experienced their first 'peaceful rotation of previous opposition parties in power'. This 'critical threshold' in democratisation (O'Donnell *et al.* 1986: 9), reached by Portugal in 1979, by Greece in 1981, and by Spain one year later, was highly important in providing the new democratic regimes with legitimacy and removing doubts about how *de facto* powers might react, particularly in the Spanish case. In Greece and Spain the electoral shifts of the early 1980s constituted historic turning-points, for both gave rise to the first ever victories for their country's Socialist party. The triumph of the Panhellenic Socialist Movement (PASOK) increased the sociological breadth of the Greek political class, while the landslide victory of the Spanish Socialist Workers' Party (PSOE) meant that for the first time since the end of Francoism a party had absolute control over both houses of Parliament. By 1979 in Portugal, there was no question of a Conservative alliance being prevented from taking office, but the Democratic Alliance's arrival in government at least showed voters that a Conservative alternative was electorally viable under the post-revolutionary regime.

Although these elections were key turning-points, democratisation still had a long way to go. By the start of the 1980s there were still doubts about whether democracy was becoming really rooted in society and to what extent political cultures were changing. At the level of attitudes and associational membership, the early enthusiasm for democracy had declined and there were definite signs of 'disenchantment' in Iberia. Moreover, it was still too early to regard the new party systems as stable, and the Spanish one was patently unstable. Finally, and especially in Iberia, it was not yet clear whether the traditional established powers, which had been buttresses of authoritarian rule in the past, had come to accept fully civilian dominance and political party rule. True, the Catholic church had been subject to liberal influences in recent years, particularly in Spain, but reactionaries none the less still held influential ecclesiastical posts in the Catholic countries. The churches had changed sufficiently to accept democracy, but it was less certain whether the same could be said of the military.

THE NEW MEDITERRANEAN DEMOCRACIES

Many observers of the new Mediterranean democracies have been initially struck most by the success and prominence of charismatic leaders whose appeal has transcended that of particular political parties. It is of more than anecdotal significance that for most of the 1980s the majority of Greeks and Spaniards referred to their prime ministers by their first names, 'Andreas' and 'Felipe'. Political success in Greece has traditionally been inseparable from charisma, and of course personal qualities can be exploited all the more effectively in the electronic age. Charisma has also been electorally profitable in modern Spain, while in Portugal rather more dour figures have also attracted personal followings as a result of their demonstrated ability.

However, if one looks beyond the élite level to view the new polities in their entirety, it is evident that their distinctiveness derives from their being parliamentary systems within which political parties play an extremely dominant role. During the transitional period, prior to constitutional revision, the Portuguese and Greek regimes were semi-presidential, while in 1976–78 King Juan Carlos in Spain possessed the power to nominate a number of senators and to select prime ministers irrespective of whether they led the largest parliamentary party. These arrangements did not last: before long power became concentrated in a single executive based on the parliamentary outcome of electoral competition. Yet this does not mean that the new assemblies, whether unicameral (Greece and Portugal) or bicameral (Spain), have enjoyed much power of initiative in the new systems. Indeed, by the early 1980s they were being widely accused of merely rubber-stamping the decisions of the executive.

Insufficient resources for members of parliament generally, in Spain the organisation of the parliamentary timetable (allowing back-benchers few possibilities to play an effective role), in Portugal the absence of linkage between deputies and constituents, and above all, in all three countries, the high degree of party discipline and dominance, have together served to undermine the prestige of parliaments[2]. Here the Mediterranean democracies conform to the Western European norm of increasingly weak assemblies and more predominant executives; they have been fully accepted as kith and kin by the other continental democracies. Nevertheless, the new Mediterranean polities differ from their northern counterparts with regard to the *extent* of party dominance.

Party dominance is greater in the south for two reasons. First, the transition from authoritarian rule created new political terrain and power vacuums that parties, because of their potential institutional relationship with the state, were uniquely qualified to occupy and exploit. Second, democratisation has occurred in countries with long histories of state interventionism, not only in the economy but also in areas such as the mass media. Thus occupants of power have enjoyed very extensive opportunities to penetrate and influence civil society. Party dominance has also been enhanced by the emergence of much more solid party systems than those which existed in the pre-authoritarian period. Societal modernisation, electoral engineering, institutional devices, and a determination not to revive practices that rendered early democratisation efforts abortive, have all combined to produce less fragmented party systems, with fewer significant parties and/or less factional strife within them. Generally speaking, anti-system parties do not play a crucial role in the newly democratised countries. The most important party of this type, the Basque country's Herri Batasuna, is strong enough only to influence the composition of the regional government based in Vitoria.

Although one cannot talk of there being a Mediterranean model of democracy, the concentration of power in the hands of party élites is something that the new democracies have in common with Italy[3]. Parties in southern Europe not only dominate state institutions but also seek with some success to 'colonise' or 'populate' other key public and social institutions and agencies as a means of extending their partisan influence. The level of political patronage tends to be much higher than in the northern democracies, and interest groups generally are weak in comparison with the political parties. Many groups lack real independence, having been created by the parties or having entered into dependent relationships with them.

With reference to Italy, it has been argued that the emergence of a strong 'party state' may facilitate the process of democratic consolidation (even if the *quality* of democracy is affected by it): 'It locks voters into stable patterns of allegiance, reducing the pool of voters available for anti-democratic flash parties which may threaten the system, and it provides the base from which established parties can effect compromises with one another in the interests of stable and lasting coalitions' (Hine 1987). However, in Italy the breadth of the ideological spectrum spanning the political parties has tended historically to counteract these potential advantages. In this respect, democratic consolidation may be somewhat easier to accomplish in the case of the more recent Mediterranean regimes, given the relative (and growing) weakness of their Communist parties and the fact that (contrary to the Italian case) Socialist movements in Spain, Greece, and Portugal have so far been largely united and thus have been able to serve as more than effective counterweights to the Communist left, irrespective of whether the latter has undergone a 'Eurocommunist' experience.

Among interest groups, trade unions have generally been the most populous and they have often been less fragmented than employers' associations. This helps to explain why they have managed to exert some influence in the 1980s. Other reasons are their ability to mobilise beyond their fairly small memberships, and in the case of Socialist unions their early honeymoon relationship with Socialist governments. Like the political parties, the trade unions grew enormously in the late 1970s, but then they declined. Apart from the organisational difficulties encountered in integrating rapidly growing memberships, their numbers and strength were hit by the recession and rising unemployment. In this context of economic deterioration, the defence of labour interests was further undermined by the partisan model of trade unionism that prevails in Mediterranean Europe (more distinctly in the Iberian countries than in Greece). This often prevented labour from taking concerted industrial action, though after feeling the effects of harsh economic policies, especially when applied by Socialist governments, Socialist and Communist trade unionists were finally driven to engage in united action during the second half of the 1980s.

Political parties have enjoyed substantial advantages over interest groups. While the funding of the latter tended to be precarious, even in the case of relatively successful unions, the parties received useful financial assistance and recognition from abroad during their difficult period of establishment or emergence from clandestinity. Subsequently, they benefited from state subsidies in proportion to their electoral strength or parliamentary presence. Moreover, the major parties were favoured by new electoral systems which tended to exaggerate their popularity when it came to the distribution of parliamentary seats. Although the new Mediterranean electoral systems vary, and that of Greece is markedly different from those of Iberia, they all share this distortion in practice of what purports to be proportional representation.

Elections in the region are also similar in their employment of party lists of candidates to be opted for *in toto* in each constituency. This excludes independents from parliamentary representation and makes dissidence within parties extremely hazardous for MPs, for their careers thus depend more upon central party authorities than upon the voters. Even in those parties that enjoy some internal democracy, local and regional branches have frequently complained about their nominations being overruled by higher party authorities, and the widespread expulsion of dissenters has been another cause of discontent. Party leaders have defended these practices in the name of unity and 'coherence', though of course internal currents, and not just the party as an electoral competitor, have often had a vested interest in them.

Additional advantages have been available to victorious parties, giving them a good chance to extend their period of dominance. In spite of the electoral success of Socialist parties that pledged to liberalise broadcasting, most recent southern European governments of both right and left have been reluctant to dismantle decades-old state monopolies in this area. Indeed, it has been argued that the partisan exploitation of the electronic media increased in Greece when PASOK came to power in the early 1980s. Meanwhile in Spain the introduction of private television to accompany the existing government-controlled channels was postponed until the late 1980s, by which time the Cavaco e Silva government in Portugal was making similar preparations.

Above all, access to office gave parties the chance to expand by clientelist means: they could recruit members by informally making membership a precondition for certain posts in the civil service, public sector, and any other area subject to public appointment; and this clientele of party loyalists would often be useful in extending party influence further. Here we are not talking about traditional southern European clientelism. Under the latter, party authority was distributed among a series of locally based 'notables' who could deliver votes because of the services they provided to supporters. For this reason, some scholars regard 'clientelism' as a misnomer in the present context, when party patronage is at stake and the role of patron is no longer occupied by an individual (Featherstone and Katsoudas 1987: 271–87; Pridham 1984: 99–118; Tzannatos 1986: 114–129; Mavrogordatos 1983: 7–8).

Irrespective of whether one prefers to describe it as 'clientelism' or as 'machine politics', the phenomenon was accentuated in the 1980s. In Portugal its growth in the late 1970s was less a function of party ambitions to 'colonise' as much public and social space possible, and more one of the huge expansion of the public sector which occurred as a result of the extensive nationalisation of the economy in 1975. However, the public sector quickly became a valued terrain of patronage for successive parties in office, especially as unemployment rose. Not only were there 'top jobs' to fill, and some not quite so elevated, but the security of employment in the public sector generally became an issue that upheld voting for the left and made parties of the right rather cautious about how to raise their proposals for economic liberalisation.

Although detailed information is difficult to obtain in the case of all three countries, it is clear that the level of public appointment greatly increased when the Socialist parties came to power in Greece and Spain in 1981–82. Previous incumbents of office had dispensed patronage but had less to fear from bureaucratic obstructionism than the more left-wing parties had. It is hardly surprising that parties whose electoral promise had been one of 'Change' (the campaign slogan of PASOK and the PSOE alike) should feel a need to make more extensive political appointments in the early 1980s in order to ensure that their policies were actually implemented. This, plus the introduction of new lower-middle-class people into a world hitherto dominated by the old liberal professions in the Greek case, were the justifications put forward for this development. However, with the use of political appointment spreading far and wide, sometimes even to include for example (in Spain) library directors, the phenomenon was bound to become controversial. The fear that gripped some imaginations was of the self-perpetuation in office of a ruling party through co-optation and occasional acts of repression. Left-wing critics in Spain even used the term 'Mexicanisation' to denote the shift in this direction, which seemed all the more threatening because of the lead enjoyed by the Socialists over the other political parties: about 20 percentage points separated the PSOE from its nearest rival in the general elections of 1982 and 1986.

In response to such criticism and to expressions of frustration from career officials, the Spanish government in 1987 finally began to specify which civil service posts mights be obtained 'politically' and which could be obtained only through normal promotion procedures. Also promising to curb the tendency towards the increased use of patronage was the re-election in Portugal in mid-1987 of

Cavaco e Silva's Social Democratic Party (PSD), now with an absolute majority in favour of a programme envisaging the scaling down of the public sector. Even so, it seemed likely that a substantial public sector would remain because of the existence of vested political party interests in its maintenance.

CONSOLIDATION IN THE 1980s

Once the powers of the Spanish monarch and Greek and Portuguese presidents had been reduced, the political parties' main competitors for influence were traditional *de facto* powers such as the military and mainstream church, and the more autonomous and politically oriented of the economic pressure groups. In order to assess the extent of democratic consolidation in the 1980s, further discussion of party relations with these forces is necessary. Equally, given the centrality of political parties in the new regimes, it is important to look at the extent to which the new party systems have become stable. And finally, even if the available evidence is rather limited, some attempt must be made to evaluate how successful the new regimes have been in putting down roots in society.

The subordination of the military to civilian authority began in the 1970s but uncertainties persisted into the 1980s. Civilian ascendancy was favoured by the dominance of democracy in Europe and the southern Europeans' determination to join the EC. Although previous authoritarian governments had been able to secure preferential trade agreements with the Community, democratic government had always been insisted upon as a precondition of membership. Once the new democracies had joined the Community, the southern European military's new sense of being politically circumscribed was reinforced, especially since the immediate economic impact of membership was positive. It was abundantly clear to the military that there could be no reversion to authoritarianism without provoking a strong European reaction.

Civilian dominance was established earliest in Greece, where the army was the most discredited. There was no significant military reaction against PASOK'S electoral victory in 1981. Here an improvement in civilian–military relations was facilitated by the persistence of tension between Greece and Turkey, which guaranteed the existence of a large defence budget and provided a 'nationalist' basis for Greek unity (Clogg 1983: 173–83; Featherstone and Katsoudas 1987: 214–52). Besides, a substantial gap had opened up between the Greek Socialists' policies and their semi-Marxist and Third-World-oriented prescriptions of previous years. Anti-NATO rhetoric and pledges to secure the removal of US bases from Greek territory had been extremely prominent in PASOK's election campaign. However, once in office Papandreou's party decided that — especially in the economic sphere — Greece had too much to lose from pursuing a foreign policy that would be perceived as 'anti-Western'. Thus the relationship with NATO remained the same and the government concentrated on improving the terms upon which the US bases would remain. This decision not to upset radically Western defence plans, combined with the near absence of a domestic terrorist problem, also helped to maintain the army's resolve to abstain from direct intervention in political life.

A similar reluctance to risk antagonising the leading Western countries was also present in Spain. As in the case of Greece with Turkey, it was feared that an excessively independent foreign policy might produce a reaction beneficial to a national rival. The González government was concerned that the US-backed Moroccan monarchy might be tempted to seize the Spanish North African enclaves of Ceuta and Melilla in the event of a decision to terminate the agreement on US bases made under Franco, or to withdraw from NATO. However, on both of these issues the Spanish Socialists' option for accommodation with the United States had more to do with a desire to maintain existing trade links and political stability, as well as access to new technology.

Military–civilian relations in Spain improved as a result of increases in military funding and the first González government's volte-face over the question of NATO membership, the PSOE earlier having stood for Spain's withdrawal. However, relations with the military were complicated by the controversy surrounding regional devolution and the related persistence of separatist violence and uncertainty about the future of the Basque country. The army feared that devolution would lead to the dismemberment of the Spanish state whose unity it had an official duty to defend, and violent attacks on military personnel by the Basque separatist organisation, ETA, were a regular reminder of this unacceptable scenario and a reason to see democratic government as weak. Until 1982 military discontent was sufficiently widespread to support various conspiracies, including the near success of 1981. Thereafter, however, defiance of the constitution was voiced only by isolated officers.

The Socialists' pragmatic policies did much to placate the military. By negotiating seriously with the moderately nationalist Basque and Catalan regional authorities, the González government managed to reduce the tensions surrounding the territorial issue. Meanwhile, ETA suffered serious reverses, particularly as a result of new extradition agreements with France, where the separatists had their leadership and logistical bases. The government even earned some military respect as a result of the firmness with which it acted against insubordinate right-wing officers, breaking with the weak precedent set by the Union of the Democratic Centre (UCD) governments. The Socialists were able to implement some significant military reforms without major opposition, though they did hold back from revising the contents of officer-training programmes until 1989.

Civilian ascendancy over the military advanced even more surely in Portugal. In 1982 the armed forces abandoned their institutional presence in the new regime without resistance, although they were disappointed by the absence of any expression of party gratitude for their role in bringing democracy to the country. Some democrats were alarmed by the subsequent creation by former leaders of the revolution of an 'April 25th Association' to defend its ideas, but this pressure group soon showed itself to be supportive of the new institutions, if critical of certain policies (Bruneau and Macleod 1986: Ch. 1). The only remaining possible avenue for extraordinary yet legitimate military influence in the regime, once a civilian president had been elected in 1986, was electoral success by the new Democratic Renewal Party (PRD). This was a pro-Eanes populist party that enjoyed some military backing. However, the party suffered a shattering defeat in the general election of mid-1987, prompting Eanes to resign from its presidency.

The ending of national isolationism also contributed to the advance of democratic consolidation at the level of civilian–military relations. European integration, sealed with entry to the EC, brought the northern Mediterranean more fully into a world in which military rule was frowned upon as anachronistic and where democratic stability was the valued norm. Membership of NATO provided no guarantee of democratic survival,[4] as the Turkish military intervention of 1980 had shown, but southern European membership was relevant to the process of consolidation in that it presupposed the allocation of greater resources to the military which was in clear need of modernisation. It thus underpinned an important means of placating, or isolating, potential military subversives.

Meanwhile, having defended authoritarian rule in the past, the traditionally established churches now generally sought an accommodation with the new democracies. In all three countries they opposed, and attempted to mobilise their supporters against, the liberalisation of family law, yet in each case they dropped their agitation when their opposition proved futile. The Spanish Roman Catholic and Greek Orthodox churches could not really afford to antagonise progressive governments unreasonably, given their heavy financial dependence on the state. Besides, they had at least managed to conserve some influence and a semi-official status under the new political arrangements (Catholic church influence in Portugal is notably weaker). In the mid-1980s the Papandreou government announced plans to nationalise church lands in Greece, thus threatening to increase further church dependence on the state, but within a couple of years and after religious protests reconciliation was made possible by means of a partial government climb-down. Similarly, relations with the Spanish church were restored as a result of concessions made by the González government. During 1987 the Spanish Ambassador to the Vatican was replaced in response to Catholic church criticism of his 'Marxist' views, and the government also decided to ease the church's dependence by enabling taxpayers to allocate a certain percentage of their personal taxes to their church. No doubt these were signs of the important new Catholic presence within the traditionally anticlerical PSOE, half of whose members were holders of religious beliefs by the mid-1980s.

Overall, then, while there are distinct signs of the *de facto* powers retaining influence, particularly in Spain, there has been a marked advance by the specifically political élites. This would not have been possible without the emergence of a degree of stability in the new party systems. The most stable so far has been that of Greece. There, following the decline of the centre parties, most loyalties have become polarised around two parties, ND on the right and PASOK on the centre–left. New Democracy's departure from government in 1981 was the result of a leadership problem (following the election of Karamanlis to the presidency) and of the party's inability to break with traditional methods and become a modern, organised, mass party. Meanwhile PASOK advanced, chiefly by occupying some of the political space once associated with the old Centre Union. With the smaller third party of the Greek system, the Communist KKE, anchored to a narrow Stalinist position, PASOK was able to poach for votes in the centre without losing support on its left flank.

In contrast, Spain's party system has been in constant evolution, at least since 1979, with successive general election results suggesting the existence of different types of system. During the late 1970s and early 1980s this was less a result of electoral volatility than of intra-party crisis. Internal party conflicts often started when electorally-minded leaderships began to pursue 'catch-all' tactics, aimed at a broad range of voters — an approach that many of the more doctrinaire members found unpalatable. Only the Socialists managed to overcome these conflicts without splintering. Benefiting from crises affecting the parties to its immediate right and left (the UCD and the Communists), the PSOE was able to attain a position of great dominance at the general election of 1982, when the previous Socialist vote almost doubled. The Socialists' 48 per cent of the popular vote left them 22 percentage points ahead of the conservative Popular Alliance and this huge lead was substantially maintained in 1986. However, the suggestion that Spain was acquiring a 'predominant' party system with the PSOE in charge looked questionable by 1986–87. The advance of Suárez's young Social and Democratic Centre (CDS) party in the general election of 1986, together with major school, student, and worker protests and Socialist electoral slippage in the local, regional and European elections the following year, all placed the PSOE's ascendancy in doubt.

Portugal meanwhile suffered far greater governmental instability, with seventeen governments being formed between 1974 and 1987 and none lasting longer than two years. Though polling figures remained remarkably high, this instability gave rise to doubts about the effectiveness of the new institutional arrangements. None the less, there was a fair degree of stability between 1976 and 1985 at the level of the party system. It was consistently dominated by four major parties which for much of the period experienced a stable rank-ing of their electoral performances (Socialists, Social Democrats, Communists, Centre Social Democrats). Shifting party alliances were the main key to governmental variation. In 1985 the dramatic success of the new PRD, largely achieved at the expense of the Socialists, threatened to transform the picture, but this maverick party soon proved to have insufficient internal cohesion to last (Bruneau and Macleod 1986; Gallagher 1986). A more definite turning-point in Portuguese politics occurred in 1987, when for the first time since the revolution a party gained an absolute majority in an election. Cavaco e Silva's PSD took the credit for economic improvements that owed much to earlier austerity measures implemented by Soares and recent falls in the dollar and the price of oil; the electorate at last also showed itself to be voting for continuity, and punished the PRD for provoking yet another early election.

Thus, of the three party systems only the Greek seemed to have become settled by the late 1980s. Even in Greece, though, the continued success of PASOK was by no means assured. Quite apart from governmental performance, the party was, and remains, vulnerable in two respects. First, although it is relatively well organised in national terms, PASOK is highly dependent for its broad appeal upon the charisma of one man, Papandreou; and second, its electorate is potentially unstable, given its broad extension across social boundaries and over the urban/rural divide. By the mid-1980s PASOK had sunk its earlier differences with the Socialist International, yet many of its voters were supporting the party on entirely non-Socialist grounds.

After a decade of democratisation, then, a number of uncertainties still surrounded the southern European party systems. In spite of them, consolidation of the new polities advanced. Sooner or later, firm majority government become feasible in Greece, Spain and Portugal and the legitimacy of governments became accepted by virtually all the opposition forces. Extremist forces generally lost ground and only in the case of the radical Basque party, Herri Batasuna, did an unequivocally anti-system force actually grow in popularity. Its combined vote with the Basque left Euskadiko Ezkerra party rose in regional elections from 23 per cent in 1984 to 28 per cent in 1986. Meanwhile, the main opposition parties often played a contructive role. It is thought by some that the Spanish Socialists' censure motion against the Suárez government in 1980 helped create the atmosphere of crisis that encouraged military conspirators to move early in 1981, yet the aftermath of the coup saw the opposition forming a common front with the government in defence of democracy. There have also been several instances of opposition parties lending governments their support over the implementation of unpalatable economic measures.

The question that remains to be addressed is whether the 1980s have seen the new regimes becoming more firmly rooted in society. Clearly, old political cultures do not die overnight. In the Iberian countries, as a legacy of prolonged authoritarian rule, many people are still reluctant to become involved in political or trade union activity, though the PSOE's membership did revive when the party began enjoying the fruits of office. On the other hand, traditional corporatism is still a problem for democratic governments: from time to time their authority has been disputed by middle-class professional groups possessing a strong sense of corporate identity and feeling that they should govern in matters affecting their own professions. Corporate resistance from within the medical profession has undermined the initial designs for national health services, while civil service obduracy has been a major explanation of the lack of reform of public administration.

Difficult as it is to measure, the vitality of associationalism is an important indicator of whether a new kind of political culture is emerging in southern Europe. Here, in relation to population, the Greek situation is in some respects the healthiest. While by the mid-1980s PASOK had a membership on a par with those of the leading parties of the more populous Iberian countries, Greece's non-civil service trade unions embraced about one-third of the workers and employees, compared with Iberian union membership rates of only 10–15 per cent of the workforce.[5] What is probably relevant here is the relative brevity of the most recent authoritarian period: 7 years in Greece compared with almost 40 in Spain and almost 50 in Portugal.

On the other hand, Greece's tradition of state intervention in society has greatly conditioned the development of interest groups. Many recent groups owe their origin to party initiative, and even the more established unions find it difficult to play an independent role (which may explain a low level of member participation). Twice during the first half of the 1980s, the Papandreou government intervened in the General Confederation of Greek Workers and Employees (GSEE) to ensure the dominance in its leadership of broadly sympathetic elements. First it acted to put an end to decades of Conservative control (based on the representation of a large number of small unions); later, it recognised an alternative, supportive Socialist executive after the previous leadership of dissident Socialists and Communists had resisted an austerity programme introduced in 1985. Papandreou's government also made it difficult for public sector employees to go on strike legally.

The Spanish and Portuguese unions claimed a similar level of affiliation (that is, about one-third) within a few years of the change of regime, but from the late 1970s their memberships declined dramatically. This may be readily understandable in Portugal, where centre–right administrations predominated, yet in Spain it occurred under a nominally Socialist government which enjoyed greater dominance than PASOK enjoyed in Greece. Committed to neo-liberal economic policies from the start, the early González administrations presided over mounting unemployment, while facilitating a major increase in temporary work contracts. Both were detrimental to the unions, whose declining affiliation levels may also have been a result of workers realising that they could enjoy the fruits of collective bargaining without becoming union members.

Government policies in Spain tended to give the impression that associations such as the employers' CEOE were influential. The reality was that although the González governments received accolades from the representatives of capitalism for implementing austere economic policies which a Conservative government would have found difficult to introduce, organized employers' influence was almost as much undermined here as it was in Greece and Portugal by a markedly fragmented structure of representation. In broad design, government policy was influenced by international economic realities and the highly technocratic composition of the González administrations, rather than by the pressures emanating from domestic economic élites.

Of course, the emergence of a more democratic political culture cannot be appraised simply in quantitative terms (and it should be remembered that trade union affiliation was also in decline in other parts of Europe at this time). What is important is that some southern European interest groups began to act assertively on behalf of their members, with considerable protection for their activities being provided by the new constitutions, and that on a few occasions they actually managed to influence the decision-making process. To differing extents, the trade unions at least did manage to play such a role during the 1980s. Indeed, because organisationally they were less fragmented than the employers' associations, and since they possessed a capacity occasionally to mobilise beyond their memberships, the southern European labour movements arguably exerted rather more influence than some of their northern European counterparts.

Initially, the Socialist unions in Greece and Spain were extremely supportive of the new Socialist governments. Although the latter were to prove disappointing as champions of social justice, they at least acted early on to consolidate trade union rights similar to those enjoyed by labour movements in other European countries. The Portuguese context was different, yet even when faced with centre–right governments the fairly new and mainly Socialist UGT favoured a moderate, conciliatory, participative approach, thus offering an alternative to the militant Communist-dominated CGTP.[6]

However, when the Socialist governments' economic and labour policies began to bite, there was growing working–class pressure on the unions to become more confrontational. Militancy in the mid-1980s seems to have helped curtail the harshest period of austerity in Greece. In Spain, meanwhile, it probably persuaded the government to accept slightly higher inflation targets than otherwise would have been adopted, and it enabled the UGT to secure a pledge that there would be no further weakening of job security.

One reason why union militancy may have achieved most in Spain is that in 1987–88 it was accompanied by the school student unrest and included middle-class professional agitation as well as direct action and strikes by workers. The 'Hot Spring' of school student unrest in 1987 won a number of educational concessions from the government and thereby encouraged workers to adopt a similarly combative approach. Government concessions were made because polls showed the unrest to be damaging to its public image, and there were even fears that a 'May 1968' scenario of student–worker unity might develop.

As time went on, the traditional divide separating Socialist from Communist unions began to be bridged. When anti-inflationary measures were hitting workers in Greece and Spain, and when the public sector and job security were under attack from the Cavaco e Silva government in Portugal, trade unionists saw no alternative to militancy and union co-operation. In Spain the UGT and the Communist-dominated Workers' Commission (CCOO) even signed a formal united action agreement in February 1988. However, it would be simplistic to suggest that the traditionally militant Communist unions have been proven right. Indeed, in Portugal in late 1987 the Communist General Confederation of Portuguese Workers (CGTP) made a move in the direction of the UGT position. In response to the Communist Party's electoral decline, the CGTP became more autonomous and announced a more flexible attitude towards participation in the Permanent Council of Social Co-operation, established by the 'Central Bloc' Soares government in 1983 to institutionalise governmental consultation of the employers and unions on socio-economic matters. Unlike the UGT, the CGTP had hitherto boycotted that body. Shortly thereafter, however, the UGT itself began to despair of the uncompromising attitude of the Cavaco e Silva government. When early in 1988 the latter refused to negotiate over new labour reform proposals that facilitated dismissals, it was the UGT that took the lead in organising a general strike, which the CGTP supported.

Notwithsanding moves towards greater Socialist–Communist trade union unity in Spain, Portugal, and Greece, it is unlikely that co-operation will lead to unification and the emergence thereby of the unions as a more influential interest group. Mutual distrust within the left still runs deep and in periods of economic growth the Socialist unions, which regard themselves as more modern and professional than the Communist unions, are likely once more at least to test the road of negotiated improvements. In principle, the Socialist unions are in favour of labour unity, but want to see it develop on a Socialist basis.

CONCLUSION

It should be clear from the above discussion that, while democratic consolidation has unmistakably advanced in the southern Europe of the 1980s, there are still areas where it has some way to go. One is deterred from regarding the new Mediterranean democracies as consolidated by the uncertainties that — albeit decreasingly — still surround the loyalty of armies, at least in Spain; by governmental interference in, and state control over, the electronic media; by the low levels of associationalism; by the persistence of bureaucratic obstruction and inertia from largely unreformed public administrations; and by the failure of at least two of the party systems to settle into stable patterns.

That said, it would be unfair to judge the new polities against the standards of some ideal liberal democracy when other contemporary European political systems approximate to this only remotely. The type of democracy emerging in the new polities is closer to the Italian than the northern European models, and it may thus be most appropriate to assess progress in terms of the consolidation of party dominance. In this sense, the low level of associational membership may be less of a problem than some pluralist theorists would have it. What is more crucial in terms of the 'party state' model of democracy is that political parties sooner or later have managed to achieve stable and effective governments, that there has been party alternation in office (and much sooner than in Italy), and that a clear majority of the people in Spain, Greece, and Portugal have at least shown sufficient commitment to the new regimes to maintain a reasonably high level of electoral participation.

Common problems remain, as do nationally specific ones such as the lack of consensus surrounding the regional question in Spain. Many southern Europeans have felt disappointed by the weak reform performances of governments formed by the Socialist parties, which were seen early on as the strongest unequivocally democratic forces. Yet, so far at least, there has not been any increase in the proportion of people who are nostalgic about life under the previous regimes, or who support radical alternatives to the new democracies.[7]

None the less, certain dangers surround any regime that seeks to operationalise democracy chiefly through the political parties. With civil society overshadowed by the state and not encouraged to develop, problems of popular alienation from regimes could well emerge in the southern Europe of the 1990s. Equally, if the recent tensions between Socialist politicians and trade unionists in Greece and Spain were to develop into permanent dissociation, we might well see the populistic features of the Socialist parties becoming further accentuated, especially if social reform continues to be neglected in the interests of economic growth and competitiveness. Perhaps only when voted out of office will the Socialist parties seriously reconsider the advantages of possessing vital and assertive, organised social bases. They may then also begin to question the quality of the new democracies which they themselves have helped to shape.

ACKNOWLEDGEMENTS

The author wishes to thank Tom Gallagher and Kevin Featherstone for their helpful comments on the initial draft of this chapter.

NOTES

1. There was direct military rule in Greece, while in Spain one-third of Franco's ministers were military men. Salazarist Portugal was a civilian dictatorship but owed its birth and demise to the armed forces, and a military officer always occupied the presidency.
2. In Spain, Felipe González was absent from the Cortes for a full seven months in 1986–87.
3. Lijphart *et al.* (1988). But see also Payne (1986), where it is argued that since 1975 the southern European countries have experienced one of their periods of strongest convergence.
4. Many Spaniards were shocked to hear that during the coup attempt of February 1981, Alexander Haig had declared that it was an internal Spanish affair.

5. Spain had the lowest European level of associational participation, according to a survey carried out in 1984 (*El País*, 27 March 1984). Bruneau and Macleod (1986: Ch. 5) reported that participation in Portuguese associations grew from 11 to 15 per cent between 1978 and 1984, but that there was a decrease in the case of political associations, while union participation fell from 31 to 13 per cent.

6. Bruneau and Macleod (1986: 105–8). In this respect the Portuguese UGT (which includes PSD supporters as well as Socialists) was closer at this time to the Italian Socialist union (which includes Socialists and Radicals, and in 1987 came out in favour of the regulation of strikes) than was the Spanish UGT.

7. In Spain by the end of 1984, only one in ten preferred an alternative regime and four-fifths saw democracy as better that any other form of government. Public opinion surveys reveal a less unequivocal picture in Portugal, though the introduction of more liberty since 1974 is clearly valued positively.

REFERENCES AND FURTHER READING

Bruneau, T. C. (1984) *Politics and Nationhood: Post-Revolutionary Portugal* (New York: Praeger)

Bruneau, T. C. (1986) *Politics in Contemporary Portugal* (Boulder: Rienner).

Clogg, R. (1983) *Greece in the 1980s* (London: Macmillan).

Featherstone, K. and Katsoudas, I. K. (eds) (1987) *Political Change in Greece: Before and After the Colonels* (London: Croom Helm)

Gallagher, T. (1986) 'Twice choosing the unexpected: the Portuguese elections of 1985 and 1986', *West European Politics*, 9, 233–7.

Gillespie, R. (1986) 'Spain's referendum on NATO', West European Politics, 9, 4, 238–44.

Gilmour, D. (1985) *The Transformation of Spain* (London: Quartet).

Graham, L. S. and Wheeler, D. L. (eds) (1983) *In Search of Modern Portugal: The Revolution and its Consequences* (Madison: University of Wisconsin Press).

Gunther, R, Sani, G. and Shabad, G. (1986) *Spain After Franco: The Making of a Competitive Party System* (Berkeley: University of California Press).

Hine, D. (1987) 'Political parties and the consolidation of democracy in postwar Italy', paper presented at the Annual Conference of the Political Studies Association, Aberdeen.

Hudson, R. and Lewis, J. (eds) (1985) *Uneven Development in Southern Europe* (London: Methuen).

Katsoudas, D. K. (1985) 'Greece: a politically controlled state monopoly broadcasting system', *West European Politics*, 8, 2, 137–51.

Kohler, B. (1982) *Political Forces in Spain, Greece and Portugal* (London: Butterworth).

Lijphart, A., Bruneau, T. C., Diamandouros, P. N. and Gunther, R. (1988) 'A Mediterranean model of democracy? The southern European democracies in comparative perspective', *West European Politics*, 11, 7–25.

Lopez-Escobar, E. and Faus-Belau, A. (1985) 'Broadcasting in Spain: a history of heavy-handed control,' *West European Politics*, 8, 122–36.

Mavrogordatos, G. T. (1983) *Stillborn Republic: Social Coalitions and Party Strategies in Greece, 1922–1936* (Berkeley: University of California Press).

O'Donnell, G, Schmitter, P. C. and Whitehead, L. (eds) (1986) *Transitions from Authoritarian Rule* (Baltimore: Johns Hopkins Press).

Payne, S. G. (1986) 'The concept of "Southern Europe" and political development', *Mediterranean Historical Review*, 1, 100–15.

Preston, P. (1986) *The Triumph of Democracy in Spain* (London: Methuen).

Pridham, G. (ed.) (1984) *The New Mediterranean Democracies* (London: Cass).

Tzannatos, Z. (ed.) (1986) *Socialism in Greece* (Aldershot: Gower).

Wiarda, H. J. (ed.) (1986) '*Southern Europe and the Mediterranean*', special issue of *AEI Foreign Policy and Defense Review*, 6.2.

Williams, A. (ed.) (1984) *Southern Europe Transformed* (London: Harper & Row).

CHAPTER TWELVE
Stages of European Development: Electoral Change and System Adaptation

Gordon Smith

A EUROPEAN FLUX?

The liberal democracies of Western Europe enjoy a reputation for political stability. In recent years there have been various signs of change, one of which is an altering relationship between European electorates and the political parties. What such a change signifies is far from certain, and the term 'flux' is often applied – a movement away from hitherto stable patterns without as yet new ones becoming clearly apparent. Is the major trend towards a general electoral dealignment in the sense of a weakening attachment to parties or is there a fundamental realignment possibly under way and with it the discovery of new loyalties and collectivities of interest? (See Flanagan and Dalton 1984; Dalton *et al.* 1984.) If the description of a flux is correct, then the existing format of party competition and even the structure of several West European party systems could face substantial alteration.

Against a background of fluctuating party fortunes and electoral movement, currency is also given to the view that there is an incipient crisis affecting party government and party democracy. Several indications may support the argument that the parties could be losing their authoritative position in society. One is the growing direct influence of the mass media on the formation of public opinion. Another is the increasing readiness on the part of disaffected social groups to resort to 'direct action' rather than rely on the efforts of parties and abide by the outcome of elections. There are also the inroads into party government made by extra–party decision-making processes which have the effect of bypassing representative institutions. This latter tendency is associated with the concept of neo-corporatism which many would see as being inherently opposed to the pluralist version of the articulation of social interests – and political pluralism is the rationale of party competition in liberal democracy. If we aggregate all these apparent threats, then there are grounds for drawing a picture of a looming crisis: the restiveness of electorates is just one symptom of a deep-seated malaise affecting the status of parties and their functioning in society and government. The legitimacy of party democracy could be subjected to a steady erosion.

It is beyond the scope of this discussion to examine all the ingredients of a possible general crisis, but the question of electoral and party system change is bound to be a central issue in any debate. One difficulty in making an assessment in this respect lies in finding a suitable perspective from which 'change' can be viewed. It is tempting to focus on the contemporary scene, since what is happening at present has immediate relevance to the idea of an impending crisis. Yet – and this is the argument to be developed in the following account – a snapshot of change at the present time is likely to be seriously misleading. One reason is that both the extent and rate of electoral and system change can easily be exaggerated; alterations are slow to come about and adjustments may prove to be marginal. But there is a more fundamental consideration involved: changing patterns, however basic they may be, may also be *incomplete*. This idea of 'incomplete change' as a feature of European development has the important consequence that a substantial 'overlayering' occurs; in other words, there is an incorporation of party characteristics acquired at successive stages.

Since we are mainly concerned with contemporary development, it is not feasible to trace the historical patterns throughout Western Europe, and yet it is essential to appreciate what the major acquired characteristics have been. The purpose of the following examination is to specify the features of three major 'stages' of European electoral and party development – one of them still under way – and further to show how the amalgam of characteristics could affect future development. To the extent that the idea of a contemporary flux is appropriate, is it a temporary phase or could the flux itself become the new normality? Do the changes pose a challenge to parties generally, or do they represent a crisis for particular kinds of party?

SOCIO-ECONOMIC CHANGE AND THE EUROPEAN 'CORE' MODEL

Two features stand out in the post-1945 development of Western Europe. One has been the pace of economic change which has brought about a growing affluence for the great majority of people, and the continuing economic growth has also had a drastic effect on pre-existing social structures. The second feature is the trend towards the homogenisation of European society which is gradually leading to the erosion of national specifics in favour of the uniform characteristics of advanced industrial societies. Both kinds of change have important consequences for what may be termed the core cleavage model of European society. This cleavage model offered a comprehensive explanation for the patterning of politics throughout Europe for more than the first half of the present century, and it is still the major point of reference against which later developments and alternative theories have to be judged.[1]

There is little doubt that the structuring of modern European politics – in a form that still prevails in most party systems – can be traced to the conditions ruling at the time of the initial mass entry into politics, that is, in the late nineteenth and early twentieth centuries. This 'primary mobilisation' of electorates, made possible through progressive extensions of the franchise, largely followed the lines of the then-salient cleavages: the parties took their places on one side or the other of the significant social divisions and conflicts. While the cleavages relating to economic issues and social-class differences were usually paramount, the existence of others – notably rural–urban and religious conflicts, especially those concerning the relationship of the churches with the secular state – gave rise to complex cleavage formations. The precise configuration that resulted in individual countries depended on a variety of factors: how far and on what terms the problems of nation- and state-building had been resolved, the pace of industrialisation and urbanisation, the timing of suffrage extension.

Given the variety of factors involved, the scope for all kinds of party system to emerge was considerable. But the notable fact is that most West European systems do show strong similarities, particularly in widespread representation of the 'historical' European party 'families' – Conservative, Christian, Liberal, Social Democratic and Communist (see von Beyme 1985). Yet to explain their resilience it is inappropriate to rely on the persistence of the origina l social cleavages as a sufficient explanation, since it is impossible to overlook the extent of socio-economic and other changes in the course of the past century. At least part of the explanation must refer to the ability of the parties themselves to preserve a form of political and electoral status quo: it appears that they were able to secure their position by encapsulating the voting loyalties of specific social groups and maintain a high level of partisan identification, despite altering circumstances, and that these loyalties were transmitted from one generation to another. In other words, the partial inertia of party systems following on from the primary mobilisation of electorates resulted from the resilience of individual parties and their ability to reinforce political cleavages.

The initial stage of European development proved to be exceptionally long-lasting, so much so that the terms of primary mobilisation looked set to become permanent ones as well. This fixity was expressed in the description of West European party systems having become 'frozen' into the shapes they had originally acquired. It proved to be a structuring that persisted well into the 1960s, despite all the changes and upheavals that Europe had experienced, not least through the impact of the Second World War.

Yet it is also evident that the continuing momentum of social change, spanning the whole era since 1945, would inevitably at some point have radical consequences for the traditional parties as the lines of historical cleavage weakened. As a result, the core model would be gradually robbed of its wide explanatory power. Structural changes in the economy have been of prime importance in affecting the nature of occupations and the mobility of labour, and for Western Europe as a whole the decline of the agricultural basis of the economy has been of great significance. The eclipse of peasant-based societies has removed a major prop – and preoccupation – for many parties. In northern Europe, and Britain in particular, this decline has long been in evidence, but the same process is now well advanced in the Mediterranean countries. Western Europe is now a predominantly urbanised society, regardless of where people happen to live.

Just as momentous has been the decline of the traditional industrial bases of West European economies: the creation of new industries along with the movement into tertiary-sector employment has made the 'old' working class into a residual force instead of being a leading protagonist. The creation of new occupations together with rising standards of living and higher levels of education has resulted in the blurring of the previously sharp lines of social-class division. Instead, the alternative picture presented is of a diffuse and amorphous 'new' middle/working class, with similar aspirations, common consumption patterns, and a homogenised mass culture.

A concurrent development is the weakening of the network of social affiliations that helped to underpin established political loyalties. In particular, this loosening of social ties has affected the bedrocks of support for two important political forces in Western Europe: the Christian Democratic parties on the centre–right, and the Social Democrats/Communists on the left. In the case of Christian Democracy, the decline in church membership and religious observance has led to an attenuation of a specifically 'Christian' appeal for the parties concerned. In addition, a particular rationale for such parties – the preservation of church interests – no longer requires the same political reinforcement as, for example, when the conflicts over church–state relations and religious education were intense. For the parties of the left, the infrastructure of support provided by organised labour, whether or not there are formal links between trade union organisations and particular parties, has been of vital importance. Increasingly, however, the shift away from old industries has led to a decline in membership and to a weakening of the bastion of working-class solidarity. There is recompense in the growth of white-collar unionism, but in new occupations union attachment is more instrumental in character and less likely to lead directly to support for a left-wing party.

Pervasive as these socio-economic trends undoubtedly are, it is important not to overdraw the picture of an increasingly undifferentiated European electorate and to imply that inherited social cleavages have become entirely residual. The leading socio-economic indicators – occupation, trade union membership, religious persuasion/observance – continue to explain patterns of voting behaviour in most countries better than other variables, even though they are far less reliable than they were thirty years ago. Despite the fact that the changing structure of society is modifying the original lines of cleavage, they need not be eradicated, and they may appear in new forms. This reservation applies to the changing basis of trade union membership: white-collar unions can be quite as militant as industrial unions. Similarly with the question of religious adherence: the decline in formal membership and attendance need not at all mean that the 'religious factor' in politics has become irrelevant, since it can be expressed in diverse forms.

How do parties respond to such changing social conditions? One possible reaction – the theory of which is examined in the following section – is for a party to discard its old representational links. On one level, it is true, there may be decisive switch affecting a party's ideology and programme, but it would be wrong to suppose that an established party, with a continuity of membership and tradition behind it, could disregard its existing clientele, whatever else it sought to do besides. The preferred strategy is to win over new social groups without at the same time jeopardising tried party support, even though a party's appeal must necessarily become more diluted as a result.

For all these reasons, the core model of European electoral behaviour continues to hold an important place. In spite of the weakening of the old cleavages and the consequent ebbing of related social polarisation, a voter's socio-economic location and social affiliation remain significant determinants of electoral choice. What this means for our present discussion is that the first stage of European development has not been entirely displaced by subsequent stages and that we have to see the evolution more as a composite whole.

PARTY ADAPTATION AND CENTRIPETAL COMPETITION

As an explanation of electoral behaviour, the pure cleavage model suggests that voters identify themselves and their interests with clearly defined social groups and that this sense of belonging largely determines their political loyalties. Since the idea of a 'cleavage' implies that the interests of one group are sharply demarcated from – and even antithetical towards – those of others, there is little likelihood of widespread voting deviance taking place. Yet, once the underlying causes and supports of tension and cleavage begin to weaken the potential for fundamental change will be revealed. The question is: what direction will it take?

There are two ways of answering this question. One is to say that an immediate fluidity in electoral behaviour will become apparent – and that should occur without any marked initiative or stimulation coming from the parties. The alternative is to see the parties themselves as the prime movers, and in this version the parties – or at least one of them – appreciate the possibilities of the changing social situation and seek to refashion their strategies and appeal accordingly. In the sense that there is bound to be a dynamic interaction between parties and voters, the two versions are clearly compatible. But there is an important difference of emphasis: whether voters act 'autonomously' or whether party adaption is the decisive factor. The latter course appears the more plausible, since voters are more inclined to switch support, for instance, if they perceive that a party which they previously regarded as ineligible has modified its position, and they will be less likely to move as long as the party battle-lines continue to reflect the old antagonisms. In this sense, the initiative lies with the parties.

Following this line of reasoning, party adaptation to a changing socio-economic environment can be taken to mark the second principal stage of West European development. Its inception was signalled in the period after 1945, since the economic reconstruction and recovery which then commenced merged with a sustained era of economic growth. The 1939–45 conflict itself speeded up the processes of social change: the dislocation and discontinuity the war brought about made many of the former social divisions redundant, and that was particularly true for countries that had experienced fascist dictatorship, for it could persuasively be argued that – for example, in the case of Nazi Germany – the impact of totalitarian rule had been integral to the 'modernisation' of societies that had lagged behind in their social evolution.[2] Taken together, the different contributions – fascism, the war, economic rebuilding, and later affluence – had a powerful, cumulative effect on European social structures.

At this point it is instructive to examine the analysis made by Otto Kirchheimer who – writing in the 1950s and early 1960s – not only sought to locate the underlying cause of party system change which even at that time appeared to be under way, but who also sketched a scenario of future West European development (Kirchheimer 1966). In his view the parties were being ineluctably drawn into the meshes of centripetal competition as a direct result of the direction that social evolution had taken. The social transformation was the key factor behind a parallel transformation of West European party systems.

Although the course to be taken envisaged by Kirchheimer did not fully materialise, or at any rate proved to be only one aspect of subsequent development, his emphasis on the changing character of parties and the kinds of strategy that they would adopt accords with the idea of the commencement of a second stage in European development. The decline in social polarisation went hand in hand with declining political polarisation, but the adjustments required of the parties were not easy, for – as Kirchheimer depicted them – they were 'the remnants of intellectual and social movements of the nineteenth century', and they had remained 'glued to the spots where the ebbing energy of such movements had deposited them some decades ago'. Party adaptation to reflect new social realities and aspirations necessitated a radical revision of ideological positions. In effect, what was demanded of the parties was a form of 'non-ideological' politics to suit the conditions of less polarised and less segmented societies.

With the parties competing in similar terms and with a considerable overlap in their potential support, centripetal competition would become the norm. If the traditional parties failed to make the required adaptation, then new ones would arise which would make the appeal to wide cross-sections of the community their leading aim. Either way, the scene was set for the rise of a new type of party. Kirchheimer, in extrapolating the consequences of this movement, went even further in regarding the new party-type as a 'competitive phenomenon', that is to say, once one such party had proved its ability to straddle old social divisions– and thus in principle being in a position to tap support from the whole electorate – then other parties would be forced to follow suit, since otherwise their electoral base would steadily be eroded and they would face the prospect of being relegated to permanent opposition. The end-result of this centripetal dynamic seemed inescapable: only a few very broadly based parties could survive, perhaps just two, either of which could realistically aim to win majority support on its own account.

With the knowledge of how West European party systems have actually developed since the 1960s, it is easy to see that this extrapolation was seriously flawed: the new-type party simply did not sweep all others aside, and there has been no sign of the number of parties declining as one might have expected.[3] Indeed, it has become apparent that the larger parties, those capable of making a society-wide appeal, are just as vulnerable as those with a narrow ideology. Yet it is important not to lose sight of the basic distinction that has to be made between, on the one hand, the centripetal nature of party competition and, on the other, the supposed transformative consequences for party systems. In retrospect we can see that the 'centripetal bind' imposed on party competition following from the social changes has only been one of the major influences at work. That there have been other influences operative would anyway be expected, and that follows from the view that the original cleavage structuring has left an indelible imprint on European politics. Furthermore, we can also expect that the effects of a new, third stage will supervene before the full consequences of centripetal competition could be realised.

None the less, the premise of the second-stage argument is surely valid: party competition has become centripetal rather than centrifugal. That need not prevent a sudden contrary lurch sparked by a crisis in national affairs, but parties are well aware that a polarising course or one appealing to a narrow sectional interest can lose more support than is gained. It is, of course, peculiarly difficult to make a certain judgement about the prevailing direction of party competition in any system, since there are various indicators which may point in different ways: party programmes may say one thing, while a party's behaviour – in campaigning, in coalition or opposition – may reveal another (See Budge *et al.* 1987).

Less equivocal evidence comes in examining the fortunes of avowedly extremist parties, since they must aim at polarising the party system. On the extreme right successful parties are a rarity, and although the National Front in France and the Italian Social Movement (MSI) have had an irritant effect on right-wing parties closest to them, they can hardly be said to have polarised their party systems. The long-term decline of Communist parties in Western European together with the efforts of individual parties to adopt a more moderate and accommodating stance is in a sharp contrast to the polarising power of the extreme left in earlier post-war years. The waning challenge mounted by anti-system and extremist parties – at least as far as those that can be counted along the conventional span of left and right – must substantiate the case for centripetal competition, even though that still leaves open the possibility of moderate parties taking more radical positions. Even if Sartori's (1976; 132–40) category of 'polarised pluralism' is not to be consigned to the history books, nowhere in Western Europe can it convincingly be applied.

DIFFUSION AND DECONCENTRATION AS A THIRD STAGE

While the case for centripetal party competition, the second stage, is in most respects undeniable, too many other features have become apparent in recent years for it to be singled out as the sole driving force. We can summarise these other features under two heads: a 'deconcentration' of party systems and a growing 'diffusion' of electoral behaviour. Neither of these tendencies is in outright conflict with centripetal party competition, but their effect – as a third stage of development – is such that no clear pattern emerges, and the incidence of deconcentration and diffusion is still highly uneven.

Most voters support particular parties on a consistently permanent basis, so that the extent of electoral change can easily be overdrawn; yet the overall West European picture has changed substantially since the early 1960s. There has been a rising trend of electoral volatility in almost all countries. Voters are now more inclined to switch their party support – or alternatively abstain from voting; from one election to another there can be dramatic fluctuations in party performance, and as a result a sense of political instability may be fostered. But it is important to differentiate between the various forms that electoral volatility may take. A 'contained volatility', that is, a movement between a few established parties, can simply result in a see-saw transfer which may leave the party balance intact over a period, and the chief consequence is likely to be on party strategies which will be geared to vote recovery/maintenance on a centripetal basis. However, within this contained form of volatility there is further distinction to be made: whether the movement is between parties that are fairly closely related or whether it is a switch between ones that are in conflict (see Mair 1983). In the former case – an intra-area transfer – the significance of the rise/decline of the related parties is limited, but in the latter – an inter-area transfer – an electoral realignment may be occurring which could have far- reaching consequences for the political system. The same is possibly true in the case of 'uncontained' volatility, that is, one leading to a drift of support to small and new or previously disregarded parties: the increasing fragmentation of the party system that results will possibly lead to an instability of government even if the regime itself is not seriously under threat.

Whatever the nature of the volatility and the direction it takes, there is evidence of a changing electoral outlook, the most characteristic feature of which is the increasing electoral detachment from particular parties – although not necessarily implying an alienation from the parties *tout court*. The concept of 'partisan dealignment' sums up this electoral diffusion, suggesting a shift away from party identification and loyalties, especially those based on old social cleavages – without new ones appearing. Since at the present time the levels of declining identification are higher than the actual rates of volatility, the potential for increasing electoral turbulence is considerable. Moreover, dealigned voters are joined by non-aligned voters as new electoral cohorts arrive who have not been 'aligned' in the first place. This phenomenon of electoral detachment gives voters a freedom of choice to support parties according to the issues involved, and issue-voting indicates a scattering of previously uniform political directions, and it is a good match with the idea of electoral diffusion.

From the perspective of party systems, the effects of the changing patterns of electoral behaviour are seen in three related components of system 'deconcentration': a dispersion of party strength, in number and relative size as measured by an index of fractionalisation; by a declining share of the vote taking by the leading parties, for instance in measures of two-party aggregates; and by the rise of entirely new parties which put new issues on to the political agenda. Although there is evidence of deconcentration of one kind or another in almost all West European party systems, only if they are lumped together does a vista of fundamental change emerge.

In the first place we should leave aside the experience of the newer democracies – Greece, Portugal, and Spain – which are arguably just completing the phase of electoral and system consolidation. The extremes in Western Europe are probably best represented by Belgium and Denmark on the one side and by Sweden and Switzerland on the other: the former showing the greatest diffusion and deconcentration, and the latter still relatively unaffected; in this assessment, of course, it is the extent of change which is important, otherwise Switzerland would have to be included in the same group as Denmark and Belgium. Countries in intermediate positions vary considerably in the kind of change taking place, and it is uncertain whether some are just in the forefront or whether they are taking a special course. Britain has shown a steep decline in the two-party aggregate, although electoral volatility has not been particularly high. West Germany also has a falling two-party aggregate, and a rise in abstention rates, but in this case the most significant change has been the breakthrough achieved by the Greens; their appeal – principally to younger voters – is of importance in signifying a generational switch away from old party alignments. The two-party aggregate is less relevant to countries such as the Netherlands, Belgium, and Denmark, since they have fractionalised multiparty systems, but all three have recorded a rise in partisan dealignment, and for Belgium and Denmark this weakening of party ties came *after* an 'explosion' of their party systems.

Austria can be taken as representative of the intermediate group, that is, in showing signs of change, but without pointing to a basic restructuring of the party system. Until the recent past Austria belonged firmly in the group of static party systems. Post-1945 development was characterised by the almost absolute domination of the two major parties, and Austria had a strong party identification with the lowest rates of electoral volatility on record. Yet in the 1980s all measures indicate a rising trend of diffusion and deconcentration: a declining two-party aggregate, increasing electoral volatility, declining party identification, and rising fractionalisation – with a fourth party, the Greens, making an initial entry. Yet at the same time the prime position of the two leading parties, although apparently made more vulnerable, is not seriously under threat.

Naturally it is fair to argue that many changes can be traced to circumstances and crises peculiar to the countries concerned. For instance, the internal upheavals that affected the British Labour Party for over a decade goes some way in accounting for electoral disenchantment and for the resurgence of the Liberal Party and the formation of the breakaway SDP. The highly fragmented Belgian party system has resulted almost entirely from the intractability of the linguistic issue. The rise of the Greens in West Germany could owe just as much to the special features of the German political culture as to the influence of post-materialism, and the Greens might have been totally unsuccessful if the SPD had not lost its radical spirit after spending sixteen years in office. Yet to plead 'special circumstances' in all cases neglects the fact that, whatever the operative factor at a particular juncture, it may be no more than a trigger for change that would anyway have come about at some stage.

STAGES AND THEIR SYNTHESIS – AN OVERVIEW.

It is helpful at this point to recapitulate the terms of the original argument. Essentially it is that the three historical stages of European development have imparted permanent features affecting both electoral behaviour and the party systems. Each stage has been governed by contemporary circumstances, but even after these have changed, electorates and parties continue to reflect some of those former conditions. If we are to understand the present-day structuring of West European party systems, the elements of continuity have to be taken into account. What results is a synthesis of the stages, and it is not surprising if the resulting picture is complex, and no single model or theory can give an adequate account of electoral behaviour or properly explain the intricacies of party competition. The legacy of past development continues to influence the nature of electoral response and to affect the structuring of contemporary party systems.

One way of illustrating the cardinal features of each of the three stages is to set the direction of the principal feature of electoral behaviour for each stage against the corresponding prevailing pattern of party competition. The variations, which of course only serve to give an overall impression, are shown in Fig. 1. The basis of the 'core model' is the stable character of social cleavages and for the most part a relatively stable electoral behaviour. This corresponds to the 'stable polarised' group in IA, although within it the extent of polarisation could vary considerably. If, in addition to the pronounced cleavages, electoral behaviour was also unstable – as was historically the case, due in part to the uneven and imperfect electoral mobilisation in some countries – then a condition of 'fragmentation' (IB) obtained. The second stage of development, with the parties in centripetal competition, implies a broad inter-party consensus with a stabilisation of electoral behaviour around the consensus (II). Finally, there is the developing situation (III) which shows apparently contradictory tendencies in electoral behaviour and party competition. Rose and McAllister (1986) have, in fact, described the contemporary situation in Britain as one of 'centripetal instability', and it is a term which is readily applicable to several countries in Western Europe, although the implication of electoral instability is increasing volatility, not instability of the party and political systems.

This formulation of electoral behaviour and party competition would be at odds with all reality if the 'stages' were presented as discrete processes, and it is only in appreciating that they merge with one another that the present complexity becomes apparent. It is possible that the conditions leading to fragmentation are no longer operative, but there is still considerable scope for an individual party

		Centripetal	Centrifugal
Electoral behaviour	Unstable	III	IB
	Stable	II	IA
		Centripetal	Centrifugal

Party competition

Fig. 1 Electoral behaviour and party competition

system to combine several features — differentially affecting sections of the electorate and particular parties.

ELECTORAL CHANGE AND THE LEFT–RIGHT AXIS

It is interesting to juxtapose the new phenomenon of 'centripetal instability' with one of the oldest of European political hallmarks – the left–right dimension – which thus far has proved immune to electoral and system change. The question is whether the current trends towards deconcentration and diffusion also point to the redundancy of left and right as useful concepts or at least point to a need for their substantial redefinition. In this connection, too, account has to be taken of the impact of the 'new politics' in Western Europe and its consequences for the left–right ordering.

There are several reasons why the left–right axis has shown such resilience. First there has been the persistence of social-class related cleavages in European society, even though they have never squeezed out the salience of other fault-lines. Second, the ability of Social Democratic and Communist parties to maintain the relevance of social-class issues should not be underestimated: most national politics still reflect the inherited pattern of left–right conflict. Third, for the most part the parties are willing to present themselves and align with others in terms of left and right despite, – or perhaps precisely because of – the cloudy imprecision that surrounds them. Finally, even though some parties may be unwilling to accept a restrictive categorisation, the force of party competition and the need to find compatible coalition partners still help to fashion their *de facto* orientation. This tendency is reinforced by voters' perceptions of the ordering of parties within the system: electoral psychology translates party competition to unidimensional framework, usually a left–right one, even though a multidimensional mapping would be more appropriate.

These factors go some way to explain the tenacity of the left–right patterning of European politics, but there are signs of change. The centripetal nature of party competition weakens political extremes and encourages parties to moderate their programmes in order to secure competitive advantage. As a result the left–right axis is foreshortened, not eradicated: socioeconomic issues remain paramount and yet do not cause intense polarisation. The electoral consequences may be more radical: transfer between the established parties is easier, but also – just because the parties are operating within a consensus – voters are more free to give priority to particular issues or lend their support to minority movements and parties, and those issues or movements may have little in common with those relating to the major, conventional divisions separating left and right. There is no shortage of examples in Western Europe: the peace movement, ecological issues and opposition to nuclear energy, the feminist movement, and diverse minority causes. Issues such as these cut across party lines, and they do not correspond at all to the old cleavage structures.

From one point of view the rise of issue-politics can be treated as a random collection of unrelated priorities promoted by disparate sectional groups, and as such they could point to a destructuring of politics. A different interpretation sees an underlying unity involved, a coherence expressed in the concept of the 'new' politics as a reaction against the 'old' politics of the traditional parties of the left and right. Linking the expressions of the new politics are the values of post-materialism which are opposed to those of industrial society, with its one-sided concentration on economic growth and material security. Instead, post-materialism (See Inglehart 1977) emphasises a non-exploitative relationship with the environment together with a priority given to self-realisation, communality, and participation. Moreover, in fostering a participatory culture there is an inevitable clash with the élitist and non-participatory structures of parliamentary democracy and the parties that uphold the system. Thus the new politics leans towards direct action, both as a means of advancing particular causes as well as an end in its own right. In its rejection of élites and established institutions, the new politics dimension can alternatively be treated as an anti-establishment one that cuts across the existing left–right axis – the 'old politics' dimension.

The hitherto modest success of Green parties in Western Europe, but with a notable impact in West Germany, indicates that they could stop short of becoming major political forces (Müller-Rommel, 1989). Nevertheless they have to be seen as one fact of social change, and in that process the specifically political elements – for instance, party organisation – could become less important, since social movements relying on direct action do not require tight party linkages. For this reason the new politics should probably not be regarded principally as a source of new party formation, but rather as having a potential for a catalytic effect on existing parties – and thus on the meanings attached to left and right.

A distinction should be made between, say, the superficial borrowing of 'green clothes' – taking on board selected environmental and related issues – from far-reaching changes. In the latter respect parties of the left are more susceptible, stemming from the traditional concerns of left-wing parties with issues such as social emancipation and equality. As an expression of political ideology the concept of 'equality' is capable of a number of meanings. Precisely because of its elasticity, the parties of the left are open to the influence of the new politics and its values. This is especially so at a time when these parties need effective appeals to counter the attractions of neo-liberalism in the wake of the severe jolt to the ruling 'social democratic consensus' in Western Europe which found many left-wing and Social Democratic parties in a moribund ideological condition. Yet it is also clear that no simple process of ideological absorption from the new politics is possible, since the priority of the old politics shared by the parties of the left – continuing economic growth – is incompatible with central post-materialist values.

Viewed from this perspective, the present European 'flux' can be seen as reflecting a difficult process of realignment on the left. It is a difficult process because at the same time as this reorientation is under way, those same parties are caught by the pressures of centripetal competition, which also means that they have to come to terms with the reinvigorated philosophy of 'market forces' that has become the persuasive doctrine of the European right.

Neither electoral instability nor centripetal competition appears to point to the irrelevancy of left and right; it rather indicates a change in their content. Yet such a change would not easily allow a restaging of past conflicts unless the social interests involved represented cohesive social groups. The former cleavage structures of European society did produce cohesive attachments, but there are now too many fragmenting influences at work for parties to be able to weld them into consistent electoral blocs. To the extent that social groups can be singled out, they are likely to be identifiable minorities, and a party that seeks to combine and reconcile divergent minority interests is in danger of being pulled in too many directions.

As the mode of a possible absorption of the new politics dimension demonstrates, the left–right ordering is strongly rooted in Western Europe. Yet it has never been absolutely dominant. Religious forces have proved to be one exception, even though the corresponding political parties can usually be located near to the centre–right. Least reducible to the uniform scale are regionalist and nationalist movements. At their extreme, they question the whole framework of the nation-state and thus represent a more basic conflict than the socio-economic conflict within the state. Such movements have led to a deconcentration of some party systems in the post-war era, most notably in Belgium and Spain. Yet although the potential of sub-state nationalism should not be underestimated, its claims cannot be entirely divorced from other demands and discontents: resurgent nationalism can also be treated as symptomatic of wider social changes, and in certain circumstances they find a focus in the form of strong localist loyalties. Hence it can be argued that challenges are best met not so much by decentralisation as concentrating on the underlying social and economic causes that led to alienation from the centralised state.

The concepts of left and right, together with formal party ideologies associated with them, have always grossly over-simplified political realities. In a sense, too, they can become a straitjacket that inhibits innovative forces: established party organisations and the strict lines of party demarcation squeeze out new impulses. This restrictive inheritance becomes more apparent when, as at present, party identification is in decline and issue-voting replaces the acceptance of a party package. Yet at the same time these negative judgements often fail to show how European party systems might otherwise be structured.

CONCLUSION: SYSTEM CHANGE AND POLITICAL STABILITY

An attempt to draw up a conspectus of electoral and party system development is bound to have shortcomings. Objection can be made to presenting the complex evolution of European politics in the form of 'stages', and at best they will be seen as abstractions that require all kinds of qualification. Yet there are compensations. Firstly, the approach helps us to appreciate contemporary change in its historical context. Secondly, the sense of continuity in moving from one stage to another gives a proper weight to gradual nature of most change. Thirdly – and related – the persistence of the concepts of left and right, the original mould of West European politics, underlines the continuity of political traditions. Lastly, the very elasticity of these concepts is of fundamental importance: they allow a continuing accommodation with new ideologies. We can put these points together: although present trends in electoral behaviour show increasing volatility and a concomitant decline in party commitment, there are barriers in the way of a destructuring of West European politics, and suggestions of an indeterminate flux have to be treated with scepticism.

This conclusion does not of itself resolve questions as to whether Western Europe is likely to become politically more or less stable, since substantial changes in electoral behaviour and party systems are only one group of factors – albeit the most immediate — affecting the standing of democratic regimes. Party government depends on the sustenance of electoral support, and electoral volatility causes system instability with the same effect on governments. Yet while a succession of short-lived governments can have harmful effects, it is more important if the discontinuity gives rise to a frustrating immobilism or to sharp and continual changes in direction. The problem is whether the prevailing pattern of centripetal instability is likely to court either of these dangers.

The possibility of a 'system crisis' emerging at some point is not entirely to be dismissed, but it is more likely that changes will present a challenge to individual parties rather than to the system as a whole or even to the party regime. Established parties have to bear the brunt of electoral change, and they must show an adaptive response along two lines. They have, firstly, to take account of the changing relationship of voters to parties. Secondly, they have to be able to redefine their positions in terms of right and left. But it is also evident that these two tasks are related: what kind of ideological stance will best attract the uncommitted voter? A massive failure on both counts by all the established parties would certainly invite the prospect of political turmoil. Yet it is also an unlikely scenario, for experience suggests that European parties are well versed in the art of adaptation.

NOTES

1. The classic statement of the 'cleavage model' is Lipset and Rokkan (1967). The theory of cleavages and contemporary Western Europe is examined in detail in Lane and Ersson (1987: 39–93).

2. Dahrendorf (1968: 412) argues that the dictatorship was integral to the process of modernisation: 'While the social revolution of National Socialism was an instrument in the establishment of totalitarian forms, by the same token it had to create the basis of liberal modernity.'

3. For an examination of Kirchheimer's thesis and an empirical examination of the evidence of fractionalisation, see Wolinetz (1979).

REFERENCES AND FURTHER READING

Budge, I. Robertson, D. and Hearl, D. (1987) *Ideology, Strategy and Party Change* (Cambridge: Cambridge University Press).

Dahrendorf, R. (1968) *Society and Democracy in Germany* (London: Weidenfeld and Nicolson).

Dalton, R. Flanagan, S. and Beck, P. (eds) (1984) *Electoral Change in Advanced Industrial Societies* (Princeton: Princeton University Press).

Flanagan, S. and Dalton, R. (1984) 'Parties under stress: realignment and dealignment in advanced industrial societies', *West European Politics*, 7, 7–23.

Inglehart, R. (1977) *The Silent Revolution: Changing Values and Political Styles among Western Publics* (Princeton: Princeton University Press).

Kirchheimer, O. (1966) 'The transformation of Western European party systems' in J. LaPalombara and M. Weiner (eds), *Political Parties and Political Development* (Princeton: University Press), pp 177–200.

Lane, J. E. and Ersson, S. (1987) *Politics and Society in Western Europe (London and Beverly Hills: Sage)*.

Lawson, K. and Merkl, P. H. (eds) (1988) *When Parties Fail: Emerging Alternative Organizations* (Princeton: Princeton University Press).

Lipset, S. M. and Rokkan, S. (1967) *Party Systems and Voter Alignments* (New York: Free Press).

Mair, P. (1983) 'Adaptation and control: towards an understanding of party and party system change', in H. Daalder and Mair P. (eds), *Western European Party Systems: Continuity and Change* (London and Beverly Hills: Sage), pp 405–29.

Müller-Rommel, F. (ed) (1989) *New Politics in Western Europe: The Rise and the Success of Green Parties and Alternative Lists* (Boulder, Colo. and London: Westview Press).

Rose, R. and McAllister, I. (1986) *Voters Begin to Choose* (London and Beverly Hills: Sage)

Sartori, G. (1976) *Parties and Party Systems: A Framework for Analysis* (Cambridge: Cambridge University Press).

von Beyme, K. (1985) *Political Parties in Western Democracies* (Aldershot: Gower).

Ware, A. J. (ed) (1987) *Political Parties: Electoral Change and Structural Responses* (Oxford: Blackwell).

Wolinetz, S. V. (1979) 'The transformation of Western Europe party systems revisited', *West European Politics*, 2, 4–28.

Wolinetz, S. V. (ed.) (1988) *Parties and Party Systems in Liberal Democracies* (London: Routledge).

Appendix: Elections in Western Europe during the 1980s

Thomas T. Mackie

This appendix reports the results of elections to the lower houses of the national Parliaments of eighteen Western European countries from the beginning of 1980 to the end of 1988 and the results of elections to the European Parliament since the first direct election in 1979. In addition, because of the importance of the presidency in these countries, presidential elections in Finland, France, and Portugal have also been included.

For each parliamentary election the date of the election, the number of registered electors, and the percentage of valid and invalid votes cast are recorded. The percentage vote and number of seats won for all parties winning more than 1 per cent of the vote at any

AUSTRIA (Nationalrat)

	Date			
	24.4.83		*23.11.86*	
Electorate	5.3 million		5.5 million	
Valid votes	91.3%		91.3%	
Invalid votes	1.5%		1.6%	
Party	Vote (%)	Seats	Vote (%)	Seats
Socialist Party	47.7	90	43.1	80
People's Party	43.0	81	41.3	77
Freedom Party	5.0	12	9.7	18
United Greens	1.9	0⎫	4.8	8
Alternative List	1.4	0⎭		
Communist Party	0.7	0	0.7	0
Others	0.2	0	0.3	0
Totals	100.0	183	100.0	183

election during the 1980s are then presented. In addition, less successful parties are included if their performance is of comparative interest, for instance small Green or Communist parties.

Except where otherwise stated the sources for all the data presented here are the official election returns compiled by the public authorities responsible for the administration of elections and the publication of election results.

The results of earlier Western European elections may be conveniently obtained by consulting the second edition of *The International Almanac of Electoral History* (2nd edn), by Thomas T. Mackie and Richard Rose published by Macmillan in 1982. Reports of national elections held in twenty-five Western countries during the previous year are published annually in the September number of the *European Journal of Political Research*.

BELGIUM (Kamer der Volksvertegenwoordigers/Chambre des Representants)

	Date					
	8.11.81		13.10.85		13.12.87	
Electorate	6.9 million		7.0 million		7.0 million	
Valid votes	86.1%		86.6%		86.8%	
Invalid votes	8.5%		7.0%		6.0%	
Party	Vote (%)	Seats	Vote (%)	Seats	Vote (%)	Seats
Christian People's Party	19.7	43	21.3	49	19.5	43
Flemish Socialist Party	12.6	26	14.5	32	14.9	32
Francophone Socialist	12.6	35	13.8	35	15.6	40
Party of Liberty and Progress	13.1	28	10.7	22	11.5	25
Reform Liberal Party	8.2	24	10.2	24	9.4	23
Social Christian Party	6.7	18	8.0	20	8.0	19
Volksunie	9.9	20	8.0	16	8.1	16
Agalev } Ecolo }	4.4	4	3.7 / 2.5	4 / 5	4.5 / 2.6	6 / 3
Francophone Democratic Front } Walloon Rally }	4.2	6 / 2	1.2 / 0.1	3 / 0	1.2 / 0.2	3 / 0
Democratic Union for the Respect of Labour	2.7	3	1.1	1	—	—
Communist Party	2.3	2	1.2	0	0.8	0
Flemish Block	1.1	1	1.4	1	1.9	2
Others	2.5	0	2.3	0	1.7	0
Totals	100.0	212	100.0	212	100.0	212

DENMARK (Folketing)*

	8.12.81		10.1.84		8.9.87		10.5.88	
Electorate	3.8 million		3.8 million		3.9 million		3.9 million	
Valid votes	82.7%		87.8%		86.1%		85.1%	
Invalid votes	0.5%		0.6%		0.7%		0.9%	
Party	Vote (%)	Seats	Vote (%)	Seats	Vote (%)	Seats	Vote (%)	Seats
Social Democrats	32.9	59	31.6	56	29.3	54	29.8	55
Conservatives	14.5	26	23.4	42	20.8	38	19.3	35
Socialist People's Party	11.3	21	11.5	21	14.6	27	13.0	24
Liberals	11.3	20	12.1	22	10.5	19	11.8	22
Progress Party	8.9	16	3.6	6	4.8	9	9.0	16
Centre Democrats	8.3	15	4.6	8	4.9	9	4.7	9
Radicals	5.1	9	5.5	10	6.2	11	5.6	10
Left Socialists	2.7	5	2.7	5	1.4	0	0.6	0
Christian People's Party	2.3	4	2.7	5	2.4	4	2.0	4
Justice Party	1.5	0	1.5	0	0.5	0	—	
Communist Party	1.1	0	0.7	0	0.9	0	0.8	0
Common Course	—	—	—	—	2.2	4	1.9	0
Greens	—		—		1.3	0	1.3	0
Others	0.1	0	0.1	0	0.2	0	0.0	0
Totals	100.0	175	100.0	175	100.0	175	100.0	175

* Metropolitan Denmark only. In addition the Faroe Islands and Greenland each return two Members to the Folketing.

FINLAND – presidential elections

	Dates				
	17–18.1.82			31.1–1.2.88	
Electorate	3.9 million			4.0 million	
Valid votes	81.0%			76.7%	
Invalid votes	0.3%			1.6%	
Candidates	Vote (%)*	Seats	Candidates	Vote (%)†	Seats
M. Koivisto (Social Democrat)	43.4	145	M. Koivisto (Social Democrats and Rural Party)	48.9	144
H. Holkeri (National Coalition)	18.7	58	P. Väyrynen (Centre Party)	20.6	68
J. Virolainen (Centre)	16.9	53	H. Holkeri (National Coalition)	18.4	63
K. Kivistö (Communist)	11.0	32	K. Kivistö (Communist)	10.7	26
J. Jansson (Swedish People's Party)	3.8	11	J. Kajanoja (Democratic Alternative)	1.4	0
R. Westerholm (Christian Union)	1.9	0			
V. Vennamo (Rural Party)	2.3	1			
H. Sipilä (Liberal People's Party)	1.8	1			
Others	0.2	0			
Totals	100.0	301		100.0	301

* Votes cast for Electoral College candidates committed to individual presidential candidates. The Electoral College met on 26 January and elected Mauno Koivisto President with the support of Social Democrat and Rural Party electors.

† Votes cast for individual presidential candidates. Changes in the electoral law before the 1988 election provided for the possibility of direct election of the President. Any candidate winning an absolute majority of the popular vote is elected. Otherwise the electoral college is convened to choose the President. As President Koivisto narrowly failed to win an absolute majority of the vote, the electoral college met on 15 February and he was re-elected on the second ballot with 189 votes. The remaining votes were distributed as follows: Holkeri 18, Väyrynen 68 and Kivistö 26.

FINLAND (Eduskunta)

	Date			
	17/18.1.82		*15/16.3.87*	
Electorate	4.0 million		4.0 million	
Valid votes	75.4%		71.7%	
Invalid votes	0.3%		0.4%	
Party	Vote (%)	Seats	Vote (%)	Seats
Social Democrats	26.7	57	24.1	56
National Coalition	22.1	44	23.1	53
Centre Party	17.6	38	17.6	40
Liberal People's Party			0.9	0
Finnish People's Democratic Union	13.8	27	9.7	16
Rural Party	9.7	17	6.3	9
Swedish People's Party	4.9	11	5.6	13
Christian League	3.0	3	2.6	5
Greens	1.4	2	4.0	4
Pensioners' Party	—	—	1.2	0
Democratic Alternative	—	—	4.2	4
Others	0.8	1	0.7	0
Totals	100.0	200	100.0	200

FEDERAL GERMAN REPUBLIC (Bundestag)

	Date					
	5.10.80		*16.3.83*		*25.1.87*	
Electorate	43.2 million		44.1 million		45.3 million	
Valid votes	87.8%		88.3%		83.5%	
Invalid votes	0.8%		0.8%		0.8%	
Party	Vote (%)	Seats	Vote (%)	Seats	Vote (%)	Seats
Christian Democratic Union	44.5	174	48.8	191	44.3	174
Christian Social Union		52		53		49
Social Democrats	42.9	218	38.2	193	37.0	186
Free Democrats	10.6	53	7.0	34	9.1	46
Greens	1.5	0	5.6	27	8.3	42
Communist Party	0.2	0	0.2	0	—	—
National Democrats	0.2	0	0.2	0	0.6	0
Others	0.1	0	0.0	0	0.7	0
Totals	100.0	497	100.0	498	100.0	497

⋆ Excluding the deputies from West Berlin who are elected by the West Berlin House of Deputies.

FRANCE – presidential elections

Dates: Round I 26.4.81 / Round II 10.5.81

	Round I 26.4.81	Round II 10.5.81
Electorate	36.4 million	
Valid votes	79.8%	83.4%
Invalid votes	1.3%	2.5%
Candidates	Vote (%)	Vote (%)
François Mitterrand (Socialist)	25.8	51.8
Valéry Giscard d'Estaing (Union for French Democracy)	28.3	48.2
Jacques Chirac (Gaullist RPR)	18.0	—
Georges Marchais (Communist)	15.3	—
Brice Lalonde (Ecologist)	3.9	—
Arlette Laguiller (Trotskyist)	2.3	—
Michel Crépeau (Left Radical)	2.2	—
Michel Debré (Independent Gaullist)	1.7	—
Marie-France Garaud, (Independent Gaullist)	1.3	—
Huguette Bouchard (Unified Socialist Party)	1.1	—
Totals	100.0	100.0

Dates: Round I 24.4.88 / Round II 8.5.88

	Round I 24.4.88	Round II 8.5.88
Electorate	38.1 million	
Valid votes	79.7%	81.0%
Invalid votes	1.6%	3.0%
Candidates	Vote (%)	Vote (%)
François Mitterrand (Socialist)	34.1	54.0
Jaques Chirac (Gaullist RPR)	19.9	46.0
Raymond Barre (Union for French Democracy)	16.5	—
Jean-Marie Le Pen (National Front)	14.4	—
André Lajoinie (Communist)	6.8	—
Antoine Waechter (Greens)	3.8	—
Pierre Juquin (Independent Communist)	2.1	—
Arlette Laguiller (Trotskyist)	2.0	—
Pierre Boussel (Trotskyist)	0.4	—
	100.0	100.0

France (Assemblée nationale)★

	Date					
	14.6.81†		16.3.86		5.6.88†	
Electorate	36.3 million		37.5 million		38.1 million	
Valid votes	69.3%		74.7%		64.4%	
Invalid votes	1.0%		3.4%		1.5%	
Party	Vote (%)	Seats	Vote (%)	Seats	Vote (%)	Seats
Extreme left parties	1.4	0	1.7	0	0.4	0
Communist Party	16.1	44	9.8	35	11.3	27
Socialist Party and other candidates supporting President Mitterrand	38.2	289	32.7	216	37.6	280
Rally for the Republic	20.8	85 }	41.0	277	19.2	128
Union for French Democracy	19.2	61 }			18.5	129
Other right-wing candidates	2.8	12	3.8	14	2.8	12
National Front	0.2	0	9.7	35	9.6	1
Greens	1.1	0	1.2	0	0.4	0
Others	0.2	0	0.1	0	0.2	0
Totals	100.0	491	100.0	577	100.0	577

★ Including the overseas departments and territories.
† Date of the first round ballot. Votes reported are for the first round.

GREECE (Vouli)

	Date			
	18.10.81		2.6.85	
Electorate	7.3 million		7.7 million	
Valid votes	77.5%		83.1%	
Invalid votes	1.1%		0.7%	
Party	Vote (%)	Seats	Vote (%)	Seats
Pan-Hellenic Socialist Party	48.1	172	45.8	161
New Democracy	35.9	115	40.8	126
Communist Party	10.9	13	9.9	12
Progressives	1.7	0	—	—
Communist Party (Interior)	1.3	0	1.8	1
Others	2.1	0	1.7	0
Totals	100.0	300	100.0	300

ICELAND (Althing)

	Date			
	23.4.83		25.4.87	
Electorate	0.15 million		0.17 million	
Valid votes	86.4%		88.5%	
Invalid votes	2.5%		1.0%	
Party	Vote (%)	Seats	Vote (%)	Seats
Independence Party	38.7	23	27.2	18
Progressive Party	18.5	14	18.9	13
Popular Alliance	17.3	10	13.3	8
Social Democrats	11.7	6	15.2	10
Social Democratic Federation	7.3	4	0.2	0
Womens' Alliance	5.5	3	10.1	6
Citizens' Party	—	—	10.8	7
Humanist Party	—	—	1.6	0
National Party	—	—	1.4	0
Others	1.0	0	1.3	1
Totals	100.0	60	100.0	63

ITALY (Camera dei Deputati)

	Date			
	26.6.83		14.6.87	
Electorate	43.9 million		45.6 million	
Valid votes	84.0%		84.6%	
Invalid votes	5.0%		5.9%	
Party	Vote (%)	Seats	Vote (%)	Seats
Christian Democrats	32.9	225	34.3	234
Communist Party	29.9	198	26.6	177
Socialist Party	11.4	73	14.3	94
Social Movement	6.8	42	5.9	35
Republican Party	5.1	29	3.7	21
Social Democrats	4.1	23	3.0	17
Liberal Party	2.9	16	2.1	11
Radical Party	2.2	11	2.6	13
Proletarian Democracy	1.5	7	1.7	8
Pensioners' Party	1.4	0	—	—
Greens	0.0	0	2.5	13
Regional parties	1.4	6	2.7	7
Others	0.4	0	0.6	0
Totals	100.0	630	100.0	630

IRELAND (The Dáil)

	Date							
	11.6.81		18.2.82		24.11.82		17.2.87	
Electorate	2.3 million		2.3 million		2.3 million		2.4 million	
Valid votes	75.5%		73.2%		72.3%		72.7%	
Invalid votes	0.7%		0.6%		0.5%		0.7%	
Party	Vote (%)	Seats	Vote (%)	Seats	Vote (%)	Seats	Vote (%)	Seats
Fianna Fáil	45.3	78	47.3	81	45.2	75	44.2	81
Fine Gael	36.5	65	37.3	63	39.2	70	27.1	51
Labour	9.9	15	9.1	15	9.4	16	6.4	12
Workers' Party	1.7	1	2.2	3	3.3	2	3.8	4
National H-Block Committee	2.5	2	—	—	—	—	—	—
Sinn Féin	—	—	—	—	—	—	1.9	0
Greens	—	—	—	—	—	—	0.4	0
Progressive Democrats	—	—	—	—	—	—	11.9	14
Others	4.2	5	4.1	4	2.9	3	4.4	4
Totals	100.0	166	100.0	166	100.0	166	100.0	166

LUXEMBURG (Chambre des Deputés)

	Date	
	17.6.84	
Electorate	0.2 million	
Valid votes	83.4%	
Invalid votes	5.4%	
Party	Vote (%)	Seats
Christian Social Party	36.6	25
Socialist Workers' Party	31.8	21
Democratic Party	20.4	14
Communist Party	4.4	2
Green Alternative	4.2	2
Independent Socialist Party	2.4	0
Others	0.2	0
Total	100.0	64

THE NETHERLANDS (Tweede Kamer)

	Date					
	26.5.81		8.9.82		21.5.86	
Electorate	10.0 million		10.2 million		10.7 million	
Valid votes	86.6%		80.6%		85.5%	
Invalid votes	0.5%		0.4%		0.3%	
Party	Vote (%)	Seats	Vote (%)	Seats	Vote (%)	Seats
Christian Democrat Appeal	30.8	48	30.4	47	34.6	54
Labour Party	28.3	44	29.4	45	33.3	52
Liberal Party	17.3	26	23.1	36	17.4	27
Democrats '66	11.1	17	4.3	6	6.1	9
Pacifist Socialist Party	2.1	3	2.3	3	1.2	1
Communist Party	2.1	3	1.8	3	0.6	0
Political Reformed Party	2.0	3	1.9	3	1.7	3
Radical Political Party	2.0	3	1.7	2	1.3	2
Reformed Political Federation	1.5	2	1.5	2	0.9	1
Greens	—	—	—	—	0.2	0
Centre Party (extreme right)	0.1	0	0.5	1	0.4	0
Others	2.7	1	3.1	2	2.3	1
Totals	100.0	150	100.0	150	100.0	150

NORWAY (Storting)

	Date			
	13.9.81		8.9.85	
Electorate	3.0 million		3.1 million	
Valid votes	81.9%		83.9%	
Invalid votes	0.1%		0.1%	
Party	Vote (%)	Seats	Vote (%)	Seats
Labour Party	37.2	65	40.8	71
Conservative Party	31.7	54	30.4	50
Christian People's Party	9.4	15	8.3	16
Centre Party	6.7	11	6.6	12
Socialist Left	4.9	4	5.5	6
Progress Party	4.5	4	3.7	2
Liberal Party	3.9	2	3.1	0
Communist Party	0.3	0	0.2	0
Others	1.4	0	1.5	0
Totals	100.0	155	100.0	157

SPAIN (Congreso de Diputados)

	Date			
	28.10.82		22.6.86	
Electorate	26.8 million		28.9 million	
Valid votes	78.9%		69.3%	
Invalid votes	0.6%		1.5%	
Party	Vote (%)	Seats	Vote (%)	Seats
Socialist Party	46.5	202	44.3	184
Popular Alliance } Popular Democrats	25.8	106	26.1	105
Union of the Democratic Centre (UCD)	6.7	12	—	—
Democratic and Social Centre (CDS)	2.8	2	9.3	19
Communist Party and allies	4.1	4	4.6	7
Major Catalan parties				
Convergence and Unity	3.9	12	5.0	18
Catalan Republican Left	0.7	1	0.5	0
Major Basque parties				
Basque Nationalists	1.9	8	1.5	6
Herri Batasuna	1.0	2	1.2	5
Basque Left	0.5	1	0.5	2
Other regional parties	2.0	0	3.1	4
Democratic Reformist Party	—	—	1.0	0
Greens	—	—	0.4	0
Others	4.1	0	2.5	0
Totals	100.0	350	100.0	350

PORTUGAL (Assembleia da Republica)

	5.10.80	25.4.83	6.10.85	19.7.87
Electorate	7.0 million	7.3 million	7.60 million	7.7 million
Valid votes	84.5%	75.8%	70.4%	70.5%
Invalid votes	1.9%	2.0%	1.8%	2.1%

Party	Votes (%)	Seats	Vote (%)	Seats	Votes (%)	Seats	Votes (%)	Seats
Centre Social Democrats	⎫	82	12.9	30	10.2	22	4.4	4
Social Democrats	48.3 ⎬	46	27.2	75	30.6	88	51.3	148
Popular Monarchists	⎭	6	0.5	0			0.4	0
Socialist Party	28.7	74	36.1	101	21.3	57	22.8	60
Communist Party	17.3	41	18.1	44	15.9	38	12.5	31
Popular Democratic Union	1.4	1⎫	1.2	0	1.3	0	0.9	0
Revolutionary Socialist Party	1.0	0⎬	0.3	0	0.6	0	0.6	0
Socialist Unity Party	1.4	0	—	—			0.2	0
Democratic Renewal Party	—	—	—	—	18.4	45	5.0	7
Others	1.9	0	3.7	0	1.7	0	1.9	0
Totals	100.0	250	100.0	250	100.0	250	100.0	250

SWEDEN (Riksdag)

	Date					
	19.9.82		*15.9.85*		*18.9.88*	
Electorate	6.1 million		6.2 million		6.3 million	
Valid votes	90.6%		89.1%		84.9%	
Invalid votes	0.8%		0.8%		1.1%	
Party	Votes (%)	Seats	Votes (%)	Seats	Votes (%)	Seats
Social Democrats	45.6	166	44.7	159	43.2	156
Moderate Unity Party	23.6	86	21.3	76	18.3	66
Centre Party	15.5	56 }	12.4	43	11.3	42
Christian Democrats	1.9	0 }		1	2.9	0
People's Party	5.9	21	14.2	51	12.2	44
Left Party Communists	5.6	20	5.4	19	5.8	21
Greens	1.7	0	1.5	0	5.5	20
Others	0.2	0	0.5	0	0.7	0
Totals	100.0	349	100.0	349	100.0	349

SWITZERLAND (Nationalrat–Conseil National–Consiglio Nazionale)

	Date			
	9.11.83		*18.10.87*	
Electorate	4.1 million		4.2 million	
Valid votes	48.2%		46.1%	
Invalid votes	0.7%		0.7%	
Party	Votes (%)	Seats	Votes (%)	Seats
Radical Democrats	23.4	54	22.9	51
Social Democrats	22.9	47	18.4	41
Christian Democrats	20.4	21	20.0	42
People's Party	11.1	23	11.0	25
Independents' Party	4.1	8	4.2	8
National Action }	3.5	4 }	3.2	3
Vigilance }		1 }		0
Greens	2.9	4	7.8	10
Liberal Party	2.8	8	2.7	9
Progressive Organisations	2.2	3	1.3	4
Evangelical People's Party	2.1	3	1.9	3
Communist Party	0.9	1	0.8	1
Swiss Auto Party	—	—	2.6	2
Others	3.7	2	3.2	1
Totals	100.0	200	100.0	200

Appendix: Elections in Western Europe during the 1980s

UNITED KINGDOM (House of Commons)

Party	*9.6.83*		*11.6.87*	
	Vote (%)	Seats	Vote (%)	Seats
Electorate	42.2 million		43.2 million	
Valid votes	72.7%		75.3%	
Invalid votes	0.1%		0.1%	
Conservatives	42.4	397	42.3	376
Labour Party	27.6	209	30.8	229
Liberal Party		17 ⎫		17
Social Democratic Party ⎰	25.4	6 ⎭	22.5	5
Scottish National Party	1.1	2	1.3	3
Plaid Cymru	0.4	2	0.4	3
Greens	0.2	0	0.3	0
Communist Party	0.0	0	0.0	0
Northern Irish parties				
Ulster Unionist Party	0.8	11	0.8	9
Democratic Unionist Party	0.5	3	0.3	3
Social Democratic and Labour Party	0.4	1	0.5	3
Sinn Féin	0.3	1	0.3	1
Alliance Party	0.1	0	0.2	0
Others	0.8	1	0.3	1
Totals	100.0	650	100.0	650

Sources: Based on F. W. S. Craig (1984) *Britain Votes 3* (Colchester: Parliamentary Research Services) and F. W. S. Craig (1988) *Britain Votes 4* (Aldershot: Gower).

Parliamentary Groups in the European Parliament, 1979–1989

Group	1979 First direct election	1981 Greek accession	1985 Second direct election	1987 Spanish and Portuguese accession	1989 Third direct election
Socialist	112	123	130	164	181
European People's Party	108	115	110	115	123
European Democrats	64	64	50	66	34
Communist	44	48	41	48	41
Liberal	40	40	31	43	44
Progressive Democrat	22	22	29	31	19
CDI/Rainbow	11	11	20	20	39
European Right	—	—	16	17	22
Non-attached	9	11	7	14	15
Totals	410	434	434	518	518

Note: The European People's Party combines the Christian Democrat parties in the Community. The European Democrats unite the British and Danish Conservatives. For a period after Spanish accession the Alianza Popular was a member. This party later joined the People's Party group. The Progressive Democrats combine the French Rally for the Republic, Ireland's Fianna Fail and the Scottish National Party MEP. The Rainbow Group (until 1985 the Group for the Technical Coordination and Defence of Independent Groups and Members) links, green, new left and regional parties. The European Right groups parties of the extreme right.

ELECTIONS TO THE EUROPEAN PARLIAMENT SINCE 1979

BELGIUM

	1979		1984		1989	
Electorate	6.8 million		7.0 million		7.1 million	
Turnout	91.3%		92.1%		90.7%	
Party	Vote (%)	Seats	Vote (%)	Seats	Vote (%)	Seats
Christian People's Party	29.6	7	19.8	4	21.1	5
Flemish Socialist Party	12.8	3	17.1	4	12.4	3
Francophone Socialist Party	10.6	4	13.3	5	14.5	5
Party of Liberty and Progress	9.4	2	8.6	2	10.6	2
Reform Liberal Party	6.9	2	9.4	3	7.2	2
Social Christian Party	8.2	3	7.6	2	8.1	2
Volksunie	6.0	1	8.5	2	5.4	1
Agalev	1.4	0	4.3	1	7.6	1
Ecolo	2.0	0	3.9	1	6.3	2
Francophone Democratic Democratic Front	} 7.6	} 2	2.5	0	1.5	0
Walloon Rally			0.9	0	—	—
Communist Party	2.6	0	1.6	0	0.5	0
Flemish Block	—	—	1.3	0	4.1	0
Others	2.9	0	1.2	0	0.7	0
Totals	100.0	24	100.0	24	100.0	24

DENMARK (Excluding Greenland)[1]

	1979		1984		1989	
Electorate	3.7 million		3.8 million		3.9 million	
Turnout	47.8%		52.4%		46.1%	
Party	Vote (%)	Seats	Vote (%)	Seats	Vote (%)	Seats
People's Movement[2]	20.9	4	20.8	4	18.9	4
Social Democrats	21.9	3	19.5	3	23.3	4
Conservatives	14.0	2	20.8	4	13.4	2
Socialist People's Party	4.7	1	9.2	1	9.1	1
Liberals	14.5	3	12.5	2	16.6	3
Progress Party	5.8	1	3.5	0	5.3	0
Centre Democrats	6.2	1	6.6	1	7.9	2
Radicals	3.3	0	3.1	0	?	0
Left Socialists	3.5	0	1.3	0	?	0
Christian People's Party	1.8	0	2.7	0	?	0
Justice Party	3.4	—	—	—	?	?
Common Course	—	—	—	—	?	?
Others					?	0
Totals	100.0	15	100.0	15	100.0	16

[1] Greenland returned one deputy to the European Parliament in 1979 and 1984. He sat with the Socialist Group. When Greenland left the European Community in 1985 its seat was allocated to metropolitan Denmark.

[2] People's Movement against the European Community. An alliance of parties and individuals opposed to Danish membership of the Community. In 1989 includes the Greens.

FEDERAL GERMAN REPUBLIC

	1979		1984		1989	
Electorate	42.8 million		44.5 million		45.7 million	
Turnout	65.7%		56.8%		62.4%	
Party	Vote (%)	Seats	Vote (%)	Seats	Vote (%)	Seats
Christian Democratic Union	39.1	35	37.5	34	29.6	25
Christian Social Union	10.1	8	8.5	7	8.2	7
Social Democrats	40.8	34	37.4	33	37.3	31
Free Democrats	6.0	4	4.8	0	5.6	4
Greens	3.2	0	8.2	7	8.4	8
Communist Party	0.4	0	1.3[1]	0	0.2	0
Extreme Right	0.1[2]	0	0.9	0	8.7[2]	7
Others	0.4	0	1.4	0	2.0	0
Totals	100.0	81	100.0	81	100.0	81

[1] Peace List

[2] Of which 7.1% Republicans who won seven seats

FRANCE

	1979		1984		1989	
Electorate	35.2 million		36.9 million		38.3 million	
Turnout	56.7%		60.7%		51.3%	
Party	Vote (%)	Seats	Vote (%)	Seats	Vote (%)	Seats
Rally for the Republic	16.3	15 ⎫	43.0	41 ⎫	28.8	26
Union for French Democracy	27.6	25 ⎭		⎭		
Socialist Party	23.5	22	20.9	20	23.6	22
Communist Party	20.5	19	11.2	10	7.7	7
National Front	4.4	0	11.0	10	11.7	10
Greens	—		3.4	—	10.6	9
Extreme left	3.1	0	3.7	0	1.8	0
Centre[1]	—	—	—	—	8.4	7
Hunting[2]	—	—	—	—	4.0	0
Others	4.6	0	6.8	0	3.3	0
Totals	100.0	81	100.0	81	100.0	81

[1] List headed by Simone Weil and consisting largely of candidates belonging to the Centre Social Democrat wing of the UDF.

[2] "Hunting, Fishing and Tradition", European list for freedom of hunting and fishing

GREECE

	1981		1984		1989	
Electorate	6.5 million		7.1 million		7.9 million	
	88.5%		87.0%		84.5%	
Party	Vote (%)	Seats	Vote (%)	Seats	Vote (%)	Seats
Pan-Hellenic Socialist Party	40.1	10	41.6	10	36.0	9
New Democracy	31.3	8	38.0	9	40.4	0
Communist Party	12.8	3	11.6	3	14.3	4
Communist Party (Interior)	5.3	1	3.4	1		
Progressive Party	2.0	1	0.2	0	—	—
Democratic Socialist Party	4.3	1	0.8	0	—	—
Greens	—	—	—	—	2.6	0
Others	4.2	0	4.4		6.7	1
Totals	100.0	24	100.0	24	100.0	24

IRELAND

	1979		1984		1989	
Electorate	2.2 million		2.4 million		2.5 million	
Turnout	63.6%		47.8%		68.3%	
Party	Vote (%)	Seats	Vote (%)	Seats	Vote (%)	Seats
Fian a Fáil	34.7	5	39.2	8	31.5	6
Fine Gael	33.1	4	32.2	6	21.6	4
Labour Party	14.5	4	8.3	0	9.5	1
Workers' Party	3.3	0	4.3	0	7.5	1
Sinn Fein	—	—	4.9	0	2.3	0
Green Alliance	—	—	0.5	0	3.8	0
Progressive Democrats Independent	—	—	—	—	11.9	1
Others	8.6	2	10.6	1	11.9	2
	100.0	15	100.0	15	100.0	15

ITALY

	1979		1984		1989	
Electorate	42.2 million		44.4 million		46.8 million	
Turnout	85.7%		82.9%		81.5%	
Party	Vote (%)	Seats	Vote (%)	Seats	Vote (%)	Seats
Communist Party	30.8	25	33.3	27	27.6	22
Christian Democrats	36.4	29	33.0	26	32.9	26
Socialist Party	11.0	9	11.2	9	14.8	12
Social Movement	5.4	4	6.5	5	5.5	4
Social Democrats	4.3	4	3.5	3	2.7	2
Liberal Party	3.6	3	6.1	5	4.4	4
Republican Party	2.6	2				
Radical Party	3.7	3	3.4	3	—	—
Regional parties	1.1	2	1.6	2	2.9	4
Proletarian Democracy	0.7	0	1.4	1	1.3	1
Greens	—	—	—	—	3.8	3
Anti-Prohibition League	—	—	—	—	1.2	1
Rainbow	—	—	—	—	2.4	2
Others	0.4	0	—	—	0.5	0
	100.0	81	100.0	81	100.0	81

Appendix: Elections in Western Europe during the 1980s

LUXEMBURG

	1979		1984		1989	
Electorate	213,000		216,000		218,000	
Turnout	88.9%		88.8%		87.4%	
Party	Vote (%)	Seats	Vote (%)	Seats	Vote (%)	Seats
Christian Social Party	36.1	3	34.9	3	34.9	3
Socialist Workers' Party	21.6	1	29.9	2	25.5	2
Democratic Party	28.1	2	22.1	1	20.0	1
Communist Party	5.0	0	4.1	0	?	?
Social Democratic Party	7.0	0	—	—	—	—
Greens	1.0	0	6.1	0	10.4	0
Independent Socialist	—	—	2.6	0	—	—
Others	1.2	0	0.3	0	?	0
	100.0	6	100.0	6	100.0	6

NETHERLANDS

	1979		1984		1989	
Electorate	9.8 million		10.5 million		11.1 million	
Turnout	58.1%		50.9%		47.2%	
Party	Vote (%)	Seats	Vote (%)	Seats	Vote (%)	Seats
Christian Democrat Appeal	35.6	9	30.0	8	34.6	10
Labour Party	30.4	10	33.7	9	30.7	8
Liberal Party	16.1	4	18.9	5	13.6	3
Democrats '66	9.0	2	2.3	0	5.9	1
Calvinist parties	2.6	0	5.6	2	5.9	1
Communist Party	1.7	0				
Pacifist Socialist Party	1.7	0	5.2	1	7.0	2
Radical Political Party	1.6	0				
Centre Party (extreme right)	—	—	2.5	0	?	?
European Greens	—	—	1.3	0	—	—
Others	0.3	0	0.5	0	?	?
	100.0	25	100.0	25	100.0	25

PORTUGAL

Electorate	7.8 million		8.0 million	
Turnout	72.6%		51.3%	
Party	Vote (%)	Seats	Vote (%)	Seats
Social Democrats	38.4	10	32.7	9
Democratic Renewal Party	4.6	1	28.5	8
Socialist Party	22.1	6		
Communist Party	11.8	3	14.4	4
Centre Social Democrats	15.8	4	14.2	3
Others	7.3	0	?	?
	100.0	24	100.0	24

SPAIN

Party	1987		1989	
Electorate	28.5 million		29.2 million	
Turnout	68.9%		54.8%	
Party	Vote (%)	Seats	Vote (%)	Seats
Socialist Party	39.4	28	39.6	27
Popular Alliance/Popular Party	24.9	17	21.4	15
Democratic and Social Centre (CDS)	10.4	7	7.1	5
United Left	5.3	3	6.1	4
Convergence and Unity (Catalan)	4.5	3	4.2	2
Herri Batasuna (Basque)	1.9	1	1.7	1
Europe of the Peoples	1.7	1	1.5	1
Left Regional Parties	1.2	0	1.8	1
Basque Nationalist Party	1.2	0	1.9	1
Workers' Party	1.2	0	?	?
Minor regional parties	3.8	0	?	?
Greens	0.9	0	2.8	0
Ruiz-Mateos[2]	—	—	3.9	2
Andalusian Party	—	—	1.9	1
Others	4.6	0	?	0
Totals	100.0	60	100.0	60

[1] Electoral alliance of centre left parties in Catalonia, Euskadi and Galicia

[2] In alliance with a minor Galician party in 1987. In 1989 the Nationalist Coalition alliance which also included Castilian and Canary Islands parties

[3] Supporters of the Spanish financier Jose Maria Ruiz Mateos.

UNITED KINGDOM

	1979		*1984*		*1989*	
Electorate	41.2 million		42.5 million		43.2 million	
Turnout	32.8%		33.0%		36.2%	
Party	Vote (%)	Seats	Vote (%)	Seats	Vote (%)	Seats
Conservatives	48.4	60	38.8	45	33.0	32
Labour Party	31.6	17	34.8	32	38.9	45
Liberal Party	12.6	0	18.5	0	6.2	0
Special Democrats	—	—				
Scottish National Party					0.5	0
Plaid Cymru	1.9	1	1.6	1	2.6	1
Greens	0.6	0	0.7	0	0.7	0
Northern Ireland parties	0.1	0	0.5	0	14.5	0
Social Democratic and Labour Party	1.1	1	1.1	1	0.9	1
Democratic Unionists	1.3	1	1.6	1	1.0	1
Official Unionists	0.9	1	1.0	1	0.8	1
Others	1.5	0	1.4	0	0.9	0
Totals	100.0	81	100.0	81	100.0	81

Notes on Contributors

Peter Byrd holds a joint lectureship in Politics and in Continuing Education at the University of Warwick. He has written widely on British defence policy and peace movements, and has edited *British Defence in the 1980s*, *Social Democracy and Defence*, and *The Foreign Policy of the Thatcher Government*.

Richard Gillespie is Lecturer in Politics at the University of Warwick. He has published widely on Latin American and Spanish politics, including *Soldiers of Perón*, and *The Spanish Socialist Party*.

Wyn Grant is Reader in Politics at the University of Warwick. He is the author or editor of numerous studies on interest politics, corporatism and industrial policy, including *The Political Economy of Industrial Policy*, *The Politics of Economic Policy-Making*, *The Political Economy of Corporatism*, *Business and Politics in Britain* and *Government and the Chemical Industry*.

Zig Layton-Henry is Senior Lecturer in Politics at the University of Warwick. He has written extensively on race and politics in Britain, including *The Politics of Race in Britain*. He has recently edited a special issue of the *European Journal of Political Research* on 'Immigration and Politics', and *The Political Rights of Migrant Workers in Western Europe*.

Juliet Lodge is Reader in European Community Politics and Research Director of the European Community Research Unit at the University of Hull. She is author of numerous studies on the European Community. Most recently she has contributed to and edited *European Union: The European Community in Search of a Future*, *Direct Elections to the European Parliament, 1989*, and *The European Community: The Challenge of the Future*.

Joni Lovenduski is Reader in Politics at the University of

292

Loughborough. She has written various articles on women and politics, sex equality policy, and comparative European politics. Her recent publications include *Women and European Politics*, *The New Politics of Abortion*, and *Politics and Society in Eastern Europe*.

Thomas T. Mackie is Senior Lecturer in Politics at the University of Strathclyde. He is the co-author and editor of *The International Almanac of Electoral History*, the *Europe Votes* series, and *Unlocking the Cabinet*.

Richard Parry is Lecturer in Social Policy at the University of Edinburgh. He has published several articles on social and welfare policy and is the editor of *Scottish Political Facts*.

William Paterson is Reader in German Politics at the University of Warwick and Chairman of the University Association for Contemporary European Studies. He has published widely on German politics and social democracy. His major publications include *The SPD and European Integration*, *The West German Model*, *The Future of Social Democracy*, *The Federal Republic and the European Community* and *Government and the Chemical Industry*.

Gordon Smith is Professor of Government at the London School of Economics. He has written extensively on West German and comparative European politics. His major publications include *Politics in Western Europe*, *Democracy in Western Germany*, and *Party Government and Political Culture in Western Germany*.

Stan Taylor is Lecturer in Politics at the University of Warwick. He is the author of *The National Front in English Politics* and *Social Science and Revolutions*, and is currently completing a book on *Unemployment Policy in Britain Since the 1880s*.

Derek Urwin is Professor of Politics at the University of Warwick. He has been editor of *Scandinavian Political Studies*, and is currently co-editor of the *European Journal of Political Research*. His several publications on comparative and European politics include *Western Europe Since 1945*, *From Ploughshare to Ballotbox*, *Economy*, *Territory*, *Identity*, and *Centre–Periphery Structures in Europe*.

INDEX

Index